W9-APL-734

The Heart of a
Servant
Leader

The Heart of a
Servant
Leader

Letters from Jack Miller

C. JOHN MILLER

Edited by Barbara Miller Juliani

PUBLISHING
P.O. BOX 817 • PHILLIPSBURG • NEW JERSEY 08865-0817

© 2004 by Rose Marie Miller

All rights reserved. No part of this book may be reproduced, stored in a retrieval system, or transmitted in any form or by any means—electronic, mechanical, photocopy, recording, or otherwise—except for brief quotations for the purpose of review or comment, without the prior permission of the publisher, P&R Publishing Company, P.O. Box 817, Phillipsburg, New Jersey 08865-0817.

Page design and typesetting by Lakeside Design Plus

Printed in the United States of America

Library of Congress Cataloging-in-Publication Data

Miller, C. John
        The heart of a servant leader : letters from Jack Miller / C. John Miller ; edited by Barbara Miller Juliani.
                p. cm.
        Includes bibliographical references.
        ISBN-10: 0-87552-715-9 (pbk.)
        ISBN-13: 978-0-87552-715-4 (pbk.)
        1. Christian leadership. 2. Miller, Jack, 1928–1996—Correspondence.
3. Presbyterian Church—United States—Clergy—Correspondence. I. Juliani, Barbara Miller. II. Title.

BV652.1.M537 2004
253—dc22
                                                                04045677

Contents

Foreword: My Most Unforgettable Christian

As a boy I enjoyed reading the *Reader's Digest's* column, "My Most Unforgettable Character." If I could write this column about a Christian, it would be about Jack Miller.

I first met Jack when I was a young seminary student. I came to seminary because I wanted more knowledge; I believed that I could help people change by skillfully reasoning with them. So I signed up for one of Jack's classes thinking that he would help me with that project. Instead he spoke on repentance and humility in the life of the believer, and I felt completely exposed in my pride and arrogance. But I knew that this was just what I needed to hear, and I went home and told my wife Valerie that I was going to get in this man's shadow and learn everything I could from him.

I did get in his shadow, and I found out that what Jack preached he also lived. He preached that the gospel of Jesus Christ is powerful enough to change the hardest heart and then he took that gospel everywhere—to counterculture young people, to the inner city, to street gangs, to drug addicts, to intellectuals, to artists, and even to some businessmen—and I and other students went right along with him. He taught us to pray and repent as we took the gospel to the world, and then modeled that for us by stopping often to pray and repent himself.

I stayed in his shadow as he planted New Life Presbyterian Church, and I watched as he preached servant leadership and every-member ministry and then put feet on that by giving everyone a job to do; I started as the youth leader. Even when I left to plant a church in the South, I stayed in Jack's shadow—often calling him for advice and then going on mission trips with him as he worked to start World Harvest Mission.

Jack's unexpected death in 1996 left many of us without our spiritual father and mentor. There are many of my peers who would say that Jack Miller was the Christian who had the greatest influence on their lives. Although I don't know how Jack found the time, he mentored many men and women exactly as he mentored me— by taking us along with him on his amazing faith journey. Jack taught us to believe the promises, trust the Spirit's work, choose humility, and above all to want the glory of God in every way. One friend of mine says that he sees Jack's gospel fingerprints everywhere.

I am so thankful that Jack's daughter Barbara has given herself to this project of editing his letters. When I read through this book I was challenged, convicted, and comforted. As you read you will meet a humble, yet joyful servant of God whose heart reflected his heavenly Father's heart for the church and the spread of the kingdom of God. These letters are heart to heart and life to life.

Jack was "my most unforgettable Christian," but he wanted everything he did to point away from himself and toward the risen Christ whom he worshipped with all his heart. Jack would say that any shadow he cast came from being in the presence of the crucified, resurrected Savior. I know that he would want these letters to be used by the Spirit to point you to Jesus and the sufficiency of His gospel.

Yet he did not waver through unbelief regarding the promise of God, but was strengthened in his faith and gave glory to God, being fully persuaded that God had the power to do what he had promised. Romans 4:20

Clyde Godwin, Director, World Harvest Mission

Introduction

This letter is written to you, the reader of this book of letters. If you are a person who likes to skip introductions and just plunge in—feel free. But if you would like some background material on the letters—who wrote them, why they were written, and what makes them useful now—then read on.

July, 2003

Dear Reader,

This book, *The Heart of a Servant Leader*, is a collection of letters written by my father, Jack Miller. Besides being a husband and father of five, Jack was an evangelist, a church planter, a seminary professor, a missionary, and an author.[1] And, although nobody used this word thirty years ago, he was a mentor to many young men and women.

Whatever Jack did, he liked to have a crowd along to do it with him (we thought that was why he had five children—a guaranteed audience and student body). We lived just outside of Philadelphia, and our large old home was always full of students, church members, and sometimes random people Jack picked up

---

1. He wrote *Repentance and Twentieth Century Man*, *Powerful Evangelism for the Powerless*; *Outgrowing the Ingrown Church*; *Come Back, Barbara*; and *A Faith Worth Sharing*.

hitchhiking.[2] He shared his faith with all of them, and when some became Christians (including a few seminary students), he started teaching them how to share their new faith. His teaching methods were very hands-on. When he went to a bar, to a city subway stop, to a hospital, to a park, or even to Africa and Ireland to share his faith, he brought along whoever happened to be in our living room the day he was making plans.

But as the church he planted (New Life Presbyterian Church, [NLPC])[3] grew and started daughter churches, and as the mission he helped to start (World Harvest Mission) expanded into more mission fields, Jack's mentoring could not be quite as hands-on. This is when he began to spend more time writing letters to the young Christian leaders he wanted to continue mentoring. Jack spent a lot of time writing letters, and he copied and saved many of them. He always hoped that one day they would be published.

The letters in this book were written to Christians all over the world. Many of the men and women he mentored lived far away from Philadelphia. Some of them were missionaries, some of them were pastors who had attended NLPC while in seminary, and kept in contact with him as they pastored their own churches, and others were men and women who sought him out after reading his books or hearing him speak. But he also wrote a lot of letters to leaders at NLPC; he liked to take the time to organize his thoughts, put them on paper, and then give someone else the chance to sit down and think over what he had written.

In these letters Jack addressed a wide range of questions and problems. Some letters focus on ministry issues. There are letters to church planters wondering how to start and grow a church; to missionaries struggling to adjust to a new culture; to leaders at NLPC about specific plans and problems; to pastors seeking to

2. For the story of how one hitchhiker became his son-in-law and a missionary see *A Faith Worth Sharing*.

3. Jack refers to New Life Presbyterian Church as "New Life," but it is referred to as NLPC in introductory and background material.

apply principles from his books to their specific church; and to Christian leaders in conflict situations (a very large section). And there are many letters that discuss the personal challenges that all Christians face: physical suffering, overcoming sin, learning to forgive, spiritual warfare, dealing with change, and persevering through hard circumstances.

As you read through these letters you will notice that Jack's mentoring did not start with planning, organizational strategies, or practical tips on how to run a successful Christian ministry and/or live a successful Christian life. Although his letters are full of such advice, he didn't believe that those were the most important things a church leader needed to start and sustain a life of Christian service. Jack believed that the Christian leader should be the chief servant—not necessarily the successful one, but the one working to make others successful. But he also knew, from personal experience, how much easier it was to work for your own glory and build your own kingdom (no matter how small).

He found that, in his own life, leadership with a servant attitude could come only from a heart that was changed by an encounter with God. In his mentoring he always began by talking about what was going on in the heart. So many (if not all) of these letters come back to the same theme of having your heart changed by understanding the gospel and then living a life of humility, faith, and prayer. He thought that these were the basics of Christian leadership; any planning and organization had to come after the leader's heart had been humbled by God. This was what had changed his life, his ministry, and his ability to lead; he believed that these things were a necessary prerequisite to all Christian leadership and service.

The letters are organized to reflect these themes. In the first section the letters address the issue of motivation for ministry. Jack emphasized in each letter that the Christian leader must always be motivated by the glory of God. He said again and again that this is the only motivation that will sustain a life of ministry and bring freedom and joy in serving others.

In the second section, the letters address what Jack considered to be the basic heart attitudes that must be in place for the Christian leader. He believed that understanding the gospel, living by faith, repenting regularly, and praying constantly were the non-negotiables of Christian leadership. This section is divided into two parts. The first stresses what it means to have a changed heart, and the second applies these principles in practical ways to different situations and problems.

The third section on perseverance includes letters on spiritual warfare, conflict resolution, and change. In these letters Jack acknowledged how hard the circumstances were, gave much practical advice, but in the end managed to sound the same themes of being motivated by God's glory and understanding the gospel of grace so that you are filled with humility, faith, and constant prayer. He believed that the way you started in Christian ministry was also the only way to keep going in ministry.

The last section includes letters to those who were suffering physically, emotionally, and spiritually. In them Jack encouraged each person to have a greater understanding of how believing the gospel expressed in Jesus would change the way they dealt with their sins, the sins of others, and the hard circumstances of their lives.

Although Jack always wanted his letters to be published, he was also concerned to protect the privacy of those he wrote to. So all names, identifying characteristics, and circumstances have been changed. In each section the letters are organized chronologically, but in some cases the date and chronology of a letter has been changed in order to further protect the privacy of the recipients. Each part begins with an introductory section that discusses the themes of the letters and gives background material provided by Rose Marie Miller, Jack's wife and my mother. Also, the letters are titled to make it easier to identify a specific letter and go back to it.

For the last year I have been reading and rereading these letters, and they never fail to encourage me, challenge me, and change my thinking about my life and ministry. I also copied many of the letters and gave them to my husband Angelo to read. He immediately used a number of them in teaching he was doing at our church. A few months later he was at a pastors' conference, and a letter he had handed out appeared as part of the seminar leader's packet. So, in an informal way, these letters are already being used in the church to continue Jack's mentoring of Christian leaders. Reading this book is your opportunity to also be mentored by Jack.

This book of letters is named *The Heart of a Servant Leader*, because I believe that they reveal Jack's heart of love for God and his people. As you read these letters, I would like you to feel as if you are having a heart-to-heart talk with an older, wiser Christian who has experienced the struggles that come with Christian leadership, yet is still filled with the hope and joy that come from knowing Jesus. In that spirit, I would recommend that you pour yourself a cup of tea (or coffee) and sit down for a heart-to-heart talk with Jack Miller.

Yours because of Jesus,
Barbara Miller Juliani

Part 1

Motivation for Serving:
The Glory of God

*What I finally came to as I walked and prayed for you
is the old, old story of getting the gospel clear in your
own hearts and minds, making it clear to others, and
doing it with only one motive—the glory of Christ.*

The letters in this section emphasize how important it is for
the Christian leader to be motivated by the glory of God. This was
a subject that Jack talked and thought about a lot. Right after he
became a Christian, he spent the summer living in a fire lookout
that was on top of a mountain in Oregon. During his time alone,
he read the Book of Romans and meditated on the gospel of grace
and how it brought God glory. The sunsets on the mountain were
spectacular. In describing them he said, "It was a glory road of amber,
orange, and yellow that started in heaven and reached my lookout."[1] He felt the same way about the gospel of Jesus that he was

1. Letter to Rose Marie Miller circa 1950.

17

studying in Romans. For him it was a glory road that came from heaven, reached into his mind and heart, and taught him to live only for the glory of God.

It was his desire to live and work for the glory of God that led Jack to become a church planter and a pastor. But after twenty years of full-time Christian ministry, Jack found out how easy it is to lose that essential focus on God's glory—and to end up depressed and burned out. He faced this kind of crisis in the spring of 1970 while he was pastoring a small church in Bucks County, Pennsylvania, and teaching practical theology at Westminster Seminary in nearby Glenside, a suburb of Philadelphia. He had gradually become frustrated in both jobs. It seemed to him that neither the church members nor the seminary students were changing in the ways that they should, and he did not know how to help them. In desperation he resigned from both positions and then spent the next few weeks too depressed to do anything except cry.

Gradually during those weeks it became clear to him that the reason for his anger and disappointment was his own wrong motivation for ministry. He realized that instead of being motivated only by God's glory, he was hoping for personal glory and the approval of those he was serving. He said that when he repented of his pride, fear of people, and love of their approval, his joy in ministry returned, and he took back his resignations from the church and the seminary.[2]

Instead of quitting ministry he took his family on an extended sabbatical to Spain and spent his time there studying the missionary promises of God through the whole Bible. He spent long hours tracing the promises of grace for sinners in Isaiah, Ezekiel, Jeremiah, Joel, Habakkuk, and Zechariah. Then he looked at how they were fulfilled by God in the New Testament. As he studied, he was captured by the vastness of God's promise to fill His kingdom with people from every tribe and nation. He also realized in a new way that

2. *Outgrowing the Ingrown Church* (Grand Rapids: Ministry Resources Library, 1986), p. 21.

the promise of the Holy Spirit's help, comfort, and encouragement was not just for the disciples of long ago; it was for every Christian. He went back to the United States full of hope, not in his abilities, but in the power of the Holy Spirit to be with him, to change his heart, and to use him to bring all kinds of people into the kingdom of God.

This marked a turning point in Jack's life and ministry. Not only did he go back to work with a renewed sense of purpose, he also had a new freedom to live and work only for God's glory. It was out of this time of repentance and renewal that NLPC was founded and missionary work was begun. But Jack never forgot how far he had drifted from his focus on God's glory, and he never forgot how that affected his life and ministry. So, in his mentoring of leaders, he often returned to the theme of God's glory. He knew that if they did not start in ministry with the right motivation they would eventually end up as he did—full of anger and bitterness.

In this group of letters Jack was writing to missionaries and pastors. Some of them were on the mission field, one couple was considering whether or not to leave the mission field, and another couple (his daughter and son-in-law, Bob and Keren Heppe) was deciding whether or not they should become missionaries. To each person Jack emphasized the necessity of living, working, and serving with only God's glory in view.

He wrote in a letter to a young missionary couple in Uganda, "What I finally came to as I walked and prayed for you is the old, old story of getting the gospel clear in your own hearts and minds, making it clear to others, and doing it with only one motive—the glory of Christ." Jack believed that this was the essence of serving God, and that when you begin with desiring the glory of God the "how-tos" of bringing Him glory will become clear.

He repeated this message in slightly different ways in each letter in this section. To the couple who was struggling with whether or not to leave the mission field, to his daughter and her husband, and to Jack's copastor who was mentoring missionaries, his message was the same: begin with desiring the glory of God, and everything else will become clear. Jack wrote to Bob Heppe, his son-in-law, "Honestly, I find it hard to believe that anyone who wants His glory will be long without some clues as to how to express that glory in a form of service to Him."

Jack began his Christian life captured by the glory of God, and he learned as a failed pastor and professor that living for God's glory is the only motivation that can sustain a life of service to God and others. He said this to one of his copastors at NLPC: "The thought that came to me was the power that comes when our vision is centered on the glory and praise of God. Practically I believe that this glory comes into its own when we self-consciously make it our anchor for what we are doing." The glory of God became Jack's motivation and his anchor through many years of doing ministry. He believed that there was no other anchor or motivation worth having.

The Glory of Christ Is the Motive for Getting the Gospel Clear

To a young couple who were one of the first missionary families sent from World Harvest Mission (WHM) to the Ruwenzori Mountains in Uganda.

March, 1984

Dear Tom and Joanne,

Today is the third day of spring here in Philadelphia, but the weather has in it the sharp fingers of February rawness. But I managed to get my walk through Jenkintown completed anyway, about a mile and a half. While I was walking, I prayed for you and meditated on how to pray more effectively for you. Yesterday we had good prayer all morning and brought you all before the Lord more than once. Then in the evening I had more prayer. But still to pray effectively is more than any human being can work up. I am convinced that prayer, effective praying, is a divine gift that comes while praying. Sounds odd, prayer comes while you are praying? But I think that really there is praying which gets results and that is fine, but then there is praying that gets into the center of God's will and gets bigger results and also leaves the soul at peace, satisfied that God's will has been contacted and God has responded with peace in the heart.

What I finally came to as I walked and prayed for you is the old, old story of getting the gospel clear in your own hearts and minds, making it clear to others, and doing it with only one motive—the glory of Christ. Getting the glory of Christ before your eyes and keeping it there—is the greatest work of the Spirit that I can imagine. And there is no greater peace, especially in the times of treadmill-like activity, than doing it all for the glory of the Lord Jesus. Think much of the Savior's suffering for you on that dreadful cross, think much of your sin that provoked such suffering, and then enter by faith into the love that took away your sin and guilt, and then give your work your best. Give it your heart out of gratitude for a tender, seeking, and patient Savior. Make every common task shine with the radiance of Christ. Then every event becomes a shiny glory moment to be cherished—whether you drink tea or try to get the verb forms of the new language.

Put quality in your lives then. In the sloppy world in which we live, try to make the most ordinary things have a special touch from God. I think Florence Allshorn used to serve tea in good silver up in Busoga district when all was primitive. Not so much as a touch of home, but as a touch of heaven.

So I have prayed that God would give you grace to seek quality in all that you do and seek to promote quality in others. We have prayed this for your language studies, for your preaching and teaching, and for your whole way of living. Believe me this is no easy battle. You will find in the world of Uganda, as in the world here in the States, "getting by" is the dominant tone. Of course, I know we are all glad just to get by with many things. Some things merit only getting by, but don't give in to it as the rule. Keep up the standards.

I'm also praying that God will give you some "quality people" with whom to work and some "quality converts." I don't mean flashy and razzle-dazzle people. Uganda and the U.S. always seem to have plenty of that sort. But I'm thinking of the solid people like John in the Kampala painting company. He's a real example of how Christ can take a raw pagan out of the marketplace and give you a life that shines for Jesus through honesty and hard work. I just glorify Jesus for such a brother!

Tom, two pieces of counsel: always try to be daring but don't be in a hurry. I'll let you think about that. Another thought: if you don't like what's going on in Uganda, wait a week. It'll be the opposite.

Rose Marie has had much physical weakness of late, for about the last two months. We are watching her diet and sending her to the doctor on Monday. She spent nine days in Florida resting with Jill and Kimberly [daughter-in-law and granddaughter] and got some rest with me when I attended a seminar at Ventnor on "Evangelism and the Poor" by Vinay Samuel.

But spiritually Rose Marie has continued to grow, really very encouraging. I think all the wear and tear of the last year have begun to catch up with her. She has closed down her Thursday afternoon Bible class. The results have been great, but my feeling is that a good foundation has been laid for these women and now they can seize the opportunity to build on it.

Naturally we are most eager to hear reports of your trip west and to learn how you are settling in. We take up an offering at New Life this week to help with your costs. . . . Greetings to Zeke and James. We also pray for them.

In Christ's love,
Jack Miller

The Power That Comes When God's Glory Is Our Vision

When Jack first became a Christian, he read an appeal from a pastor in Ireland for Christians to come and preach the gospel there. He was very moved by that appeal and decided that one day he would go to Ireland as a missionary. He was never able to be there on a full-time basis, but NLPC began sending short-term mission teams to Ireland in 1977. From that small beginning grew a team of missionaries that World Harvest Mission sent out. This letter is to a pastor who is preparing to go to Ireland to encourage the team of missionaries there.

April, 1984

Dear Steve,

This is our first morning at Ventnor by the sea. Our hope was for warmer weather, but this morning we awoke to gaze upon a new blanket of snow. But we praise God who is sovereign over all weather and rejoice that already His gracious Spirit is refreshing us. This day we began by reading Psalm 115—the great "Not unto us, O LORD, not unto us, but unto thy name give glory." It was health to our souls to renew our vision of God's glory as the great reason for our being here in the world and the inspiration for every task given us by the King.

We had prayer this morning for you and your journey to Ireland. We also had in view your request that we pray that you be a leader with vision. We are praying that for you more and more.

The thought that came to me was the power that comes when our vision is centered on the glory and praise of God. Practically I believe that this glory comes into its own when we self-consciously make it our anchor for what we are doing. What I would really urge upon you is to dedicate this trip to God for His glory, that God would be honored during it by a marvelous demonstration of His grace and saving power.

I say that in the light of the depression that seems again and again to gather over things Irish—and probably in some degree over our team. What we need is a greater vision of Christ increasing until He has changed Ireland and then to give God no rest until this takes place. I think that means a new call for prayer for Ireland, the land where Christ's name has been shamed and is being shamed.

What I would stress, then, is that a man of vision gets his vision only in and through prayer. Only prayer with a goal of glorifying God at any cost can give God's vision to a man or a woman. I covet this for myself—and for you.

I would encourage you to remember that such a desire for vision is already a gift of the Lord, and what He has begun to give He wants to increase. Hindrances there are. One of these happens to be reservations in our hearts about the nature and character of His will for our lives. We secretly suspect that His will might be more demanding, more crucifying of our desires, than we can handle. But daily surrender to His will as you pray, and it will bring a freedom from anxiety that you cannot believe.

Recently I was caught up in a spirit of anxiety. Nothing would shake it. But I simply gave myself to thanking and praising God for everything I could think of. Result? As I increasingly gave Him the glory for all His great works, my faith recovered from its near death and I ended up walking on water and singing a song as I went. Praise and glorying are mysterious visitations of the King and the moving of His kingdom.

The times we have spent together as a staff recently have been profitable and confirmed me in the conclusion that Christ is in our midst. Praise the Lord for the wisdom God has given you for doing His will. I commend you for your really seeking and learning from God during these past months as we worked through the selection of a new staff member. I think you have handled matters very well indeed. Thanks for being my good friend.

Again, you go to Ireland with our prayers.

> Most warmly in Christ,
> Jack

Discovering Our True Motivation: God's Glory or Our Self-Interest?

To a young missionary couple who is unsure whether they should stay on a mission field.

September, 1984

Dear Jim and Anne,

Warm greetings to both of you in the Lord Jesus Christ! You have been much in our prayers over the past two years. Too, you are in our hearts as we have prayed for you during this time of re-examination of your role. . . . I was a bit concerned that you might quickly return without thinking through the issues of your call—or lack of call to

26

that land. But your correspondence to Charles [another pastor who had been mentoring Jim and Anne] has been encouraging to me.

In what way? Mainly in your growth in self-knowledge and honesty. One evidence of the Spirit's presence in our lives is our seeing where we really are and admitting it to others. One cannot make progress in life or ministry without being a forthright and forthcoming person. Probably each one of us has tons of kinky motives and loads of self-deception—or at least we do until we begin to ask the Holy Spirit to search us out. So, I am really pleased at your openness with Charles and encourage you to continue in it. That is of the Holy Spirit, I do believe. I was pleased as I reflected upon it that you made your innermost thoughts known to him. Believe me, we don't love you the less for that. We accept you just as you are, just as we want you to accept us just as we are.

I am in accord with what Charles has written to you. He is a wise brother, and I have full confidence in him. Would I add anything to his advice? Perhaps a thought or two along the lines mentioned above. It's vital that you not stay to please Charles, or me, or anyone else. That would please us, but the crucial thing to get hold of is your own identity and call. You can make decisions only out of that kind of grip on reality. So don't stay just to please us, but only because you believe the Lord of the church wants you there to do something for him.

Now I do not think such a disclosure of His will is gained on the cheap. It requires prayer and fasting and some earnest and painful heart-searching. When I do this, I ask the Holy Spirit to search out my innermost heart motives. Guess what I often discover? That my motives are usually mixed. Especially I am likely to discover I am not doing things for God's glory and out of delight and fellowship with Him, but out of half-concealed self-interest and self-glorying. I do not mean that no heavenly motives go into the mix of my inward thoughts, but often because I can detect some good motives in myself, I feel that this is the last and only word. Don't believe it about me or

Charles or yourselves. The scriptural emphasis on our encounter with the flesh needs to be taken seriously. I am thinking of some of the underscoring of things like "ambitions" in Galatians 5. It's there in all of us and cannot be ignored.

So especially ask yourself: what is my concern for the glory of God in my life? How much am I led by concern for my own comfort and feeling of well-being? Do I witness out of enjoyment of God? Do I love people—not just on the mission field, but people? Am I willing to imitate the Good Shepherd and die for them? Do I really know the power of the Holy Spirit as I daringly witness? Do I really confront the lost with heaven and hell? Am I repenting regularly?

Once you wrestle over a period of time with these questions, you can much more easily decide whether you should be [on this field] for a longer period of time. Take great care not to be hasty. "He that is hasty in spirit exalts folly." But it just may not be God's will for you to be there as long as we might like. But the reason must be related to His purpose for your life. You might decide that your calling is not to be there because of a revelation of Christ's will to you. This is not to say at all that I am encouraging you to come home sooner, but to get you to put the matter of your whole personal relationship to the Father before God and to decide based upon a clear dependence upon Him in the light of your careful evaluation of your gifts, calling, motives, etc. In other words, to quote my dear wife Rose Marie, "It's important not to decide hastily like an orphan in flight, but like a son who knows the Father's unconditional love."

I think I also need to apologize to you both for my failure to help you more. Actually, here at New Life we see that we have been far too casual in some of our training and preparation for ministry. I don't say this to run ourselves down or because I am guilt-ridden about it. I am not at all, but I think the "flesh" in me kept me back from giving better leadership to you and your ministry. So forgive me please.

Let me assure you how much more seriously we are beginning to take this whole enterprise. All of us here are seeing it as a much more demanding undertaking than hitherto. We also see how much we needed to have much more prayer behind it. Let me counsel you, too, to pray much more. Pray and keep praying and then pray some more.

You are in our hearts. Very much so.

Most warmly in Christ,

Jack

Surrendering Our Will Reveals God's Glory

These next two letters are written to Jack's son-in-law and daughter who are deciding whether they should become missionaries to Ireland. They eventually become missionaries to Asians in London.

April, 1986

Dear Bob,

Greetings in Christ, dear brother! I was very happy to talk with you on the telephone when Keren called. It is my hope that the specialist will find nothing when he examines me on Wednesday. But as Rose Marie put it when she had a similar procedure, "Whatever is there is there, and my trust is in God to heal me if that is needed. So why worry." I can learn from that undaunted spirit.

29

I also wanted to add a few thoughts to our conversation. My sense of things is that God is speaking to you, and using your need to make a decision on future direction to impart to you a deeper knowledge of Himself. If I understood you aright, you are wondering why you don't have more of a sense of call to a work for God, whatever it may be. Certainly that is a good question.

Perhaps my thoughts may not be all that helpful. You can sift them to see if they have any worth. But when I find myself without guidance from God, one of the first things I check out is the question whether or not I want guidance from God. That is often the big issue for me. Put simply, why should God give me guidance when my mind is closed to some aspect of His will?

I may have reservations in my heart about a path that I suspect He may want me to take. Or I may fear that He wants me to undertake a work that is beyond my capacity to handle. I look at myself and say, "It is impossible for me to do this thing. I lack the gifts for it, or at least I lack the sanctification that it requires." Tied in with this can also be a fleshly love of comfort and honor, or the security of a life where it is clear that I have things somewhat under control. In other words, my attitude is: "Don't disturb me, God. Don't call me to walk on water or something else that is contrary to good sense."

But how do I disentangle myself from conflicting and confused aspirations, some of them partly unconscious? You were a big help to me at the time you were so sick with the kidney problem. You did not see God's hand and presence until you surrendered your life and your healing to Him—and sued for healing on the basis of His glory and not a self-centered desire to get well. That really helped me. Indeed, I especially remembered it when God left me helpless at the first onset of my heart attack. I found it very liberating to surrender my will to His and commit myself to live for others, not for self, and in this way to reveal His glory.

Honestly, I find it hard to believe that anyone who wants His glory will be long without some clues as to how to express that glory in a form of service to Him. So—back to the basics.

Ask yourself, what is there in my generation that Keren and I can do that perhaps no one else can do? I think you can see that as you enter more fully into the joy of the Lord, which always accompanies those who live for His glory.

In the past your faith and perseverance have often been an inspiration to me. Expect that the Lord who has shepherded you so faithfully in the past will do so in the future.

Much love,

Dad

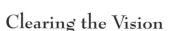

Clearing the Vision

To Jack's daughter Keren as she and her husband are praying about going on the mission field.

April, 1986

Dear Keren,

Greetings through the grace of the King! I have missed you and your team here in Malaga. Give Gillian and Natie a hug for me, and tell Gillian I have not forgotten about our plans to have lunch together

31

in Dublin. Lord willing, we shall have a fine lunch together. There is even a McDonalds there if she wants a hamburger.

The weather continues to be on the cool side here; the Spanish say that the coldness of March is a historical first. No one can remember it being like this. Actually it's not all that cold, only when it gets windy or rains a bit. Your mother has been praying for warmer weather, and now that the land has had an unprecedented soaking I expect her prayers will be heard. I think of it this way. If the land here and in Morocco needs the rain, we tourists can put up with some coolish weather for a while. You wouldn't believe Morocco between Casablanca and Fez. The valleys are just splendid with green grass and flowers. The verdant land is singing the praises of its Maker, and so shall we in fullness when Jesus brings in the big springtime of His new world. This old world is such a mess when you get to know it: so much hatred in it, so much revenge, so much greed, and an almost endless supply of human foolishness. It makes it a mystery that we mortals cling to it with such strong fingers when we are really holding on to winter's fog, mist, damp, rot, and mud. Lord, give me a longer view. Help me to see springtime in Your return. Help me to long for the green land to come!

Yet in the meantime before He comes or I go to be with Him, my prayer is that I may fulfill His purpose for me. I want to serve Him with my whole heart in my generation, and do my part to further the interests of His love working in the world.

Well, as you and Bob struggle to discern His will, there is nothing that can clear the vision faster than the discovery that all things are temporary and so am I. So what I do with my life should center on working with matters that will remain unshaken at the return of the Lord Jesus. Get a good view of the temporariness of life and—believe it or not—you will enjoy it more. When we get our footsies so mired down in time that we think it is eternal, we become subject to all the ups and downs, the vagaries, of time. Our loves are so easily disturbed because we are loving only what is changing and finally will be replaced altogether. But to see this temporariness of many of our dreams isn't bad. We cannot remain adolescents forever. God's will is for us to become adults, and the heart of being an adult is the capacity to put away the toys and put on the love and joy and peace of Christ. The mind of Christ brings such quietness where otherwise the life would be ruled by discontent and all kinds of defenses and ambitions.

But then Christ gives the surrendered Christian good dreams, beautiful visions of His glory working in lives, and gives us a simple trust that He will grant us the deepest desires of our hearts. Think of how He will answer our prayers for Gillian and Natie. As we agree in prayer for them we can expect them in turn to become images of Christ, renewed by the inbreathing of the Holy Spirit. What a comfort that must be to you!

Think too how your being in Christ confers on you as a wife and mother, as a colaborer with Bob, an inexpressible worth and dignity. You are the daughter of the Highest. You are of the royal line through adoption. . . . Amazing grace!

We do miss all of you here, and look forward to our reunion in Ireland. It is a privilege to have you for a daughter. You bring much joy to my heart. Keep the faith.

> Much love,
> Dad

Part 2

The Basics of Serving:
Faith, Humility, and Prayer

Matters of the Heart

Let me urge upon you the importance of cultivating faith if you are to be able to walk in love and spiritual power. Without faith it is impossible to please God, but those who believe are given more grace than they can handle. Believing is to expect God to be with you and change you and change others. Therefore expect great things from God; attempt great things for God.

In this section Jack's letters expand on the theme of being motivated by God's glory by considering how this is expressed in the life of a Christian leader. For Jack, living for God's glory meant first acknowledging the real Head of the church—Jesus Christ—and then going on to do "Christ's work Christ's way."

35

Jack believed and taught that doing Christ's work meant sharing the gospel with the lost. He said this about the Great Commission: "The command to go to the nations with the gospel is not one command among many, it is the master command of Jesus the Master. If we do not obey this command, we are living out of accord with our whole reason for being in this world."[1] In many of the letters in this section Jack discusses the Great Commission, calling it the "master purpose" of the church.

But Jack also thought that Christian leaders were often in danger of attempting to do this great work of Christ out of their own strength and for their own glory. He knew this was a danger because this is how he spent the first twenty years of his Christian life. Before his ministry crisis in 1970 Jack had dedicated his life to doing Christ's work. When he became a Christian at the age of nineteen he started by sharing the gospel with anyone he could persuade to listen, went on to seminary to get theological training, planted a small church in California, and then moved to Pennsylvania where he was teaching and preaching.

But despite all that hard work for Christ, he saw few tangible results. This was underlying the anger and bitterness he felt when he resigned from teaching and pastoring. Through this painful time Jack realized that not only his motivation for ministry had been wrong, but he also had been relying on the wrong person to do ministry—himself. After studying the promises of God on his sabbatical, he understood more clearly that the work of Christ was way too big for him to accomplish in his own strength. As he reflected on his own ministry, he came to understand that it was his pride and self-reliance that was keeping him from having a significant part in this great work of Christ.

As he studied the fulfillment of God's promises in the gospel, he noticed that he had missed the most important qualification for entrance into the kingdom of God—being poor in spirit. He saw

1. See Appendix on p. 307.

that doing Christ's work in Christ's way meant giving up all dependence on himself, acknowledging how poor in spirit he was, and then relying exclusively on Jesus and the gift of His Spirit. That is why the letters in this section keep returning to the Christian leader's need for personal humility, vital faith, and constant prayer. These were the concrete ways that God had provided for the poor in spirit to be full of His Spirit. Without these basic qualities there could be no power in life or ministry.

Jack saw in his own life that growth in these basics happened only as he admitted every day that he was a desperate sinner in constant need of the grace of God. As he studied what the Bible taught about faith and humility, he understood that repentance is not a once-in-a-lifetime experience, but a whole way of life. It is this life of ongoing repentance that the Spirit will use to bring faith and humility to the heart of the leader.

Jack's letters reflected this emphasis as he modeled repentance to young leaders by acknowledging his sins and asking them to pray for him. He also challenged them to have lives characterized by ongoing repentance. He did not think this was optional in the Christian leader's life; without daily repenting for sins, he knew that Christ's work would not go forward. He said in a letter to a young missionary, "A pastor really needs to be broken before God every day, or he will break up the church of God with his willfulness or let it slip into spiritual death through his sloth."

Even though Jack often preached and wrote about the necessity of repentance, he did not believe that Christians should spend all their time thinking about their sins. Instead he taught that knowing yourself as a desperate sinner should drive the Christian to a deeper dependence on Christ. For Jack, knowing Jesus as your friend was what the life of faith was all about. He wrote in a letter to Richard, a pastor at a nearby church, that knowing "your Friend (Jesus)" is the most important thing in life—even more important than knowing your sins. Jack knew that there was no power to change unless the repentant sinner was attached to Jesus by faith.

When Jack talked about understanding the gospel, this is what he meant—knowing that you are a great sinner whose only hope is to be found in Jesus Christ.

In this context it was only natural that, for Jack, prayer was an essential element in the Christian's life of humility and faith. To do "Christ's work Christ's way" was impossible using human resources; the leader must be connected to Christ through prayer. Jack said in a letter to Bill, a young missionary in Africa, "Remember the only real leader you have is Jesus Christ. . . . To get to Him you need to pray." Prayer was how he confessed his sins and how he asked for the Spirit to do what he could not—apply the message of the cross to his heart and to the hearts of those around him.

Prayer became central to Jack's life and ministry after 1970. NLPC began as a prayer meeting in his home in 1973, and through the years Jack kept one day a week set aside for prayer. He also made it his habit to pray as he met with people. He rarely said, "I will pray for you," without stopping and doing so on the spot. Then he would go on to ask for prayer for himself, for the church, and for his family.

But Jack thought of prayer as more than praying with and for other Christians. Instead, like repentance, he thought of prayer as a whole way of living. He said in another letter to Bill, "Vital corporate prayer . . . involves more than gathering as we do at New Life Church each Thursday morning for our five hours of praise, adoration, intercession, and petition. It is really, on our human side, a whole way of life as a group of shepherds and Christians, a way of constantly surrendering to Jesus Christ, to be freed of all human nearsightedness so that the life of the Spirit can flow through us with freedom."

Jack spent the first half of his Christian life attempting to do Christ's work Jack's way, and he spent the last half of his Christian life repenting of this tendency and asking the Spirit daily for the faith and humility to do Christ's work Christ's way. This is what he wanted to pass on to the young leaders he wrote to. He saw in them the same tendency to live for themselves and for their own glory that he was constantly fighting. His letters in this section are meant to encourage them to humbly rely on Jesus in every part of their lives and ministry. He knew that there would be no lasting fruit in their ministries if they did not daily learn the basics of doing Christ's work Christ's way.

The Marks of True Spiritual Revival

Jack first became interested in going to Africa when Ugandan refugees arrived at NLPC in 1975. They were fleeing Idi Amin, a cruel dictator who had killed many Ugandans and among them thousands of Christians. They challenged the church to expand its prayer meetings into all-night sessions and to pray with them that Amin would be overthrown. When Amin was deposed in 1979, the Ugandan Christians asked NLPC to send people and resources to Uganda to evangelize and be a part of the rebuilding of the country. Jack ministered there by preaching in the marketplace, helping to paint rooms in the orphanage, and teaching the gospel and the doctrines of grace. He also taught the Ugandans about the Presbyterian form of church government. When they heard this they said, "We need this so that we don't all act like kings!" This letter is written to a young Ugandan pastor that Jack had mentored. He had shared with Jack about a revival that had taken place in his village.

June, 1982

Dear Brother Jacob,

Thank you for your recent letter about God's blessing on your "bush prayer fellowship." It sounds like the Holy Spirit is doing a gracious work in your lives together, and I give the Lord Jesus all the glory for this. There is nothing more freeing than taking time to be alone with God and giving the sovereign King an invitation to subdue our proud and restless spirits.

About a dozen years ago, several Christian men and I went away for a period of prayer and fasting, and I believe God used that time to begin a new work of grace in my life. The full results didn't appear for a couple of years, because God took His time in showing me the depths of my sin, but He sure did, and was it powerful and humbling and renewing. I had been so busy in ministry that I had lost sight of God's Word and Spirit and desperately needed a conviction of sin that would lead me to see anew the power and glory of Christ's atonement.

One of my problems was a combination of busyness and self-pity. I wasn't studying the Word enough and was not bold enough in discipling men, really getting down to their sins. Too, I was all filled up with pride and conceit and didn't know it. Really, Hebrews is right. There is "a deceitfulness of sin" which "hardens the heart" and makes us think everything is just fine when in reality we are living for our own glory and praise. I became heartily ashamed of myself, and as a result God gave me a true awakening, and people were converted on every hand. It was out of this working that God saved Bob Heppe [a son-in-law who had been in Africa with Jack] and many others.

So I would urge you to test this awakening among the brothers and sisters along similar lines. If it results in a deeper conviction of sin, true humility, growth in love for one another, and joy and clarity in proclaiming the cross, then you can be sure that the Holy Spirit has sent this work. Outward signs of revival can mean many things. Some come out of our own emotions and frustrations and do not mean that the Holy Spirit has done a permanent work. I have seen people—and I know you have—who felt that they had the Spirit and didn't need to

41

study the Word. Never let people think that is a true filling with the Spirit. It just isn't. A true work leads men into the Word, gives a very tender conscience about obedience to God's will, and much humility. I suspect that what may happen in such circumstances is that the Spirit begins a work and then we become proud of His working and quench Him without knowing we have done so. I know that I have done this. What a danger there is in human pride! Pray for me on that matter. I long for a truly humble heart, because I know that God dwells in such a heart. I love Jesus very much and want Him to live in a clean, humble dwelling within me.

I also want to thank you for your prayers for me. Nothing could be clearer than that what has happened to me has come in answer to many prayers, and I am sure you have been interceding much for me and the church here. I want to list these answers for your encouragement:

1. My faith is much stronger and my ministry is much bolder and yet more tender.
2. The preaching has been very searching, convicting of sin and bringing to bear the power of the gospel.
3. My organization and use of my time has greatly improved. I am actively discipling about twelve men every Thursday morning.
4. My knowledge of people and the will of God has deepened, and I have grown some in love and patience for my wife, Rose Marie.
5. Rose Marie has grown a good deal in her knowledge of the power of faith and in doing the will of God in full surrender.
6. Both of us have improved health and more vigor, though we still need more prayer for this.
7. People are being saved here. Praise God!

In the church as a whole here is what is beginning to happen:

1. New growth in leaders. . . .
2. New daring in planning. We are now expecting to have at least five couples come to Africa over a two-year period.
3. Finances are rapidly beginning to improve. . . .
4. New zeal in our whole mission and evangelism program.

You also have my prayers as a dear band of beloved brothers and sisters in Christ. We love you in Jesus.

In Him,

Jack

The Only Real Leader You Have Is Jesus Christ

To a young missionary in Uganda who is just beginning his work there.

August, 1985

Dear Bill,

Just a few quick thoughts for you, dear brother. Remember first that I love you and keep right on loving you. We all have you in our hearts. Not because of your faithful work—which is truly wonderful—but because you belong to us in Jesus. You are first His work, and we praise Him for that.

My second thought is to make sure you are enjoying yourself and not taking your work too seriously. You don't have anything to prove to us or the world. The work is finished at Calvary, and that work alone has unlimited meaning and value. Keep your focus there. And then read Robert Ludlum and/or go on vacation.

My third thought is help others relax and enjoy the work. Like the American Express TV ad, "Relax, American Express is on the way." The checks will be replaced, eh? as we Ugandans say.

Fourth, major in giving thanks for what has been accomplished and don't spend more than one-half hour looking at your sins. Keep the praise constant. Imagine, in a little over two years a green mission has fielded a whole new team in Uganda and is now fielding another in Ireland. Amazing, really!

Fifth, do some evangelism with someone every week. Watch out for the saying "There is a lion in the streets, and therefore nothing can be done today." Don't wait till it is perfect, just go. Jason White [a retired executive who had been working with Jack and the staff at New Life] tells the story of the young executive who replaced the veteran head of the corporation board and asked the veteran the secret of his success. The older man replied, "Good decisions." The younger man said, "Fine, how do I make good decisions?" The older man replied, "Bad decisions." Bear with me if I have told you that before, but no question we have to make our share of mistakes and learn how to turn failure into training for making better decisions.

Sixth, remember the only real leader you have is Jesus Christ. Unless you are daily taught of Him you will not be able to make the right decisions. To get to Him you need to pray, but it needs to be prayer of a unique quality. You can pray all night and all day and still not be in touch with His will. Prayer is not full and effective unless it adds up to our learning to wait upon the Lord for Him to make known His will. He needs to break down our tendency to cry out in prayer, "Your will be done," and then to get up and still try to impose our will on circumstances.

Finally, remember that almost any time you feel the need of a good confab with me we can meet in Switzerland or London and wrestle through issues that burden you. That is a sincere offer, and one you should take me up on when the need arises, for you do have some tough issues before you on many an occasion, and I wish to be responsive to your need to talk some things over.

In general, here is a way I would suggest we proceed. The smaller decisions really are yours and the team's. The main thing is to try to hold to the plan. But suppose the plan needs major modification. The thing for you and Ed [a missionary Bill was working with] to do is, in cooperation with the team on most occasions, draw up a proposal and get it to me and the leadership here.

My only real concern about your working with other churches and groups is simply that you take the time beforehand to get to know the territory, wait on the Lord, and don't form any hasty covenants with the Gibeonites. The goal of the work is to establish churches that hopefully will be faithfully pastored after you leave and not put into the hands of the hirelings. Compared to that value, money is worth nothing. We must love the dear sheep for whom Christ died and not, if at all possible, leave them to the tender mercies of hirelings or wolves. But how to fulfill this goal is not so easy. My feeling is that as you wait on the Lord, and cultivate people in a gracious and respectful manner, over a period of time you will discern the spirits—who is open and teachable and who wants merely to bring our team into a Babylonian captivity, to paraphrase Ralph Winter.

We are still praying that you will be able soon to work out regular itineration into the mountains—even if you have to walk more than you ever dreamed. Keep plugging away.

So you have many of my thoughts here. God bless you and yours. Other letters will contain news and updates.

Most affectionately in Christ,

Jack Miller

Christ Plants Churches through Prayer

To the same young missionary in Uganda. This letter shares many of Jack's thoughts on the connection between church planting and prayer. Jack believed that many churches were doomed from the start because of the prayerlessness of their leaders.

January, 1986

Dear Bill,

Tomorrow I fly on to the U.S. and leave Ireland behind. It has been a delightful time, and I do not know when I have found a warmer welcome here in this dear land of chilly weather and warm hearts. I do believe that I have found a new openness to Christ's gospel here. For instance, Wednesday morning, Richard [a missionary working in Ireland] and I were waiting near a pool in a shopping mall and struck up a conversation with a young unemployed Irishman named Sean. We talked for about an hour concerning Christ and His salvation. He was willing to make a commitment, but I suggested that he wait until he had studied the booklet "A New Life." I wanted Sean to be persuaded by Christ and not by the words and personalities of Richard and me. It was obvious that he had a hunger for God, but he needed to find Christ in the quietness of his own life. Actually, in evangelism we stand before the heart's door and knock, but then we must be prepared to wait until the Holy Spirit moves the man to open that door to the inner self and welcome Christ into the living room.

Today while surveying Dublin to decide upon our outreach location with Richard, John, and Dave, I shared some thoughts on church planting with them. You may have heard these ideas before, but let me take this opportunity to focus on these concepts more sharply in this letter. The basic idea is that release for the leader (or leaders) comes through doing Christ's work Christ's way. As mentioned in my previous letter, Christ is the exclusive Head of the church and has His own methods for planning and developing congregations. To ignore His methods is to put the leader's work into a straitjacket and to generate frustrations and tension of the wrong sort in the leader's inner life.

The beating heart of Christ's planting of churches is found in corporate prayer. It is through corporate intercession that the leader and the team of shepherds find release from fears, misconceptions, prejudices, pride, and self-will. This release comes as Christ Himself visits them. He makes them one in heart and mind as they pray together. What are they seeking? For God to work in others, of course, but as a presupposition of His working they *must* be seeking a manifestation of Christ's presence in their own hearts and lives.

An example of this working through praying together can be seen in the unity Christ gave us as we prayed during our two weeks in Nairobi. At the end of our time, we were all thrilled by the people converted in Kibera and Mukuruu, with the beautiful bonds established with the leaders of the church, and our agreement on evacuation policy and plans for missionary outreach to the Bakonjo and Bwambe peoples in the Ft. Portal area. But probably the greatest evidence of Christ's presence was His making us a fellowship of shepherds as we prayed together. This was the one big thing, a coming of Christ to His church, humbling us through corporate prayer so that He could express His personality through our oneness.

Such prayerful unity releases us from our crippling personal concerns and suspicious anxieties. It also releases Christ's spirit to work among us powerfully, to teach us to love one another with a love issuing from the heart of God. It gives us an attachment to one another in shared compassion, yet also gives us a detachment that enables us to see each other with clear-eyed honesty. We have a love for each other that does not overlook faults and sins, but leads us to accept correction and rebuke from one another. As we pray, correction from one another ceases to be a threat and becomes a way of release from the bondages of our small visions, self-centered motives, and lust for pre-eminence.

Personally, Bill, I cannot tell you how life-changing—how cleansing of the fountains of my life—I found our times of praise and intercession together there on the lawn of the Fairview Hotel. I also know that the communion service you led the evening of our arrival was one of the sweetest hours of my life. Though I was a little groggy from the long flight to Amsterdam, in my unconscious self, it became an unusual working of God, a fresh introduction to Christ's tender rule manifested in my willingness to surrender all things to His will.

You see, there is "prayer" and there is God-given prayer. The former is superficial, the work of orphans who may be religious people but are unwilling to surrender human independence to the leadership of Christ. God-given prayer and praise have as their essence a waiting on God, a willingness to be wrought upon by the hammer and the fire of the Almighty, until the chains of self-centered desires fall away from the personality, and the love of Christ becomes the deepest hunger of the inner life.

Dear brother, vital corporate prayer of the New Testament sort involves more than gathering as we do at New Life Church each Thursday morning for our five hours of praise, adoration, intercession, and petition. It is really, on our human side, a whole way of life as a group of shepherds and Christians, a way of constantly surrendering to Jesus Christ, to be freed of all human nearsightedness so that the life of the Spirit can flow through us with freedom. From God's side our constant seeking of His face is nothing less than the establishment of Christ's rule over us, His conquest of us, His equipping and empowering us to serve Him in a manner that we are ourselves miracles. I am thinking of an absolute trust in the Father's will, a childlike devotion to Jesus in love, and a humility which puts others first.

Such simplicity of devotion enables us to see our work with clear vision and to plan and act with sanity. It also enables us to bear with the routine of daily work, with the knowledge that many of our tasks are left half done and even those that are completed are highly imperfect. For prayer teaches us that we are sons of God with a Father who loves us not because we are perfect, but because we are in union with Christ. It opens our eyes to see that God is not a harsh Judge, but a loving Parent who is delighted even by our imperfect efforts to obey Him.

When I arrived in Amsterdam, I felt I had to gear up somehow for the Ireland ministry. I felt really alone as I boarded the flight for Dublin. Peter had already gone home from Nairobi, Steve left me in Amsterdam. I keenly missed the sweet embrace of Rose Marie. Then I remembered that you and the team in Kenya were praying for me. I also knew that Rose Marie and others at New Life had prayed for me the previous day in our home prayer meeting. Almost immediately I knew a release in my spirit, and I also began to pray for a mind of faith and a heart of love.

I arrived in Dublin with a tired body, but God did give me a strong spirit. Really extraordinary things began to happen: first, an honesty and openness took over among us, and the love of Christ dominated our times together. Then it became clear that personal bondages of a long-standing nature in the lives of members of the Ireland team began to be recognized and to fall away. Our hearts as a team were knit together in love.

The vision I held before the team in Ireland was that of the first few chapters of Acts. It is this part of Scripture that has done so much to influence my own thinking about Christ's headship and prayer. Actually, the book of Acts is the story of the acts of Christ done in history in response to the constant corporate prayer by the leaders of the church (Acts 1:1–8, 13–14; 2:1, 42; 3:1; 4:23–31). I pointed out to Richard, John, and Dave that the early chapters of Acts follow a clear pattern: first the church is pictured indoors where prayer prevails; then the church is pictured outdoors where the Spirit of Christ prevails through preaching and mighty deeds. I suggested to them that this should be our model for ministry.

So we began our week in Ireland with a time indoors where the Word and prayer prevailed. Then we saw the Word and the Spirit prevailing in all the issues of action that followed. One brief example will give you an idea how God worked in answer to your prayers and ours. Wednesday morning we had arranged to meet with Dave at a downtown shopping mall. We were hoping that Dave might get at least one of our three friends of the past to come. Since they have had some intense spiritual problems, we hardly expected all three of them to show up for lunch. Six months ago they certainly would not all have come. But at 12 o'clock there they all were and as delighted to see us as we were to see them.

To crown it all, Richard and I had started witnessing to Sean, the man we met at the pool in the mall while waiting for Dave to return. It turned out that he had been remarkably prepared for our encounter with him. He had studied four years with the Hare Krishna people and was left dissatisfied. Then about two weeks ago he started to read

Norman Vincent Peale's *The Power of Positive Thinking*. He liked Peale and enjoyed what seemed to be one more secular solution to his problems. But in the book he came across a verse that haunted him and faced him with the Christ-question. It was Philippians 4:13: "I can do all things through Christ who strengthens me."

He said, "That was my *first* thought about Christ, really thinking seriously about Him. Now you come and tell me all about Him. It must be God doing something—my meeting with you is like it had all been planned."

Certainly it had all been planned, and came about through much prayer. We see again what an unhurried freedom comes to us once we learn to wait on Christ to act. For that reason I did not encourage Sean to rush into a premature "decision" before he really understood what Christ was saying to him. Christ will move into his life soon!

It is fun to be a Christian.

In His name,

Jack

Most Problems Are Faith Problems

To a pastor who is disappointed both by his church and by his own ministry. He is struggling with his calling as a pastor and is considering leaving the ministry.

July, 1987

Dear Joe,

Warm greetings in Christ. We are now home in Jenkintown after our lengthy time in Europe. You will be glad to hear that Christ really put His hand on our time in Spain, our Switzerland conference, and the work in Ireland. We have almost completed a new book—entirely a gift of God's grace. You have also probably heard that Zondervan accepted *Come Back, Barbara.* This was a very encouraging answer to prayer. Thank you for your prayers for us and your financial support.

Your lengthy letter about your calling and your ministry finally reached us in Spain, and I have done a good deal of thinking about it. At first I didn't know what to reply since the issues you raised sound pretty complex. But as I kept going over it in my mind and prayed for you, I came to several conclusions that you are welcome to have for whatever they may be worth.

First, I would encourage you to take some special time away to go over the issues. I am thinking of a day of fasting and prayer where you are alone and you can put these issues before God. It appears to me that the answers to the problems that are confronting you can be found only in a meeting with the living God. From what you have said, the weaknesses in the church are many and complex and very discouraging. You also feel disappointed over lacks in your own ministry. You especially noted that after all these years of ministry, you don't know of anyone becoming a Christian through your work. I think all this needs to be searched out before the Lord. Looking back over my own life and ministry, I would say one of my greatest weaknesses has also been trying to figure things out on my own without taking the time to be alone with God and opening myself to what He wants to teach me.

Secondly, as I studied your letter, it seemed to come to me that God may be trying to heal some weakness in your life. I don't mean to impute to you all my weaknesses and sins, but I discovered that at bottom most problems are faith problems. For example, you don't usually have people converted unless you believe they are going to be converted. If you really, in your heart, don't expect people to be converted, usually they won't get converted. Therefore, I would urge upon you the importance of examining your faith. Please don't misunderstand; I know you are a man of faith, probably in many ways of stronger faith than mine. Nevertheless, ask yourself, "Do I witness with strong confidence that people to whom I speak will be converted? Do I preach with expectancy, believing that the Holy Spirit will regenerate hearts as I declare His Word?" Or, "Do I have secret feelings in my heart that God isn't going to use me? Do I have confidence that God really means the free offer of the gospel and wants to take people to His heart by saving them?"

Third, do you see the congregation by faith? Do you have a picture of the stubborn ones changed by grace as you pray—or have you mentally given up on some of them?

Fourth, closely allied to the problem of faith is the need to avoid focusing on secondary issues. Take church finances for example. If you take them too seriously, this awareness can cripple your ministry and work havoc with your faith. This may be a bit extreme on my part, but I have certainly found it liberating. I have always been willing to work part-time or full-time to support myself and my family. Probably some of this willingness stems from my own spirit of independence and this is not so good. But this willingness to support myself at least in part has had a beautifully liberating movement on my ministry. It has authenticated my faith to people and to my own conscience. From the bottom of my heart, I do not want to serve God because I am paid to do it. I am not sure how this applies in your situation, and I can only tell you what I would do in your situation. As it is necessary, I would get a part-time job to help support myself and do it gladly out of love. My reason is that finances just shouldn't be that important to me.

Fifth, at the same time, the church apparently needs to be taught and exhorted to have a stronger faith in the matters of finances. But this takes time and great patience. Sometimes you can't get people to see basic issues overnight. Also by pressing matters too hard and too soon you sometimes can make them worse. This is where the prayer and wisdom come in. You need wisdom to know when and how to deal with this financial matter in the church. My thought is that probably there are even deeper issues in the church. Issues of belief and unbelief and of stubbornness of heart. I think you ought to go after these issues before you go after the financial issues.

Sixth, you may also need to learn a deeper forgiveness for those who don't really concern themselves about your family's welfare, particularly in the matter of financial support. When the church doesn't act in faith in the area of finances and the pastor's salary is not met, then this brings deep hurt to the pastor and his wife, usually leading to an alliance away from the church. Guard against this with your whole heart. Forgive and forgive and forgive. Don't let your emotional life be controlled by the sin you see in others.

Finally you asked me to help you evaluate whether you were called to the pastorate. I can only share with you my impression, but my impression is that you are a good pastor, a good preacher, and you love the congregation. You are also a good discipler and work well with the elders. If that impression is correct, then you are called to the gospel ministry, and this severe testing is God's burning so that your faith will be made pure as gold. This doesn't necessarily mean that God is calling you to stay on at your church. I cannot know that for you. But it does seem to me that your gifts seem suited to the congregation and the community. You should also not overlook the possibility that you are under satanic attack and this is an issue of spiritual warfare.

Don't let Satan take you away from the church of God. Entreat more and more people to pray for you. Don't rest until you have at least twenty people who pray for you and your ministry daily. Ask them to pray for you to be able to lead five people to Christ in the next six months. Then put feet on your prayers and go out and find them. Use the gifts that God has given you to get to their conscience with the gospel. But you have got to work at this and work at it. Then when you have five new people in the congregation, it will help balance your budget.

Joe, I know how all of this must hurt and I really feel for you, and I pray much for you. I have you, dear brother, in my heart. Pray for me. I have the same struggles, the same weaknesses, and the same sins. We also have the same Holy Spirit and the same gospel of Christ.

Be daring. Take risks. God be with you.

Most cordially in Christ,

Jack Miller

Endurance Depends on a Life of Repentance and Praise

To a pastor of a church where Jack had recently spoken about renewal, using some of the themes from his book Outgrowing the Ingrown Church.

July, 1987

Dear Doug,

Warm greetings in Christ. Since our visit with you earlier in the year, we have kept you and the church in our prayers. It was so encouraging to be with you and to see your response to the gospel of Christ. The Lord has given you and many in your congregation a heart for God. That is a very precious thing. My spirit was really knit to yours in love as I prayed with you and saw your concern for God's glory. When I see that in a pastor's life, it makes it much easier for me to pray for him. . . . So do be encouraged.

One thing that can be hard for a pastor is just the enduring. After you are in the pastorate for a decade or more, you begin to see many weaknesses and sins in yourself, many failures in the ministry, and become increasingly aware of the resistance in God's people to change. As our insights grow, so do our temptations to increase in despair. As a friend in Christ I would urge you to resist that temptation. Frequently take time to look over the church, your ministry, your family, and give God thanks for each good thing you see. So not only endure in the ministry but blossom with thankfulness and praise. Perhaps you have heard me say this before, but I like to think of repentance and praise as allied to each other—both forms of sanity. Repentance is a return to God as my center. Praise is the lifting up of God in honor as my center. But to move out away from the center without repentance or praise is to be eccentric, irrational, and insane. But what a simple thing it is to humble the heart and return to sanity by repentance and praise.

By now you are probably beginning to think about our time with you. What was that all about? And how does the biblical teaching found in *Outgrowing the Ingrown Church* apply to us right where we are? Let me throw out a few suggestions, first for yourself and then for the church. To have power in your life as a pastor, it is supremely important that you make it a first order of business for the rest of your life not to do things to impress people or to gain a reputation or protect your reputation. It is very clear from the Gospels that Jesus is calling us to deny some basic things in our personality—things that need to die. Jesus says in Matthew 16:24 to deny yourself; take up your cross and follow me. And I think that means dying to our fleshly love of impressing people in this way for glory for ourselves.

I would like to tell you, Doug, that I have solved this problem once and for all; but this is a struggle that is intense, like tearing the flesh off of your own bones. Unless we resist with all our might, we fall again and again into our love of the praise of men or we are inwardly fearful of their disapproval. This was the whole point in the chapter "Preaching by Faith" in the book *Outgrowing the Ingrown Church*.

It is also important that the church be led by you to have some concrete goals for outreach ministry. What does this mean practically? I would like to urge you to have either Tom from our New Life staff come to do some preaching or Roger [pastor of another NLPC]. Both of these men are thoroughly sound in doctrine and gifted in training churches for outreach. Roger's specialty is hospitality evangelism, and Tom's specialty is training people to witness one on one. Both men are really godly and practical.

I would also encourage you and the church to expand your missionary vision by supporting in some degree in your budget one of our Ugandan missionaries. . . .

In this letter I have been very open with you and would now like to share with you some of my own needs for prayer. I really need much grace myself to have my heart humble before God, to deny my pride and follow Christ. I especially yearn to have a heart that glories only in the cross and is fearless before men. I entreat you to pray this for me, thinking of me as having a desperate need. I am often like the man who had a visitor at midnight and discovered he had no bread. I need to know how to pray to get my bread from God. Strange as it may sound, I need prayer for my prayer life that I will grow strong in faith and walk in love. Warm greetings to the congregation. I remember the people with all affection and love in my prayers. May grace abound among them.

Most cordially in Christ,
Jack Miller

An Emphasis on Grace Leads to Repentance

To a pastor with whom Jack had been discussing the doctrine of grace and talking about how understanding the gospel of grace changes hearts. Richard had encountered some resistance as he taught these truths, and Jack is responding to that. As Jack writes he is recovering from the onset of lymphoma and the chemotherapy treatments that followed.

June, 1988

Dear Richard,

Warm Greetings in Christ! I was so glad to hear from you and to learn that you have continued to pray for me. I do pray for you and your church, but must admit my praying for you needs to become much more consistent. Your prayers for me have certainly been answered in a remarkable way. The Lord has given me a dramatic physical recovery, and, I do believe, a spiritual renewal too.

Your sharing about your burden for the church helps me to pray for you. I'm glad for what God enabled you to emphasize—that God has a gracious heart toward us in our sins and that sanctification as well as justification is of grace. You would think that would be self-evident, wouldn't you? But obviously the response you received to your emphasis in the "long-range plan" indicates that something is awry in Reformed circles.

One irony that strikes me is that so often people who emphasize the third use of the law are really not great law-keepers themselves. For example, I have noted that sometimes church members given heavy doses of the third use of the law have little idea of the inner nature of the law as a delighting in God. I have also noted a tendency to exclude the tongue and a critical spirit from consideration as well, so that you can get the irony of believers defending the law with a harshness that itself breaks the law! What sinners we can be!

But I do think that the Heidelberg Catechism and the Belgic Confession have an excellent emphasis on faith and sanctification. It is also interesting to see that (as best I can recall) the Larger Catechism speaks of the third use of the law and relates its role to breaking us and driving us to Christ. Add that emphasis, and grace follows.

Anyway I suspect that Reformed people, especially in the English Puritan tradition, have been especially prone to nomism. You know, I have often wondered why English Presbyterianism died so quickly in the 17th century, and maybe this was a factor. I am thinking of excellent men like Richard Baxter. Baxter drifted in an Arminian and nomist direction in his later life.

For what it is worth, here is how I see the theological emphasis of English Puritanism: 1. Know your enemy—sin, the devil, the flesh; 2. Know your personal limitations—your own particular fleshly characteristics and habits; 3. Know your Friend—the grace of God in Christ and the Holy Spirit.

Personally I cannot deny that sometimes churches need that order and such an emphasis has led to revival. Still, I find myself overwhelmed when I pick up a 320-page book by John Owen and find 308 pages devoted to points 1 and 2, and only 12 pages given to point 3, grace and the gospel. Owen, of course, doesn't always do this, but it seems pretty typical.

My own heart likes this order better: 1. Know your Friend; 2. Know your enemy; 3. Know your personal limitations. And I would keep the controlling theme of point 1 even when talking about points 2 and 3.

At the same time I do not think that an emphasis on grace leads to a soft ministry on sin and the severe demands of the law. Actually, it seems to me that such grace teaching makes it possible for sinners like us to hear the hardest things said about our sin patterns, and that can lead into a healthy sorrow which then leads back to sanity, i.e., repentance.

You can tell your words struck a responsive chord with me. I treasure you personally and remember with much joy my time there with you and the church. I felt I was welcomed to your hearts, and who can ask for a better gift?

Would you pray for:

1. The blessing of the Holy Spirit to be on families that will be reading *Come Back, Barbara,* soon to be issued by Zondervan. We are praying that God will use it to glorify Himself in family renewal and salvation of many young people.
2. An article I am writing for *Leadership* magazine on pastoral priorities.
3. Grace for Rose Marie and me to walk close to the Lord and for us not to live in fear. The cancer is in remission, but we

can only rely on God to keep it away or for holy endurance if it returns. The doctor says that the chemotherapy protocol he has given me has excellent statistics in putting lymphoma in remission, but the treatment is so new there are no statistics on durability. Ah, me! I live on the edge—but don't we all? Jesus, help me live moment by moment in You!

Much love in Christ,
Jack Miller

Those Who Believe Are Given More Grace

To the team of missionaries in Ireland.

August, 1988

Dear Ireland Team,

Warm greetings in the Lord Jesus Christ from the home office. We are sorry we could not be with you at this time, but you are much in our prayers, and we are delighted that we can send Bob [Jack's son-in-law] and Steve [a copastor at NLPC] to encourage your faith.

You are all very precious to us and are very much in our prayers. Some of you we do not know well, but the Spirit of grace has mysteriously given us a love for all of you. And we pray with fervency in the Spirit for the holy Father to do a mighty work in your lives and through your ministry to the Irish.

Thank you each one for being our friends, co-laborers in Christ, and our missionaries in Dublin. You are out there on God's frontier, and we are with you in our hearts and prayers.

Thank you all for your many prayers for Rose Marie and me. God has certainly heard them in a wonderful way. [The Spirit has given us] healing, spiritual strength, renewed power in ministry, conversions, opening of doors, and deepening repentance. I have a strong desire to get rid of any hidden idols in my life, and believe that it can only be an answer to your prayers for me.

One central conviction has come to me: it is that pride and self-centered ambition crowd the love of God out of my life. Therefore I constantly need to repent of pride and self-importance and to have the love of God as seen in the golden message of grace crowd out wicked stuff like self-importance. I pray; I believe; Lord, help me with my unbelief!

Let me urge upon you the importance of cultivating faith if you are to be able to walk in love and spiritual power. Without faith it is impossible to please God, but those who believe are given more grace than they can handle. Believing is to expect God to be with you and change you and to change others. Therefore *expect* great things from God; attempt great things for God. When the work is dull and routine or people are slipping away, go forth with new boldness and preach Christ until you are filled with faith yourselves and God works faith in others.

Think of it this way. All the powers of hell and earth are ranged against the gospel and your ministry. They will not compromise. Therefore don't expect it from them. Don't expect the enemy to coddle you. He will continue to attack from every quarter. At night. On the streets. In your meetings. Wherever. This is a take-no-prisoners kind of war, and we must not compromise with the uglies and with evil in any form.

Therefore resist, fight with all your heart against evil in yourself and others, seek holiness through faith in the blood of Christ, and live boldly out of your union with Christ. You are in Him and He is in you.

Don't doubt it. On that basis keep at it. Persevering is the expression of His caring love. First Corinthians 13:4: "Love is patient . . . love always perseveres."

Bob will be speaking to you about repentance and what God has been doing in many of us and in the Amsterdam team. Rose Marie and I are sending some copies of *Repentance and Twentieth Century Man* to you. Our earnest prayer—our constant intercession for you—is that Christ will visit you with grace and so strengthen you and deepen your joy in the gospel that the whole world will wonder about your turning from idols to serve the living God.

Please don't be afraid of the working of God. He calls us to repentance, but in that call supplies the Spirit to bring us to the cleansing of the Lamb. There is no greater joy than leaving our idols at the cross and walking away freed of these cruel bondages. Expect, welcome, and treasure repentance in yourselves and others. Let Christ break down sloth, lusts, pride, coldness, prejudices, despair. He has had a great deal of experience cleansing His temples, and you can trust Him to overturn in order to fill you with songs of gladness.

Let Steve help you in these matters. Steve is a wise and loving brother, a gifted church planter, and he has a good knowledge of Dublin and how things work there. Lean on his outstanding gift of wisdom and accept his encouragement as you would accept me. Let Bob help you too. Bob is a humble brother who has a spirit of discernment and understanding and is a gifted church planter and a sympathetic encourager. Please receive him as you would me.

I am sorry my time and strength did not permit me to write a letter to each of you personally, but be assured you are all in my heart.

Yours in Christ's grace,

Jack Miller

Repentance Is Just Humility

To a missionary who is recovering from a serious illness. Jack had almost died from lymphoma almost a year before this letter was written. That is the "ordeal" he is referring to. When he writes this letter he has been finished with chemotherapy for about four months.

August, 1988

Dear Sam,

It was with much joy that I received your letter, telling about God's working in your life during a very hard time. You have been very sick, and we rejoice in God's great kindness in restoring you to good health in answer to many prayers. We love you, dear brother. Your family needs you, and we need you. So take good care of your health, as much as is consistent with faithfulness to God and with living fearlessly and without undue preoccupation with our physical condition.

God has been bringing to us here at New Life and the home office [World Harvest Mission] a spirit of healing too—that of a deepening repentance. That is why your letter speaking of your own repenting struck me as part of a pattern of God's working. I know God granted me the grace and joy of repentance during my ordeal last October and November. Paul [Jack's son] and I did some deep repenting together. God really convicted me that pride crowds out the love of God. The group taking leadership training this year has also been undergoing much repentance and with many lives being changed, really in a basic way. Then some of these same folks and others under Bob Heppe's guidance in Amsterdam experienced a similar repentance as they read *Repentance and Twentieth Century Man* together in preparation for a very fruitful ministry time.

So God has shown great kindness to us—and most certainly to you. I praise Him for healing you and restoring you to your ministry. I especially honor your repentance, which you described to me. Cotton Mather has said, "Every man upon earth may find in himself something that wants mending." Calvin also describes repentance as a gift from God to the church, a gift that is especially to be treasured as we see the Spirit working it in Christian lives. Thank you for sharing with me this gift. I treasure you as a work of God, most precious to Him and to me.

May God grant you grace to deepen in your repentance! Pray that He will do the same for me! For repentance is just humility, and humility stands in the low place, not on the mountains of pride. Therefore humility gets much grace because grace runs downhill! Bear also with a little counsel about your experience of severe illness. Don't take lightly having been very sick. When you have been seriously ill— as you have—afterwards you may have to struggle to balance care of your body with a holy self-forgetting. When cancer came, my temptation and inclination was to give up being a careless extrovert in matters of health and become an introvert, preoccupied with my physical life. Well, God has helped me to repent, in some measure, for both tendencies. At present, though, I am still waging war in this area of my life. For this is the anniversary of my illness. About this time last year I first noticed the onset of lymphoma symptoms—abdominal swelling and sweats. Well, any time my body is slightly overheated or a bit feverish or I just feel sweaty in the heat, I have a fight with a satanic attack of fear. The feelings whisper, "Maybe your lymphoma is coming back."

Perhaps you don't have precisely the same kind of struggle, but we all need to labor to see that our lives are controlled by God's will and the gospel of hope and not by our anxieties.

But the Lord has helped me. I have been able again and again to confess my anxieties—really deep ones—and ask God to take them away because I cannot. They are simply too deeply rooted in me and my past. But once the Spirit shows me the self-centered unbelieving core of my fears, then help usually comes to me very quickly in the form of release. Essentially I need to confess to God that I have a deep-seated need to protect and control my life and ministry. Once I acknowledge that hard, painful fact to Him, grace seems to stream into my life. Somehow the Father delights in honesty. Usually when my anxieties dominate and will not go away, I need to face the truth that my devotion is not being given to God with all my heart, soul, strength, and mind, but to myself.

But His cleansing through the blood of the perfect Lamb has been so powerful and freeing for both you and me. So let's not be afraid to confess and forsake our ugliest sin and rely on the Spirit enabling us to put on Christ's love for others.

Since you shared your struggles with me, let me acknowledge that one of my battles is with my constant tendency to forget what God has done for me, to ease off on my repenting, and to rest on my past humblings under the impact of chastening. Here I am almost fully recovered from my severe chastening of the past year and amazing deliverances, and already my heart is drifting into complacency. Forgive, O Lord!

But Rose Marie and I took today (Saturday) to pray together and put the priority on thanksgiving and praise and letting intercession flow out of that. We have especially been praying for you and the Ireland team and for us in the church and mission here to experience revival, and maybe that revival begins with the recovery of thanksgiving and praise.

Today has been a wonderful time of joy and freedom—and we believe an opportunity to shift our faith from circumstances and appearances to the Father's holy and absolute sovereignty, His all-conquering grace, and the sweet hope of Jesus' sacrifice revealed in the preaching of the cross.

Finally back to Mather and the joy of repentance, which is closely related to the joy of praise. After he stated that every one of us has something that needs "mending," he added that "the work of repentance is to inquire, not only, what we have done, but also, what we have to do."

What the staff and I, and others, have been doing here is trying to deepen our oneness of love with members in the church and fellow elders. We think this is what we have to do! Sometimes it means that people who are really different in style and personality have to work harder at developing oneness. Sometimes it means getting rid of prejudices or prejudgments about others and especially getting rid of attitudes of superiority toward those who seem less enlightened than we are!

I am thrilled by what I see happening as we work on what we "have to do" in order to mature in Jesus' love.

Will you join us in this work of the Spirit? Why not labor with all faith and hope and joy to deepen your relationship with your team leader first?—and then with each of the other team members? Make it your goal, the burden of your labor and the intensity of your devotion—to fulfill the law of Christ in serving them in love. For me, I like to translate this into practical terms: one of my primary jobs is to make others successful. Make it your joy and your task to see that the team succeeds. Rest when you need to, but work very hard when you work. Gather the fuel by meditation in the Scriptures when you rest, but when you work burn hot for Christ!

I write these things to you with confidence that you are not neglecting them. You are laboring with zeal in the heat of harvest. I have seen you many times burn hot for Christ. Let grace abound and joy abound and let loving work abound. These next six months are crucial. Give it all you have as your praise of Christ. As we repent, we magnetize the world with our hope, love, and, joy. You are already a magnet, grow in your magnetism. Warm greetings to your family.

Much love,
Jack Miller

Personal Humility and the Obligations of Grace

To a missionary in Ireland.

December, 1994

Dear Matt,

Greetings in the love of Jesus! It's early in the morning here in Spain, very quiet, not even the sound of a bird. I've been praying for you this morning; actually I've been praying for you for over two weeks, and this morning I'm including your family. It's such a privilege to have all of you as part of our World Harvest team, and I have enjoyed interceding for all of you. Thank you for putting yourself at God's disposal!

I have meant to write to you earlier, but regrettably my good intentions were wiped out by character weaknesses. I managed to get so overscheduled in the fall that time and energy were pretty much eaten up by constant speaking. It's now clear to me that my zeal for making Christ known must be tempered by a humble willingness to recognize my limits as a weak person who constantly falls into the temptation of thinking that he can do the work of the Holy Spirit.

Rose Marie and I arrived at the Arrow Leadership Seminar (Leighton Ford and Tom Hawkes) so tired that we just leaned on each other as we prayed for strength. I apologized to Rose Marie for my letting the schedule get out of control, and she forgave me. It was very humbling to be so exposed, both in my proud assumption I could handle speaking around thirty times in a month and in my obvious foolishness in not saying no to some requests to speak.

Still, looking back, I can see how the Holy Spirit used this set of circumstances to teach some basic lessons to my heart. I'd like to share some of them with you. The first one concerns an ongoing discussion that James [a pastor and board member of WHM] and I have been having about the crucial importance of humility in the life of the Christian leader. James has been urging on me the value of meditating on the life of Brownlow North, a major evangelist in northern England, Scotland, and Ireland during 1858 and afterwards. North was the great torchbearer of the revival, mainly because he set himself the goal to practice *constant humility.* One way he did this was in his preaching. He self-consciously labored to speak from a heart knowledge that he was chief of sinners.

North began his ministry with the burden of a dreadful reputation. Who would listen to a man whose character was infamous? When he first attempted to enter the ministry, someone sent the church authorities information detailing all of North's public sins. In shame he withdrew. But then Christ did a powerful work of conversion in his life. He came once again to the church, this time to preach. Before he preached, he received another letter detailing all of his sins. He was denounced in it as "such a vile sinner."

North took the letter into the pulpit and read it for all to hear. He said, "I am the man described here." He then used the letter's indictment of his character to exalt pure sovereign grace. He exulted, "It is a correct picture of the vile sinner I once was; and oh how wonderful must the grace be that could quicken and raise me up from such a death and trespass in sins, and make me what I appear before you tonight, a vessel of mercy, one who knows that all his past sins have been cleansed away through the atoning blood of the Lamb of God."[1] The very thing that Satan hoped to use to destroy North became a powerful evangelistic weapon in his daring hands. He did not go from place to place reading this letter, but he frequently "took his hearers into his confidence" concerning the man he had been. His deep grief over his past, and his use of his own example as a demonstration of the awesome power of grace, were used to bring many people to Christ.

Perhaps you don't drift the way that I do, but I constantly forget the deep hole of depravity from which the Lord's mighty love rescued me. Drifting does not take any effort at all; just stop cultivating the knowledge of Christ, and the evil current of secularism does the rest. All passion for the lost seems increasingly a fading memory. Jesus weeping over Jerusalem, Paul willing to be cursed for the sake of his countrymen, those things become very remote to the point of being unreal. But North kept the memory line open to what he once was all the days of his life. This recollection was not at all crippling. His mourning over his sins, both past and present, enabled him to keep climbing down from his pedestal and walking with humble fear and trembling before the Lord and before people. Tens of thousands of people were stunned by his preaching of Christ; many were converted.

I entreat you to pray for me that my memory of my former lost condition will also be fresh and green, and that I will have the Spirit

---

1. *Life of Brownlow North* (London: Banner of Truth, 1961), pp. 46–47.

teach me a second lesson. This one follows from the former lesson. It is a right sense of obligation based upon a clear understanding of the purpose for which we are saved. We have an incredible rescue from lostness increased by our privileged destiny. Our pilgrimage will climax with us coming to resemble Christ exactly, flawless images of the Lord.

Now, I'm sure every true Christian agrees that the ultimate goal of our lives is to become Christlike. But is the glory of it understood? The privilege? The honor? And the compelling obligation?

Well we are stirred to think about it now and then. Sometimes we hunger for the hour of our glorification in the image of the Son of God. But it's a longing that fades. Our minds are lazy; busy lifestyles have little place for deep thinking about the very reason for our existence.

Too, we assume that we are more in touch with our destiny than we are. We know that we have some love for God and for people. And to love God and our neighbors as ourselves is the essence of being Christlike. Are we not already then reasonably far down the road toward Christlikeness? It is easily said by us. We have taught it to others and been praised for our teaching of the centrality of Christlike love.

Why then study, pursue, and long for that which we seem to have substantially attained already? Nevertheless, the Spirit of grace woos us from self-congratulation. We go to work and find we have little power to do it God's way and see God's results. We sense our lack of grace and the weakening of fellowship with the Father. We face a temptation. We feel the power of jealousy or lust or hatred or despair and realize unexpectedly how unlike Christ we really are. He lived in perfect submission to the Missionary Will of the Father. He did not choose to be in control of His own life. In the hour of fiery trial He cried, "Not my will, but Your will be done!"

71

But in my inner heart I find that my ego constantly wants to take control away from the Father. One of the deepest compulsions of my flesh is to say to my Father, "Let me be in control. Let my will be done now. I'll do your will later."

Two nights ago I had to confess to Rose Marie at midnight that my soul was carrying all kinds of burdens—that I was inwardly trying to be in control of many things by worrying about them. Led by the Spirit, I said, "Please pray for me! I'm carrying all kinds of weights and anxieties tonight. I did not know it, but I've been trying to be in control of my life, work—future. But I'm repenting of wanting to be the Holy Spirit. Ask the Lord to cleanse me!"

Her effective praying led to a cleansing and release for my needy soul. It was not that all my cares immediately fell away. But the good beginning was granted by the Father. I rested in the promise of the Spirit's presence and not in my own ability to redeem myself. I also gained a clearer understanding of what it means to be like Jesus, my elder brother, and the joyous obligation my oneness with Him imparts to me.

The Lord in His life on earth had a single-minded passion for doing the saving will of God. In His incarnation and atonement he provided the "alien righteousness" that became the good news for sinners. He came without self-interest. His only purpose was "to seek to save that which was lost" (Luke 19:10) because this was His Father's will. The house of salvation was open to all nations through Jesus' one great work of atoning sacrifice (John 2:19; 4:34; 5:36; 14:31; 17:4, 18; 20:21).

Our minds may be like well-arranged file cabinets or overturned wastebaskets. But it's all small stuff, pitifully shriveled if it is disconnected from Jesus' one great master work. His joyous obligation concentrated all His powers. Note how His public ministry begins. He forgets Himself. He cleanses the temple with holy indignation. He says, "How dare you turn my Father's house into a market!" (John 2:16). Why the wrath? It is neither polite nor politic. But Jesus knows only the Father's will. The Father has purposed that His house be a salvation house for the Gentile sinners, the unwashed, the "all nations" promised to Abraham and made the subjects of Jesus' Great Commission (Gen. 12:3; Matt. 28:19).

What was going on? What stirred the fierce anger of Jesus?

Listen, dear brother. Here is the core issue. The church of God again and again gets in the way of "the nations" coming to salvation by its busyness and business—and forgets this master purpose. We forget. I forget; you forget; New Life Church forgets; Hope Christian Fellowship forgets.

The court filled with moneychangers and the market for the sale of animals was the welcome court of the nations. It had been built by the people of God anticipating the fulfillment of Isaiah 56:6–8. It was the welcome court for the lost, the missionary part of the temple complex, the setting for sinners to taste of His redeeming grace.

My own heart is stirred deeply by the Spirit of Jesus as I write these words. My mind's eye can see Jesus standing there. He sternly takes it all in, the haggling over money, the bleating of the sheep, and the confusion of the Gentile worshippers. No one welcomes these strangers, no one teaches them the promise of grace or calls them to brokenness over their sins. Jesus' great heart is deeply grieved. He moves through the tumultuous scene, making a whip of cords and driving "all from the temple area." The sheer violence of the action astonishes me. No wonder that the disciples for once remember a Scripture verse describing Jesus' act: "Zeal for your house has eaten me up" (John 2:16–17). Jesus' soul is full of salvation fire, and He will not tolerate obstacles being put in the way of the recovery of the lost.

S. Kierkegaard once said that "purity of heart is to will one thing." His statement is not true at all if that one thing is to do our own will. Then we end up little Hitlers, Jeffrey Dahmers, or like the man who launched the subtle, deadly attack on the Bible study [in

73

Dublin]. But when by the Spirit's aid we will God's saving purpose, in purity of heart, then we may even burn with holy indignation.

As you may have guessed, I have not written this at one sitting. It's now December 10, five days later. Rose Marie and I took a walk on the beautiful beach at Cabo Pino (Cape of Pines). It's about as lovely a beach as any in Europe, a favorite spot for walking breaks. While there we found ourselves in the presence of a number of nude men deliberately putting their bodies on display. We ignored them, just talking together as we walked near the sea's edge. We looked down or across the Med or toward the mountains of Africa. But one middle-aged man, completely naked, walked toward us as we tried to avoid him, and then he determinedly walked between us. It was a willful attempt to force his lifestyle on us, a crude attempt to cause offense, and something of a crusading attempt to force his willful exhibitionism on us. He was sold out to his own will and glorying in it.

I was angry and upset. Stayed that way for a time, till I remembered my obligation to Jesus and his will. He had made me debt-free from sin and guilt. But as a debt-free child of the King I now had a new debt, to love others as Christ loved me. I owed this love debt to Jesus and to these men, forgiving them, blessing them, and asking Christ to save them. It also cleared the air of its poison. Rose Marie said, "Probably we are the only ones to ever pray for these men." Poor lost souls, the Lord's Missionary Spirit enabled us to see them with the Father's compassion, a true miracle of grace because my anger at the beginning was unholy. It came from a divided heart, a heart half committed to Rose Marie's and my well-being and half committed to the will of our Missionary God.

Think of it this way. The message of the cross takes away the burden of guilt and sin, removes forever the divine wrath from us; then it also takes away the heavy burden of our selfishness and self-preoccupation. I am offended because a beautiful beach has been taken over by homosexuals from northern Europe. I think about what

I have lost, about my feelings concerning their blatant self-assertion, etc. But the Holy Spirit rebukes me. He questions, "Where will they spend eternity? You give up your daily walk on a lovely beach, but they will perish forever unless they repent."

Then He leads me to repentance, to will one will, to taste the sweetness of His mighty love and to long for these men to experience the same self-forgetting peace.

It is now December 14, a Wednesday. This past Monday Tom [another missionary in Ireland] called and reported on his ministry and mentioned how God had been speaking to you and him. It was a most encouraging account of the Lord's giving grace and wisdom to you both. I told Tom that it was really strengthening to my faith because I had been having a special time of prayer for you for the past two weeks and was now praying for Laura [Matt's wife], planning next to concentrate on Anne, Edward, and John [Matt and Laura's children].

There was momentary silence on the phone. Then Tom told about Laura's testimony on Sunday. She apparently had a new touch of grace that was most liberating, encouraging her in serving Christ. I was thrilled.

What is my method in praying? Am I a prayer warrior? Not at all. Rather, the older I get the more I know how hard it is to pray. Therefore what I do is to try and maintain as much as I can regular prayer for all our missionaries, home staff, pastors in the churches, and especially for a core group of WHM churches and pastors. But my praying is always drifting, marred by coldness, forgetting, and apathy. Accordingly, I need to press forward or my prayer life will shrivel to nothing. One way the Lord helps me do my prayer work is by having me take an individual missionary couple and pray for them intensively for two weeks or more, sometimes a month.

The effectiveness of this approach can be seen in several ways. Altogether apart from what it accomplishes in their lives, the practice of praying for them trains my mind to keep on praying for them after the concentrated period is completed. In fact, it may mean that the concentrated prayer will keep right on. That's my hope!

This approach also clears my vision, especially my sensitivity to God's will for the ones being prayed for. For instance, I have prayed for you, Matt, and for me that we would have the truths of redemption *become deeply felt realities in our inmost being, that we would hate the sin of apathy in ourselves and others, and passionately love the lost with boldness, tenderness, and brokenness.*

I want the Spirit to grace me with much patience, a willingness to take each small step necessary to make friends with the lost person, and then boldly stand before the heart's door and knock. And then to stand with tears before the person's inner citadel and plead for the lost one to grab hold of the only salvation there is. The Father must give much new grace if this is to happen. I am often so far from this kind of total commitment to the Lord Jesus. Pray for me, my brother, pray for me!

Last fall, I mentioned, we were overscheduled, including some extra meetings slipped in by churches that were not on my schedule. But the Holy Spirit used my desperate awareness of weakness to force me to rely on the gospel and prayer with a holy recklessness once and again. I did a number of ridiculous things. At one seminar I spoke with the Spirit's brokenness about wrath and justification. I was driven by the Father's Spirit to dramatize the peril to sinners as they seek any other righteousness but Christ's by faith alone. Hell for a good number of people became a felt reality, so much so that one of the pastors there, with three of his elders, went to their congregation with a heaven-sent brokenness. The pastor, for instance, could not begin his Sunday sermon. He stood before the people and wept and wept, almost for ten minutes, and was able to fully compose himself only at the end of his sermon.

In another church I challenged the large congregation to send forth 400 missionaries!—via World Harvest! At Sonship Week at least two people were powerfully convicted of their practical atheism and were converted. Henry's [a pastor who was helping to lead the Sonship Seminar] prayer time the next evening began with great gentleness on his part after 9:00 and apparently did not end until 3:00 a.m.! Great workings of God were afoot! I also believe new missionaries are coming forward because of the moving of the Spirit. . . .

Brownlow North was an Anglican who loved the Presbyterian Church as few of us do. Most of his preaching was done in Scottish and Irish Presbyterian churches. He was much loved by them in return. However, when invited to the General Assembly to address it, he gave four rebukes. Two of them were: 1. The Presbyterian Church is essentially a *prayerless* church, and 2. Its elders are nonentities as Christians and leaders, *without real soul care.* I think these rebukes were Brownlow's "primeval scream." Really the moving of the Lord of the church. The Assembly applauded him, of all things.

I have prayed for you that God will make you a new Brownlow North. That you would feel a grace obligation to fulfill the Great Commission and to disciple praying men who feel the reality of hell and long for the appearing of Jesus, and who give themselves to the people of God without reservation in their love for them. I pray that you will conquer by prayer, privately and publicly as you daringly disciple men, calling them to give up a divided will to will only God's will.

I also want to encourage you and Tom to pray much together, to put it into your schedule, and plan to pray twice as much as you think that you have time for.

Christ is on the move. . . . May the presence of the Father carry you where your own feet never could.

In Christ's great grace,

Jack

Our Grace Obligation to Share the Gospel and Love Others

To a missionary in Ireland. This letter is a follow-up to the previous letter. Jack explains more clearly here what he means by "grace obligation" and what the character of a church planter should look like. As usual he comes back to the need for much sustained prayer. He says that prayer is what "connects cross and character."

March, 1995

Dear Jeff,

How good it feels to be back at work on the computer! Yesterday I began working again on it and did about three hours work, probably a bit too much. Today I feel stronger. My left hand had just a touch of weakness yesterday and now it's mostly gone! Jesus is good and He is strong.

Thanks for your Ireland update on the Compuserve. I'm sorry, though. I only started working on it yesterday. . . . I expect to improve, but . . . I think I sent back your update and not my response to it. Anyway, be assured that I was thrilled by your report and prayed immediately for the things you mentioned. I loved the report on the trip to Cork and the possibility of recruiting Irish leaders for mobilization. I want to hear more.

During the past two-and-one-half weeks life has been hard for Rose Marie and me. On March 6 in the evening I had a small stroke that affected my left arm, numbed my neck and face on the left side, and for a short time also numbed my lower leg. I then spent nine days in the hospital, with real progress being made. At times there were struggles too—tough ones. But the gospel of grace really caught me up with the power of the Holy Spirit so that my sense of humor and love were triumphing over my weakness and fears. One nurse seems to be near conversion, and another promised to visit New Life Church in Glenside. . . . I also gave a copy of Rose Marie's book to a young German doctor. He promised to read it. Rose Marie and I left the hospital with a little book-signing ceremony.

Praise the Lord God of mercies and miracles! I have the use of everything. The doctors were especially interested in my left hand and its weakness. But on Monday the doctor told me that my fingers were now stronger than his. It will, though, take another month, he said, for me fully to resume my normal life.

There will be a thinning out of my schedule, i.e., cutting back the Sonship weekends and long overseas trips to places like Kiev and Africa. The cardiologist also says that I cannot go overseas for three months because that's an important period for people who have had strokes. Heavy-duty work and travel should not happen till at least June 1. That is a shock because this eliminates the missionary retreat.

Jeff, I really am committed to listening better to Rose Marie about not doing too much. But both the cardiologist and the internist say that I should get back into my work. The internist said to me privately, "Your body is strong and you have good confidence; don't lose it by turning yourself into a neurotic."

I am sending you a copy of the letter I sent to Matt [the previous letter] a few months ago. I have his permission to send it to all the missionaries and the members of the Board and other interested friends. Members of the executive committee of the Board have asked me to write team leaders on a regular basis as part of my work in the mission. With your permission I will include this letter with his letter.

I also want to explain the contents of the letter to Matt more fully, filling in some broader vision and methods of mobilization.

First, I did not mean to offer the example of Brownlow North as a kind of exclusive model of piety and renewal. He has his personality and story, and you have yours and I have mine. There is no intention either to exalt conviction of sin as more important than the message of the cross. But what the Spirit of grace did for the man is instructive and applicable to all of us. He was a man overwhelmed by the wonder of grace through the conviction of the greatness of the forgiveness of his sins. His own transformation by grace made him convinced of the conquering power of Christ and His gospel. He had a deep conviction of sin, both in respect to his past and the present. But the depth of his depravity was not his primary concern: that concern was grace. The marvel of grace transforming him and other sinners dominated his consciousness.

In other words, there is in North a vividness of praise because of mercies received. It is this vividness that made the Bible live for him. The Spirit of God made the Bible to be seen for what it really is, God's living and powerful Word inscripturated. And it was this awareness that gave him courage to confront the Scottish Presbyterian Church G.A. [General Assembly] with what he believed were typical Presbyterian sins: on the one hand, we do little in the kingdom because we do not pray very much; and, on the other, we do not mobilize and train elders to do the work of soul care.

This Episcopalian evangelist was charging us Presbyterians with not knowing how to train and use elders, because of our lack of prayer.

Now we know these things already, and certainly they are becoming vivid to you. . . . We really don't know how to train and mobilize leaders effectively. It seems to me that this is what North wanted from his beloved Presbyterians: the humbling of our hearts over our failure to mobilize elders for evangelism and soul care. He wanted his Presbyterian friends to seek and find the grace to train and equip Christ's servants for passionate service in the harvest. . . .

Secondly, I am concerned with the issue of conceptual clarity in respect to the biblical character of the churches we want to plant and the kind of leaders that we wish to plant them. Our aim is to gain a bigger vision for what God can do in church planting and mobilizing leaders. As I believe you have put it, "I have been thinking too much about planting a single church, when I should also be thinking about how we can mobilize and train our own missionaries and [local church] leaders to plant 200 churches. . . ."

The rest of us share your vision, I do believe. But if North is right about us, then we have problems. It simply cannot happen unless we learn to pray better and train better—and also to think more clearly. We all have a heart burden to plant churches in the world's darkest places. But think for a moment. This requires sacrifice, suffering, endurance, even death on the part of American and national missionaries. Are we really ready for this?

I do believe that of ourselves we would never be ready. But in spite of our many weaknesses I am persuaded we are moving in the right direction. The glory is all God's.

I think in our training and mobilization we need to find the cutting edge for this work. What is that edge? It has to do with our sense of obligation, getting it clear and then acting upon it. We learn in our Sonship training that we are free from the curse obligation of the law as multiplied commandments, really a covenant of works condemning the conscience (Gal. 3:10–14). There is nothing more delightful than to taste the wonder of this justifying/adopting grace. J. I. Packer says that if he was looking for the three words to summarize the message of the N. T., he would likely choose these: "adoption through propitiation." No more wrath, no more curse, a son or daughter and free at last. But what we now need to do is stress equally the grace obligation that goes with the liberation given through the gospel. Of course, we have always done this, but we now need to banner it forth as a glorious thing, to be called into union with Christ and to be identified with Him in His sufferings, death, and resurrection.

Paul uses grace-obligation words in two ways: in respect to the obligation to take the gospel to others (Rom. 1:14–15) and the obligation to love one another (Rom. 13:8–10). In 1 John 4:7–16 the obligation words are used in respect to the incarnation and the cross. Leon Morris in his *Testaments of Love* says that these obligation words are always connected to the atonement and the cross. Christ loved us, therefore we love others; Christ died for me, I die for others. He also insists that loving one another includes non-Christians, a conclusion confirmed by Jesus' remarkable call for the sons of the Father to love their enemies the way He loves the just and the unjust.

In summary, then, we need a clearer idea of the nature of the church, its leaders, and the nature of the leader to be trained. Here are my thoughts:

1. The church is a missionary community of love. (John 13:33–34)
2. The leader/mobilizer is a Christian controlled by the love of Christ. (2 Cor. 5:14)
3. The Christian (church planter, etc.) being trained and mobilized for discipling and church planting must have a desire to be ruled by a Christlike love. (1 Tim. 1:5)

Leon Morris thinks that we have lost something important here—really lost touch with our kingdom identity. He says that Christians today are out of the loop of Christ's love. They cannot seem to connect cross and character. They don't seem to grab a hold of Christ's love as a creative power transforming us into lovers of others, Christians and non-Christians. He says bluntly, "There can be few places—at least in the western world (and none that I know of)

—where outsiders spontaneously comment on the love Christians show to one another." I believe this is overstated somewhat, but if you think of it in terms of inability to reach into the dark places of the earth, then maybe our loving is more superficial than we think.

For example, Greg Livingston of Frontiers once said to me, "If we could transfer a church like New Life to North Africa, its love would attract all kinds of people to Christ." I think that is true. But if we had a church like New Life in North Africa we would all have the immediate temptation to flee the country because the leaders would be in jail, members would be killed by extremists, and few of us could find jobs. Now—would we have love strong enough to walk with Jesus in such a situation—or would we be tempted to hunker down in self-protection? Love would not do that. Love would stand and die for Jesus.

Here is our big vision. The church is a community of love. That's the heart of the matter, and the leader is a Christian controlled by the love of Christ. We *must* choose to train people to evidence the love of Christ in a way that impacts others.

To apply to method:

1. We must see that we have a typical fault as Presbyterians. In church planting we get the order wrong. We try to perfect the church before we get it planted. We pay more attention to the organization than we do to the organism, not realizing that the order must arise out of a healthy organic life of community love. And a manifestation of this confusion can be seen in our disastrous tendency to make the elder a maintainer of visible order rather than a person who cares for souls and evangelizes.

2. We should not try to train as workers people who are not being visibly transformed by the gospel of grace. A character mark of the leader: He knows the glory of the cross and loves his family ardently and tenderly from the heart and then loves the lost with the same passion.

3. In forming small church groups on the Alliance model we ought to have clearly in view what we want to plant. Are we trying to plant something from North America or the U.K.? I am a convinced Presbyterian, but we also are under the authority of Scripture and want to work out of the model of the book of Acts and the epistles, where elders are shepherding house churches that reproduce themselves spontaneously. Not maintainers of organizational structure.

4. Each new cell church being planted ought to learn the whole implications of Sonship, freed from the curse obligation in order to follow the grace obligation to reach the lost.

5. At least forty percent of the time in new church meetings should be spent in prayer. It is this constancy in prayer that turned Herrnhut into a missionary community of love. See John Weinlick's biography of Zinzendorf. Prayer connects cross and character, God's love for us, working in us a sacrificial love for others.

6. We must plant and nurture churches with tears of repentance. See Paul's self-description in Acts. In Spain I tried to mediate between two angry men. They almost came to blows. What did I learn? I found the same fleshly anger arising in me that was in them when one insulted me. I kept my temper—on the outside. But horrified at my own secret rage, I was broken before the Lord. This humbling became, though, a powerful instrument for exalting the grace that cleansed me. It was a tremendous help upon my return and time in the hospital. A little bit like North I saw the cesspool from which the Spirit and the gospel rescued me. How precious does the cross appear when I recall what depravity was in my heart before my new birth and how much corruption still lurks disguised in my soul!

I'd recommend three books treating character and work of the pastor/elder/missionary: Charles Bridges's *Christian Ministry* (especially the section called "Hindrances to Pastoral Efficiency"), Richard Baxter's *Reformed Pastor,* and Eugene Peterson's *Under the Unpredictable Plant.* They fit in well with Ralph Neighbour's *Where Do We Go from Here? A Guide to Cell-Group Church Planting.*

I'll really miss you and all our missionaries at the retreat, but here is my ongoing labor to keep partnering with you in the cause of the gospel.

Remember: The cross towers over all the wrecks of time. May it tower over us, the wrecks being salvaged by the kingdom working of the King!

In his abundant grace,
Jack

The Mature Leader Is a Gentle, Kind Learner

To a missionary who is preparing to plant a church. This letter begins with a discussion of a counseling situation that both Jack and Chris are involved in with a missionary couple.

January, 1996

Dear Chris,

. . . Looking back over the situation, my guess is that you probably came on too quickly and aggressively for the Carters [the missionary couple Chris was counseling] to handle. I am not trying to defend them, but would suggest that a slower, more deliberate pace would have helped. Or let me put it another way, the mature leader is the person who takes time to build confidence first, last, and always. Building trust is the key to getting people to follow you . . . in the church and church planting you cannot presuppose that this trust factor is in the picture . . . [important qualities like] zip and enthusiasm—can fall flat in the church, especially if the enthusiastic leader like me does not take time to build relationships before launching the program. . . .

I am so much this way—the aggressive personality—that for a long time I questioned whether I could function as a pastor, whether I would not overwhelm people with my personality. Enthusiasm was not just my middle name: it was my first, middle, and last names. Eventually the Holy Spirit began to tame my spirit, and out of these changes I discerned that pastoral ministry was actually much easier than I thought. *Basically at the beginning of a ministry, the leader should humble himself and not try to do too much.* Really, even later a good pastor is pretty much a good listener, a patient, deliberate questioner; and at the beginning of a church-planting enterprise you will be astonished how well things will go if you are just *a gentle, kind learner.* The trouble comes in when the leader tries to be and do too much, perhaps unconsciously trying to have the power of the Holy Spirit and the Lordship of Christ. Inevitably what the leader is trying to do is to prove himself or herself and to own the ministry. This kind of approach frightens people, and flesh responds to flesh and conflicts follow.

My own conviction is that the flesh is still so strong in the Christian leader that each of us needs a healthy fear of our own capacity for ruining the work of God with our *unconscious* pride. Dear Chris, I am very, very much afraid of myself, and I think that is a good place to be—provided I take my fears to Jesus and ask Him to cleanse me of my "will to power." Indeed, a pastor really needs to be broken before God every day, or he will break up the church of God with his willfulness or let it slip into spiritual death through his sloth. I am horrified, no, terrified, by what I saw happen between the pastor of [a local church that split] and the other leaders and members of the congregation.

It was awful and could have been prevented by humility, by listening, gentleness, and mutual teachability. I am convinced that I could do the same, and you could too.

Therefore, I would ask you not to go on the mission field full of the plans you have in your mind, or any feeling you have to be the manager of the work. Your agenda will simply clash with the agendas of others. Take time to let it all become "our agenda." Here is the approach I take and would ask you to follow it. For three to six months do the following:

1. Listen and listen and gentle and gentle yourself, and then listen and gentle yourself some more.
2. Ask many questions and express appreciation for others' wisdom. Learn to accept people where they are, and work with them there.
3. Build friendships within the team and within the emerging church without putting undue pressure on the people. Some people just take time to make close friends. So let the Holy Spirit unite them to you and one another.
4. Make very few unilateral decisions, don't change things that are working, don't feel being the team leader means you have to be the sole Bible teacher. I would urge you not to take over [ministries that are already in place]; respect others' Bible teaching even though it might not be as effective as yours. Build the confidence [of others] by encouraging them as Bible teachers.
5. Center your aggressiveness on building your own life of prayer and the corporate prayer of the team and church. Do nothing without much waiting on the Lord with the brothers and sisters.

If you do these things, you will find that your American intensity will not overwhelm brothers and sisters who are easily threatened or frightened. Now—who can do these things? Not me! Yet I can do them. Why? Because in honesty I can learn to hate my egocentricity and its many manifestations, and when I do that I really cry out with sincerity for grace. Jesus always helps me when I humble myself in that way. May He grant us both grace to humble ourselves so that we do all things for His glory and not our own. "I can do all things through Christ who strengthens me."

There are a few other things I want to ask you to do:

1. Read carefully the material you will be receiving called "Striving to Plant a New Church." Pray for grace to take it into your mind and heart.
2. When you get onto the field, take the first six months just to get acquainted with the country and the other Christian ministries.
3. For the first three months have fun and enjoy yourself until it gets to be a habit. Help others enjoy themselves too.
4. When you get there don't make any heavy-duty plans for at least nine months.
5. Instead, study the plans I have already laid out for the ministry there and improve upon them. We can do this together on the phone and by mail.

My idea is that if you are going in the direction indicated in this letter, you may be almost ready for heaven as well as the mission field. I am partly serious. A gentle, quiet spirit is really heavenly! . . . you must seek to do the things mentioned in this letter with your whole heart. What I am offering is not merely good advice. To do anything less I believe is a prescription for grave trouble. I have been in on the planting of many churches and am fully convinced that there is nothing easier than destroying a new church by human haste.

I also wish to affirm you, Chris, my dear brother, and assure you that I am fully behind you and believe that you are just the right man for [this mission field]. The WHM staff here and the New Life staff have been convinced from the start that you are God's man of the hour. We all agreed that your zeal, warmth, and energy are greatly needed for our team and for the field there.

. . . Well, you know how these letters grow. Bear with the length. Warm greetings to Lynn.

In Jesus' triumphant love,
Jack

The Work of the Holy Spirit and Why Hearts Resist

To a church that Jack had recently spoken to during their missions conference.

Dear Brothers and Sisters,

Most affectionate greetings from Spain! Rose Marie and I remember with all joy your warm welcome of us at the recent Missions Conference. We also thank God for your willingness to hear the gospel from the other speakers and ourselves. You have a heart for God. But may you not rest in what you have attained by grace, but press on to lay hold of all the riches of Christ.

The theme of the conference has stayed with us: "Awake, Christian, to the Spirit."

You will remember how I said at the conference on Sunday morning that Jesus knocks at the front door of the heart (Rev. 3:20). In response we do not immediately open the door via our free will. Instead, we quickly put locks on the door and push furniture against it. The Lord then sends the Holy Spirit to slip in the back door. He goes down into the basement, where He turns up the heat and sets fires until the rising heat forces us to remove the barriers and open the front door and let Christ in. I believe that the Lord keeps right on using this backdoor approach in our growth in grace.

He sets fires in our basements by putting us in limiting and painful circumstances. Right after our return to Jenkintown from the missions conference, I woke up one morning with a swollen foot, really sore. In answer to your prayers and those of others, Christ healed me, but for more than two weeks I certainly felt the "heat from the basement." I had so much to do, both working on support-raising and getting ready to go overseas. It became a hard but good time. I meditated further on the ministry of the Spirit, especially on the tension between our assertion of independence and the Spirit's yearning to bring us to a *powerful dependence upon Himself.*

Speaking to a pastors' group I stood on one foot much of the time. Very humbling. The foot kept getting worse. So to protect it, I preached on Sunday while seated on a barstool! During this time I suggested to Gene [the pastor of this church] that I write a follow-up letter to all of you on the subject of the Spirit's ministry. He graciously welcomed my proposal. Here is the idea. We have an obsessive need to feel in control of our lives. Such a hunger is a primary obstacle to the Spirit's working mightily in us and through us.

Busyness is a hindrance to fellowship with the Lord. But what lies behind our need to fill up every last moment with activity? The answer is that we want to be in charge of our lives, and our constant activity gives us the feeling we are mastering our world. There are certain key areas where we hold on to control and weaken the Spirit's working in ourselves. Some of us want to retain control of our tongues and use them to defend our rights, gossip, and shift blame to others.

Others of us determine to say no to extreme suffering, both for ourselves and for our families. Many cling tenaciously to self-centered ambitions, material possessions, and reputations. Then inwardly most of us want an escape clause in our obedience to the Father. We want "to be free" to say no if at any time in life we find the Lord putting us in a position where we must give up our treasured idols. Has not even a great gift like the family today become a major idol for Christians?

Many would like to be missionaries or other servants of the King, but they do not wish to make their families suffer for the kingdom (Luke 14:26–27).

Why, then, is the Holy Spirit not leading more of us into a maximum Christian life? The answer is that we are letting Him have only a minimal control of our life choices, both as individuals and families. We do not want Him to lead us too far along the paths of righteousness for fear that we may get hurt or someone we love may get hurt. But the concern of the Holy Spirit is contrary to our self-protective agendas. He has a holy passion for glorifying Christ. He wishes to honor Christ for His complete self-giving in His suffering. He also wishes to bring us into partnership with the Lord's work of filling up His sufferings in His disciples. His supreme task as Christ's spy in the heart is to bring us to say, "Abba, Father, not my will but yours be done, not my control but yours."

How, then, shall we understand the call: "Awake, Christian, to the Spirit"?

It is supremely a call to abandon self-protective strategies and awake to the truth that Christ's ascension now defines us and defines our whole universe. Look up, dear brothers and sisters, to Jesus upon the throne. Christ has ascended and in the process taken total control over human history, the world, and our lives. Believe it! Act on it! In His ascension as the Mediator at the right hand of the Father, Christ became the Loving Controller of all things, working everything together for His glory and our good. Our Ruler/Intercessor exercises control over us by His Spirit. According to Acts 2:32–33, the risen and ascended Christ "received from the Father the promised Holy Spirit" and then "poured out" the Spirit on the church. The Holy Spirit has been sent to act as the executive presence of Jesus Christ (Matt. 28:20). He is the primary means for Jesus' conquest of ourselves and the universe.

His normal method is to work secretly within the self. He is God's spy in the heart, opening doors that we would keep closed, stirring us up to do impossible things contrary to our nature and training, and leading us away from self-protection and from abusing others with our tongues. Above all, the Spirit is leading us to discover empowerment through giving up control of our lives. He is calling for complete surrender daily. Such surrender does not always immediately deliver us from pressures and burdens. It may even increase them. But it does bring us empowerment in the form of personal sanity. How so? It is simply that our crippling anxieties are so obsessive because our wills have not been constantly surrendered to the Father's. But once the will is submitted to the Father the fundamental cause of our anxieties is now removed. The details may need to be worked out, but the right medicine for the soul has been found!

An example will help explain this principle. In the early 1980's one of our WHM missionaries and I stopped over in Geneva on our way home from Uganda. We went into a cafe and ordered lunch. A Swiss man in the cafe helped us in the ordering of our meal. He said he was a banker. When he found out that we were missionaries, he told us that he no longer went to church because "I never heard anything in the sermons I could not have thought of myself."

Having acknowledged the weaknesses of the church, I then said, "But I think I know something about you. Your inner life is full of deep anxieties."

Our new Swiss friend looked astonished. "How," he asked, "could you know that about me!" He did not for a moment deny the accuracy of the insight.

My answer? "It is not difficult to know. When you left the church you were taking control of your own life. You were no longer relying on God's control. Now you have to control your life by yourself. That is anxiety-producing because no human being can do it!"

His next words were, "Let me pay for your lunches." Was this a banker's way of repenting? I do not know, but I do know that left to ourselves we will make the banker's foolish choice. We will try to assert our independence of God and take charge of our own lives in ways that are often too subtle to detect if we do not take care to walk in the Spirit.

There is a release of God's power when control is surrendered to the Spirit of Christ. This is not a matter of mere feeling but of faith relying on the word of Christ. Get down on your knees in prayer and then get up and take the risk of humbling yourself by apologizing to that brother or sister you have sinned against. Is not such a liberating act a giving up of your own defensive will? Or go to a friend and say, "I have a critical spirit and a loose tongue. Will you pray for me?" Here we have the beginnings of a deep surrender.

Sometimes the surrender to Christ's sovereignty calls for patience. Ray Stedman in his book *Spiritual Warfare* tells about a believer locked into what seemed to be unending depression. Finally the person began to pray daily, "Not my will but yours be done." At first not much seemed to change. But after a year of surrendering the will in this way, the depression lifted.

Now apply this principle to witnessing. A friend of mine had moved into a new neighborhood. He became so busy that he felt he had no time to meet his neighbors and share the gospel with them. After almost two years the Spirit convicted his conscience. After repentance and prayer, the Spirit led him to visit each one of his neighbors and apologize for his failure to meet them. His humble apology was accepted; the neighbors began to visit his home; and two couples soon became Christians. The man humbled himself, gave up his own agenda, and the Holy Spirit moved.

The Father sends the Holy Spirit to do impossible things through us when we freely acknowledge our deep weaknesses. Speaking at Redeemer Presbyterian Church in Manhattan on the dangers of "A Comparison Righteousness," I said that we Americans have some crazy ideas about ourselves and God. We (like the Pharisee) have an attitude of self-righteous superiority toward others because we can see faults and sins in them (the tax-collectors) which we do not see in ourselves.

I explained, "Our idea of our own 'righteousness' is based not upon what we really are in God's sight, but upon how we stand up in comparison with others." Then I flung caution to the winds and confessed that I was naturally one of the Pharisees. I admitted I like the role of a self-appointed judge and that I thought America was full of such self-appointed judges—and that this was crazy stuff because our holy Maker looks upon our condemnation of others as a deadly hypocrisy. I concluded with a broken-hearted plea for the proud judging person to humble himself or herself and rest their hope of salvation only on the shed blood of Christ.

I was tired; I felt foolish. But a new Christian afterwards told me, "My husband and daughter have been opposed to my faith, but they were here this evening. Amazing! They cried through the whole sermon!"

Amazing grace! On the way to the Kennedy airport, I again felt tired. But Juan, the Puerto Rican taxi driver, said, "My three daughters are Jehovah's Witnesses, but I listen to a radio program—

'The Gospel.' I don't understand it all, but is that OK?" His last words were, "Where's your Redeemer Church?"

Amazing grace! On the 747 flying to Holland we were seated among a group of orthodox rabbinical students on their way to Jerusalem. Rose Marie asked one of them about law keeping, since they seemed so burdened with getting the right kosher foods. Finally I heard her ask, "Have you ever read Isaiah 53?"

Amazing grace! Its working is utterly humbling. In the fall you heard preaching on the Holy Spirit in Acts. You then chose that theme for the missions conference. Sinners were almost knocking you down wanting to talk about the gospel. What is the Spirit doing? Is revival coming? Let's wake up together!

In the bonds of grace,
Jack Miller

Practical Applications

What does it mean to serve one another in love? Practically it means to labor to make others successful.

What do living for God's glory and doing Christ's work Christ's way look like on a day-by-day basis? How does living a life of faith, humility, and prayer affect your leadership style? Does it change the way in which you talk and relate to others? These are some of the questions that the letters in this section address.

Jack's letters in this section were written to a variety of men and women: missionaries, pastors, church planters, and some who were in training for those roles. He emphasized to them the importance of learning the basics of leadership—personal humility, vital faith, and constant prayer. Then he applied these principles to the specific situations that each person was facing.

Jack believed that the humility that comes from knowing that you are a great sinner entirely dependent on the grace of God should affect every area of life. One way he practically applied this was to encourage those he was mentoring to be good listeners. Many people (including his own wife!) had challenged him to be a better listener, and he had come to see this as one of the essential qualities of a Christian leader. He often shared his own struggles with listening as he encouraged others to become better listeners. He said in a letter to a WHM team leader in Uganda, "Once [another elder] gently admonished me, 'Jack, you are a born persuader as a leader. It's a good gift, but persuasion should *follow* listening and asking questions. Give balance to your leadership by delaying your persuading until you have had time to ask questions and to listen closely to the answers.' " Jack was happy to pass on this bit of advice to others. In one letter he counseled a young pastor to be willing to hear criticism about his preaching and grow from it. In another he challenged a man who was impatient to become a missionary that "a leader must have more evidence of a broken will and the humility that has gone deep into the soul with it. . . . One evidence of the need here appears to be in the area of listening to those of us who are older."

But, as important as Jack thought listening was, he also believed that Christian leadership meant sometimes encouraging people to do things they might not want to do. He wrote to a small group leader that he was mentoring, "A pastor is someone who leads, an undershepherd. He loves the sheep and is willing to die for them. That means at times he is willing to lead them where they are not prepared or willing to go." Jack knew from his experience in church planting, evangelism, and missionary work that often God wants His people to go into situations where they are totally out of their depth. It is when they feel helpless that God's power will be seen most clearly. Jack taught that it was the role of the Christian leader to be willing to go forward despite weakness and then to encourage others to go forward despite their weaknesses.

Jack believed that the key to balancing listening and action is for the Christian leader to first submit his will to Christ and then to listen, plan, and move forward according to the wisdom that God supplies. It is this submission that will guard the leader's heart from pride and also from being judgmental in dealing with the sins of others. He said in a letter to a young missionary in Uganda, "You see the 'raging of the kingdom of self' in Uganda and . . . you discover the kingdom of self is raging within you. . . . In all this I take the greatest comfort in simply surrendering to the will of Christ. . . . But what in broad terms is the will of Christ? It is to be gentle and lowly in heart. It is to cast your burdens and anxieties upon Him, and to find rest for your souls as you labor to make Christ known. In this resting in Christ comes wisdom."

This theme of the Christian leader learning from Jesus to be "gentle and lowly" is highlighted in many of the letters in this section. Jack took seriously the idea of servant leadership. He believed that Christian leadership, at its most basic level, is simply working to make others successful. Whether he was interacting with missionaries on the field, small-group leaders, or his copastors at NLPC, his main goal was to encourage and support them in their ministry.

As you read these letters you will notice that Jack was always working to turn upside down our culture's notion of what makes a leader successful. Instead of using leadership as a way to establish identity, significance, and power, he taught that the role of the Christian leader is to be the chief servant. He summed up his philosophy of leadership in a letter to a team of Ugandan missionaries, "The danger that comes up when we talk about leadership roles is that we forget that all of this has a servant character. Leaders must lead with authority, but their purpose is always to be a servant of Christ and then of the others on the team." Jack knew that only servant leaders will be successful in God's kingdom.

Preaching with Power

To one of Jack's copastors who has just begun to preach regularly at NLPC. This letter includes a fragment of another letter that was probably a first draft of this one.

July, 1980

Dear Will,

For my devotions this morning I went over these passages which concern the Spirit as the means of power for ministry and teaching. These verses all focus on the Spirit and reliance on Him as the cause of ministry:

Luke 24:49, "clothed with power from on high."
Acts 1:8, "You shall receive power."
Acts 4:33, "With great power the apostles gave their
   testimony to the resurrection of the Lord Jesus, and great
   grace was upon them all."
Acts 6:8, "and Stephen, full of grace and power."
Acts 8:19, "Give me also this power" (Simon).
1 Corinthians 2:4 "And my speech was not in plausible words
   of wisdom, but in demonstration of the Spirit and power."

1 Thessalonians 1:5, "Our gospel came to you not only in
word, but also in power and in the Holy Spirit and with
much authority and conviction."

I believe that these passages directly relate to our conversation
[about preaching]. The act of preaching is a daring proclamation by
faith which both admonishes and teaches at the same time so that
men's souls are really confronted by Christ and His Word. It appears
to me that the fundamental issue in preaching with power and
authority finally gets down to the power of the Spirit indwelling the
preacher in response to a total life of prayer, a holy walk in obedience,
the keeping of a good conscience by faith, and a careful cultivation of
moment-by-moment fellowship with Jesus.

Power in preaching comes from a strong faith that is qualified by
wisdom. Preaching is faith speaking; that is what it means to preach in
the power of the Spirit. And faith and confident praying are two sides
of the same coin. Basically I am convinced that men who do not make
praying their first priority in life and ministry should not preach or
pastor. As preachers they will be confusing models of a Christian man,
and as shepherds they will not show willingness to die for the sheep.
Their spirit will inevitably drift in the wrong direction.

As we seek faith and pray together, the power will be in the
preaching, and other matters such as style will begin to take their own
course. However, I don't mean that the models we imitate, the
decision whether to use a manuscript, effectiveness in eye contact,
and tone of voice are not important. They can reveal some hang-ups
in us, specifically a hanging on to some kind of false self-image, or
officialism, which quenches the Spirit in us.

But I do think the chief thing in effective ministry—as a total
endeavor—is the presence of the Spirit in the man—changing him
through the gospel, breaking down our idols, and building us into the
glorious image of Christ. Often a wrong self-image or a distorted one,

which hinders liberty in preaching, is simply a life minus much real
fellowship with Christ through the Spirit. When preaching is blandly
intellectual, contentless exhortation, or heavily doctrinal, usually there
is also missing the Spirit's presence. The man is only a man preaching
to men—not a "bush aglow."

My own struggles in this area have been utterly humbling. When
believers come and entreat me to talk with their pastors about the lack
of excitement in their preaching, I remember well how crushed I felt
when a brother said to me, "I'm sorry, but your preaching doesn't
edify me." Those are the words a member of New Life spoke to me
about four years ago. But God made this comment into a great
blessing. I asked the brother to pray for me. He later came and said,
"Your preaching has really helped me." God used his words to shock
me awake, to cause me to simplify my messages, to recruit people to
pray for me, and to make my preaching more Christ-centered.

Also, I have been gifted with Rose Marie, who not only speaks
about my failures with clarity, but is not afraid to tell me that the
message "sounded more like Jack than the Holy Spirit." Almost always
she is right. There is a mystery in the Holy Spirit's presence, but the
mystery should not be overstated. Most non-intellectual types can tell
intuitively whether the Spirit is present in preaching. They feel His
wooing, a conviction, a desire to be changed, and a longing to be holy,
and they know deep in their conscience that God Himself is speaking
through the preacher to them personally.

Of course you must evaluate both praise and blame, and when it
comes to non-intellectual types, they need to be taken seriously.
When they say, "I'm not being changed by your preaching," one must
do some soul-searching and be driven to new earnestness in prayer.

I do not, of course, think of prayer as retirement from the battle
to the isolation of a remote study, but the vertical aspect of vigorous
shepherding. Usually when our praying is weak, so is our shepherding
spirit; we have more in common with the hireling than the Shepherd

who died for His sheep. To me this is probably my worst sin—lack of love for God's sheep, a holy passion to see them kept from the cliffs and wolves, and fed in green pastures.

The reason I'm sharing these thoughts is to encourage you to make reliance on the Spirit a top priority in your life and encourage you to challenge me to do the same. Prayer will reflect such reliance.

Some suggestions:

1. Not only make prayer the top priority, but use your prayers to search out any unconscious areas of self-dependence, including the written sermon, preparation, training, official position, past successes or failures, the opinions of others, and your own self-evaluation as to your own appropriate style. Then shift all your confidence away from these things to Christ. Remember: sin is a deceiving power in the preacher. "Little children, keep yourselves from idols."

2. Pray specifically for the power of the Spirit in all your life and ministry and recruit others to do the same. Greatly increase this.

3. Pray *confidently* without any doubt that the Spirit will empower you.

4. Then make each sermon a daring proclamation of Christ, not just of the text, but of Christ in His glory and power. If I were to say what I see in many men who foster the bland saltless model that I mentioned, they just do not lift up or herald Christ Himself in their sermons. Since they are not heralding Christ, they do not receive Christ's power. Will Christ empower a man to make an intellectual discourse when the preacher has no real intent to preach Christ? He can give the intellectual content via his own strength and zeal. The delivery is his own and he can do what he intends to do. I have had some experience of this. But this is not the preaching of the New Covenant. We are a city of good news. We are commanded to lift up our voices with

strength and to get up to a high mountain to proclaim this good news. Exposition minus the heralding has all of Christ's foolishness in it, but none of Christ's power.

5. Relate preaching to soul care. We must repent for falling dismally short of the true model, that of our Good Shepherd who lays down His life for the sheep. Die for the sheep as you study the Word, die as you agonize in prayer for them, die as you look at some backsliding, die as you wrestle with your own sinful self-love. And then you will find daily a resurrection of power in life and ministry.

I think the test of this dying and rising from the dead as a shepherd is our willingness to give ourselves for the flock without calculation on our part. To do this we need to see ourselves in a mighty battle for souls and that our every move is in need of the presence of the Great Shepherd's love. This awareness powerfully affects our preaching. Take it away and preaching loses its salt and its soul care.

Please save this letter. I want it for my own instruction and admonition. I need your prayers that everything in here will be fulfilled in me as well as in you. I have prayed a great deal for you this week that God would give you plenty of honey and salt in your preaching.

Much love,
Jack

Leading a Small Group

To a young man who is leading a small group at NLPC that Jack and Rose Marie are also attending. This young man has recently finished school and is now working full-time. He feels overwhelmed by the challenges of doing ministry while he is working.

September, 1982

Dear Mark,

It was a fine time calling together on Saturday. We can give God all the glory for the openness of people to the gospel and to us, but I am also thankful to all the people who prayed and for the children's prayers in particular. The prayers of seven-year-olds go straight to heaven, I do believe. Too, I appreciate the zeal that brought you to go with me. . . .

Our time together also emboldens me to make some suggestions that you will want to consider for your own ministry and that of the mini-church [this is the name for the smaller house churches into which NLPC is divided]. At this time one of the central problems in the group is that people don't know how to use their gifts and are waiting for leadership. In the past their efforts have tended to cancel out the functioning of each other's gifts. From our point of view, it's hard to get a handle on the situation so as to know how and where to start.

Too, at present the group in its meetings has fallen into consumerism, i.e., passively receiving the truth, enjoying it, and being personally helped by it, but not ministering with it to others beyond the circle of the group. We need "to get the salt out of the saltshaker and into the world." But how?

I think we need to begin with defining your and my roles. I see myself primarily as your coach, your servant committed to encouraging, counseling, and, yes, even directing you in the work. I also see myself as one of your prime prayer supports. You are in my prayers and I am dedicating myself to prayer for you. On your part, I see you as the pacesetter-leader in the group. You have already begun this work with the fine presentation based on the book of Acts. I say "begun" because the application to the group has yet to be spelled out by you and defined for them in a way that they can get a handle on in the setting of the life of the mini-church. My prayer is that God will give you a spirit of wisdom like that of Stephen and Philip. My guess is that wisdom will take the form of using the gifts of someone like Joe [another young leader] to help you do some simple planning for the group. Just some simple plans that mobilize gifts, but do not exhaust people with ambitious undertakings beyond the abilities and capacities of those present. Simple strategies can also benefit you. A discerning pastor learns not to attempt everything at once, but to concentrate on a few things and do them well. As Jay Adams says, "We don't try all at once to chop down the whole forest, but begin with a single tree."

My guess is that you may have some reluctance [to see] yourself as the "pacesetter-leader" for the mini-church. If I'm reading you right—and I may not be—you appear to be expecting the group itself to be doing the pacesetting. In a way I agree with that. The Word taught should inspire them to action. But Steve [a fellow pastor] once pointed out to me that this can make sense only if we as leaders provide the channels for this energy to pass through. To use an illustration from the book of Acts, Paul is sought out by Barnabas quite aggressively. That is, Barnabas does not consult with the whole church in Antioch so far as we know. He may have done that, but what stands out is his initiative in getting Paul and putting him into the work. It's what you might call being selectively aggressive—making choices based upon prayer and the gift of wisdom imparted by the Holy Spirit. I am persuaded that you have much wisdom, but you must believe that the Spirit will give it to you and me as we wait upon Him.

105

Against that background, I want to recommend a few simple actions that call for your selective aggressiveness:

1. Join with me and let us choose and train at least three deacons for the group . . . the main thing is for us to have a program. At this point almost anything is better than nothing. Not to do anything is dangerous.

2. The second thing necessary is to develop a program for the meetings that gives us the means to implement what you have been teaching. Again, I think the strategy for doing this implementation could be really simple. You prepare questions—or have someone else do it—which deal with implementation, and twice a month we break down into small groups with an appointed leader for each in order to discuss and plan how to implement what we have been taught as individuals and as a group.

3. Too, my recommendation is that each time you teach you shorten the teaching and then let the group discuss implementation or report on past implementation. My thought is that your teaching is really great and much appreciated, but, like me, it does not hurt to learn to condense and summarize quickly. Well, it does hurt. I hate to do it because it requires more work, but it benefits me and others. You could almost look at it this way: this gives the believers the opportunity to become teachers with you.

4. Finally, the brothers and sisters need to become more welcoming and more concerned about others. It seems to me that we can minister beyond ourselves in two directions: one is to the children. We need regular meetings oriented toward them. The other is to seek out and welcome older folks, both saved and unsaved. Many are willing to come, but we lack any planning for handling them. One thing I believe would help,

which again is very simple. I know it will sound wiltingly traditional but it's one of the things that is traditional and makes sense. At the close of the meeting on Wednesday night you can accomplish much if you simply go around the room and shake everyone's hand. Especially if there are older people present, a warm shake, a tender touch, makes them know that you really mean what you say and you care for them. It costs very little. Ten minutes time, fifteen minutes. If necessary we can close the meeting earlier just to do this.

A pastor is someone who leads, an undershepherd. He loves the sheep and is willing to die for them. That means at times he is willing to lead them where they are not prepared or willing to go. He is willing to put up with their opposition and complaints just because he loves them, but he still does not let himself be guided by them in their stubbornness. What he wants is to learn from their wisdom, but he must also take up their wisdom and combine it with his own and then move forward. If he does not do that he is not really being their shepherd. I am confident that God is helping you in these matters, and I believe that your job is helping you. I've noticed a tie-in. Since you have taken on this employment and have matured as a worker, your teaching has also strengthened. I do understand your need for physical and emotional strength to bear the responsibility for your "secular" employment and the burdens of our little fellowship. But do let me assure you that hard as it may be it has really strengthened you. And through its strengthening you, it has strengthened us. It has also confirmed me in the conviction of the importance for most pastors and church leaders to have a significant period of work out there with ordinary people. They need to understand the feeling of life pushing them into a corner, of being overwhelmed by having too much to do, and should even try occasionally to work with people who are not nice but impossible.

In a way that you might not expect, your working has helped the rest of us. Sometimes, I suspect, it makes you feel overwhelmed with what seems to be so much to do. But this has an effect of breaking you down, softening you, and making you more daring in your teaching. One person who doesn't like New Life elders, who feels that we are self-righteous and self-sufficient people, admitted the other day that you were showing signs of brokenness before God. I doubt very much if that person is entirely fair, but even an unfriendly critic is compelled to admit that there is some wholesome humility being evidenced in your life. When even our enemies can see the Spirit of Christ at work in us, then God is certainly doing something great.

I know you will wait on the Lord in prayer and consider these matters before Him. May God give you much zeal, wisdom, and tender love as you minister to us and before Christ in our midst.

Most warmly in Christ,

Jack

The Prerequisites for Mission Work

To a young man who is anxious to get onto the mission field. Jack is explaining why the elders want him to wait another six months before leaving.

March, 1983

Dear Philip,

It seemed wise to me to continue our conversation of the other evening and attempt to spell out my thinking and, I believe, the thinking of our elders in general.

I'd like to begin by drawing a profile of what I see as your strengths and personality traits. As I mentioned the other night I see you as strong in the area of Christian family, and believe that this is the most precious gift you can bring to the team [the mission team that Philip and his family want to join]. You have an excellent family, and your son's friendliness shows it. This naturally puts you into a position of opportunity in the area of family hospitality.

The other thing that stands out is your practical skills. I see you as able to use this calling as an open door for helping others and witnessing. Combining this with your natural friendliness, I believe that Christ can use you greatly in developing contacts. . . .

Another area that I see you as strong in concerns the development of projects—especially study projects involving the organization of ideas. This has been seen in the good work you have done in educating others about "unreached peoples." You have also shown a high degree of commitment to Christ in doing this work.

I'd also like to say what I don't see in the profile at this time. It does not seem to me that you have the calling of elder—or team leader. Perhaps in the future, but not now. You asked me not to hesitate even if it meant rebuking you. Well, I don't see this as a rebuke, but a leader must have more evidence of a broken will and the humility that has gone deep into the soul with it. I don't mean you have no humility, but there is a need for growth in this matter in your life. One evidence of the need here appears to be in the area of listening to those of us who are older. What comes across to us is a sense of your mind having been already made up. Often we get the feeling that when we try to communicate a thought to you, the answer comes back with the thought that we really don't understand you.

The problem that creates for us is that whether we do or don't understand we are still left feeling that you didn't put yourself out far enough to answer what we asked. At times it has come across to me so strongly—that we didn't understand you—I had the impression your convictions were that it was almost a breach of God's will to question some things.

Let me explain what I have in mind. For most of us we would draw a distinction between the validity of opening up a mission field and the readiness of any person or persons to go there at a particular point in history. I understand that these questions are not completely separable. Obviously if no candidates are approved for a mission field, then it may not be opened up. Yet there is a distinction to be made between the case for a particular mission field and the discussion of personnel readiness. It was our failure too, but it did seem to me that it was hard for us to be heard on this distinction.

Another area where I wondered whether I was being heard has to do with the need for team structure, authority spelled out pretty clearly for the field, and some lines of responsibility drawn for the home base. It seems to me that it is a major lack to develop a team without more work on the decision-making process within the team at the very least. My experience has been that teams need at least one elder type, that a majority vote or consensus makes sense only if you have one senior leader whose responsibilities are pretty clearly defined. My impression is that I have not been heard by you on this— not at least very deeply.

Too, I don't think we as elders have quite been heard in the matter of evangelism. What we are after is not something fancy, but something straightforward that would show that you can do evangelism in our culture as well as in a cross-cultural situation. What

I mean is that you can adapt skills learned here, but it is hard to adapt what you have not mastered. My thought is that some of the basics have not been mastered by you personally, and that it is going to be very hard to learn cross-cultural skills if you haven't learned the easier ones in our culture. Somehow I do not think I have been heard, and a mark of a leader is ability to listen.

The reason I stress this point is that our elders' evaluation has been that at this time your calling is to learn in the areas I have mentioned. This lies behind our recommendation that you wait six months [before going to the mission field. This does not come] from a lack of love to you or . . . any lack of confidence in you, but only from the desire that you have an opportunity as a team to differentiate your gifts and that those who are still here have the opportunity to develop other skills and grow in maturity.

We do pray for you, Jane [Philip's wife], and the whole team very faithfully, and for [the country that they were going to]. We love you and are delighted by your burden for the lost. We have learned numerous things from you and the team. You are all very much appreciated, and I do believe that you will find a very special blessing coming on you and the team as you submit to what may appear to be different from your own hopes for going right away. How you submit now will have much to do with the unleashing of the Spirit in your lives together later on. And all of us long for the release of the Spirit of harvest to empower you with His mighty presence. We love you very much.

In Christ,
Jack

The Authority of Elders

To a pastor who is arguing that elders need to take a more active role in deciding who can take communion and who cannot.

May, 1983

Dear Jim,

Your communication about the complaint to the G.A. [General Assembly] arrived the other day, and I want to take this opportunity to respond to it.

My point is a simple one. On the one hand, I do agree with you that elders in our circles do not exercise enough authority in disciplining and discipling the members entrusted to their care. On the other hand, I believe the direction you are going has in it the danger of putting the wrong kind of emphasis on the elders' work. I am fearful of creating a church situation in which the elders may fall into the practice of becoming lords of believers' consciences. I do not think anyone would do this intentionally, but I believe in practice that where a severely restricted communion has been practiced the people of God have increasingly come to feel very little freedom and joy in coming to the Lord's Supper. In particular, brethren with weak faith and distressed consciences seem unconsciously to have picked up from the elders' severity a feeling of needing some super qualifications before coming to the Lord's Supper.

Another concern of mine is the complicated argumentation that is developed for the authority of the elders. Honestly, I have trouble finding a biblical basis for believers in a local church being responsible

for passing judgment on each visitor's preparation. We exercise proper
authority by explaining Christ's qualifications for coming to the table;
we do our best as elders to find out each visitor's heart relationship to
Christ in so far as circumstances of time and place permit, but can we
go beyond this in many instances? I think the basic responsibility does
go back to the general office. It is a matter of the individual conscience
and of the whole body to practice mutual discipline in order to prevent
scandalous persons from coming to the Lord's Supper. As elders we
alone can hardly do that for our own members without the people of
God mutually discipling one another under our guidance.

I am also concerned that zeal for the purity of the Lord's
precious ordinances not cover over how many sins we all have and the
truth that grace is for sinners. What the Lord's Supper is must not be
obscured by our proper quest for purity. We want the purity but we
must not forget that daily we all are very impure and that it is the
hope of grace that is set forth in the ordinances that impels us to
forsake our defilement. Your heart and mine in the Lord's Supper are
being welcomed by Christ to His grace. Faith can only respond to
such a welcome. I do not want us unwittingly to sin against Christ by
obscuring not only the grace character of the communion of Christ's
body and blood but even the cross itself.

Again, my difficulty with your complaint is not with the question
of authority of elders as such. I think we often fail to exercise
sufficient authority in very many ways. I want to see this strengthened.
But I also do find that in the New Testament the burden is put on the
general office. The command in 1 Corinthians is not for the elders to
examine the people but for each person to examine himself.

I have written to you in a bit of haste out of love for you. I need
to take more time to study your document and give you a more
detailed response. But I am getting ready to depart for Uganda and
I'm afraid I might never get to it. And just because I have you in my

heart as a dear brother I wanted to express my concerns with whatever imperfections my letter might contain.

> Most cordially in Christ,
> Jack Miller

Coping with Culture Shock

To the wife of a missionary couple. They are just beginning their work in Uganda, and she is overwhelmed by the new situation and the needs around her.

September, 1984

Dear Debby,

By now you will have received Rose Marie's letter and had time to think about it. Our prayers have been many for you that God will use this letter to bring strength to your heart and courage for serving Christ.

I also want to comment on culture shock. I have never been all that fond of the expression, since it seems to me to cover such a wide variety of things. One of those things is what Jim [one of Jack's copastors at NLPC] has called situation shock. What he has in mind is a human situation which seems either threatening or overwhelming. This is more than just the culture, but it is the problem that you face when you must decide when and how to say no to people who descend on you with great regularity and you are not sure how to do it. You also are fearful of coming across as colonialistic or as a budding imperialist. But there they are—descending on your household early in the morning, eating up Bill's study time, keeping you back from your work, and draining off your energy and time to be alone as a person or as a family. The situation shock is increased when you discover that most, perhaps even all, of the visitors for the week have had some selfish purpose in view or at least it looked selfish.

Result: You eventually begin to despise people inwardly without admitting it. You see the "raging of the kingdom of self" in Uganda and—what is frightening—you discover the kingdom of self is raging within you. Intensifications come through other aspects of the culture, constant delays, people always late, and people you set your hope on failing you.

In all this I take the greatest comfort in simply surrendering to the will of Christ. You need most desperately a centerpiece, an anchor in the storm of feelings and inward turmoil. That is the will of Christ. How did you get there in Uganda? Through the will of the Lord. How will you do your work? Through discerning the will of Christ. How will you learn to say no when you need to? Through trusting in the will of Christ. Get it deep into your mind that your only master is Christ, and that He has power to show you what to do in situations that are overwhelming or boring or draining.

But what in broad terms is the will of Christ? It is to be gentle and lowly in heart. It is to cast your burdens and anxieties upon Him, and to find rest for your souls as you labor to make Christ known. In this resting in Christ comes wisdom. Practical wisdom. Are you besieged with visitors? Well, you establish a plan for visitors, perhaps even stated hours for visiting. I know James [a Ugandan pastor] does this, though I think he has too many of the choice hours of the day open to them. Then also evangelize the visitors. And with that go about your work and with it give them some work to do. If they eat your food, then let them do a little work without paying them and test their characters. Ask them to pray for you.

Too, some of them are bound to be tricky people. Everybody knows that new missionaries attract multitudes of this sort. Don't be intimidated at such times. Tell them you see through them. Rebuke them with the warnings of the gospel about those who do not repent. Indeed, preach to all your visitors, and put some fire in it, and you will find it sifts them out. Be kind too but don't quickly credit every story you hear about hard luck and all that. Pray each day for wisdom in these matters: the Holy Spirit can give you special discernment. And when in doubt don't do anything.

Then also expect the situation shock to expose weaknesses in your relationships with Bill which were covered over by a Western lifestyle. Rose Marie and I were married for twenty-three years before we realized that our relationship was so much built around our children that we had failed in areas to cultivate our relationship with one another.

So take any strains on your marriage as an opportunity. Get away alone monthly for two or three days without your children and just get to know each other. You will find that a great blessing, perhaps one that will make many things come into a beautiful perspective.

And whatever you do, cultivate your own faith in Christ as the One who loves you to the uttermost. Soak yourself in a book like Philippians until every word is written on your heart.

But now I must close. Today is Rose Marie's day off. She tries to take Friday as her time to be by herself. Usually she forgets or things come up. But she is beginning to see that if you are in ministry as a woman you need some time when you shut out everybody and just be by yourself.

One last thought. I talked with your dad on Sunday. He is in excellent spirits and health. But he said he thought so much money had gone into medical expenses they would need to wait a time before coming to Uganda. They are most dear people.

Most warmly in Christ,
Jack

A Leader Raises Others Up

To the three missionaries who form the leadership team for the mission work in Uganda.

December, 1984

Dear Bill, Joe, and George,

At the moment I am sitting in my study looking out the window at the first snowfall of the season. It is coming down with a beauty that has a touch of heaven in it. Our big cherry tree is covered with it, and without its leaves the snow forms a lovely white decoration.

Rose Marie has been doing very well indeed in her growth in Christ. Really, it is a most amazing thing to see her so filled with faith and the Spirit! I give Jesus the glory for it all the way. She does need your prayers for her strength, for when she gets busy she tends to forget to watch her diet and then her problem with low blood sugar surfaces. That is her state right at the moment. You can imagine how Thanksgiving does not do anything for someone who must watch out for sweets and all carbohydrates and keep them at a minimum.

But in this letter I do wish to set before you my thoughts on Joe's role on the team and how his future ministry might develop. I know that clueing you in overly much to all my dreams for the future could be confusing, since so much needs to be done to concentrate on what is right before you without getting distracted. So I appeal to you for patience with me as I try to say some things about sharpening Joe's role and give you some idea about what may lie ahead for us, God willing.

First, I see Joe as really a co-leader with Bill but concentrating on a different area. Bill should be the overall team leader, but there are areas where Joe should be given the priority. I am thinking especially in the sphere of pastoring the team. Joe really must have full authority here in Christ to give active leadership to everyone. He is the pastor of the families and needs to be recognized in that role and given due honor by all. I do not mean that Bill is not also the pastor of the families, as team leader over all; he is. But Joe ought to have priority in the areas of family life. . . .

Bill's role is essentially that of a servant. . . . The danger that comes up when we talk about leadership roles is that we forget that all of this has a servant character. Leaders must lead with authority, but their purpose is always to be a servant of Christ and then of the others on the team. So do beware of hidden restlessness and a spirit of independency when these matters are thought upon.

I think to some degree the model God has given us at New Life helps. We have always under my leadership aimed at consensus, but it just has not been true that all leadership has been equal. For a long time I have been the team leader, and to some degree still am. But my purpose has always been to raise up the gifts of others for the service of Christ. At present I am doing everything in my power to develop Steve, George, and Chris to further replace me in the work. Many things they now do much better than I. . . . It's not so easy to hand over authority to others, and sometimes to watch them stumble a bit, and sometimes stumble badly, but in the giving up of authority to others by the team leader there is a freedom and a peace and a liberation to work in new spheres.

I anticipate the same kind of thing happening with Bill and George. As George learns to relate to Bill personally and as a team leader, he will himself be learning how to become a more effective leader. It's true that a mission must have more definite lines of authority than a church, and that makes it sometimes harder to bear when you see weaknesses in leaders over you. But, what I would expect George to be doing and I am sure he has done, is not to major in seeing Bill's weaknesses—which I am sure are not as many as mine—but to learn from his strengths and support him in areas where his limitations are visible. Going through this kind of submission is what prepares you to be a leader yourself. . . .

Finally, brethren, what really matters is serving one another with a spirit of love. Concentrate on that, be patient with one another, recognize that all of us need a Father who accepts many half-done and even poorly done gifts. Praise God for free forgiveness and the blood of the Lamb. I cannot say how much I treasure you all.

In Christ,

Jack

Learning to Be a Positive Person of Faith

To a young woman who has gone to Uganda to teach the missionary children on the team.

June, 1985

Dear Sharon,

We praise Jesus very much for your letters. It is so encouraging to learn how He carries you where your own strength could not. I have been learning the same thing. Yesterday I had to work on a chapter in my book, which was a big unorganized pile. Would you believe that by prayer in a few hours it was completely redone and simplified? I could never have done that in my own strength. I am touched by what Christ does for me through your prayers and the prayers of others.

I don't see how I could be happier about your being in Uganda with the team. Sure, it will be hard, maybe impossible, but think of the adventure in it all. I am not thinking mainly of the adventure of being located in Fort Portal. Obviously that is an adventure of a sort. Rather, I have in view the splendid adventure of becoming gentle like Christ, of having a dignity which grows out of humility, patience, and giving up one's cherished rights. Too, the adventure of talking through problems rather than withdrawing. That is noble, finding Christ's courage to communicate, to suffer, to learn as a free daughter of the Most High.

Remember what Florence Allshorn said about "saving the situation"? She learned that she could always be a positive person of faith when she didn't care "two hoots about what happened to me." Once she became dedicated to fostering Christ's love in others and helping with their welfare she was free from the burden of a hard unyielding ego.

We have also prayed much for your safety. Last Thursday and for the whole week we have prayed that angel legions will camp around you. May the angel of the Lord who is Jesus go before you and give you courage at all times. May your heart constantly move from fear to faith through awareness of His presence.

We also have a good sense of what it is to be crowded together in one house with lots of people. On Saturday, Barb and Angelo and AJ [Jack's daughter, son-in-law, and grandson] moved in with us and they are working with the young people and singles. So the house is full up, and you get up early to get your shower. We find that it is an opportunity to grow in thoughtfulness, especially as you discover a cherished hour of privacy is washed away in the general flow of visitors and people living together.

But it does make it important that you begin to plan regularly to get some time away. I'm not sure how you do that, but it is important to get some time alone each week and to plan longer vacation times also. . . .

Greetings to your little flock.

In Christ,
Jack

A Leader Delegates

To one of Jack's copastors who is getting ready to return from sabbatical.

July, 1985

Dear Steve,

Rose Marie and I are at the PEF [Presbyterian Evangelistic Fellowship] conference. Bernie Kuiper has been saying that Peter's great mistake on the Mount of Transfiguration was to put Jesus on the same level as the superstars Moses and Elijah. That leads to a life centered on shadows, not on the substance. Oh for grace to hold to Christ, the Substance, and to forsake all shadows. I am appalled by the way indwelling sin blinds me so often to the superlative glory of Christ, but my prayer is that you and I will have our eyes opened to see the inheritance and hope and power we have working in our behalf in Christ.

My prayer is that the Spirit will strengthen you with power to take in Christ's life by faith. The devil's strategy is to get us problem-centered rather than Christ-centered. That will be your biggest struggle "after sabbatical." I can't believe what a war that is—to not shift from God's praise to people and their endless problems. You will be receiving a letter from me about Fred [a pastor that they both had been counseling]. Beneath it all, I think this is Fred's biggest problem. Under the intense pressure of ministry, he has lost something of the praise that has characterized his ministry. It is so easy to write daily our own little book *From Praise to Prison* or *How to Cultivate Ministry Paranoia*. I have found it in myself, seen it in others and now in Fred. Sure we may have failed him in more ways than we can count, but let's not fail him now by not drawing him back to a spirit of praise. . . .

I have been seeking to help Peter [another pastor at New Life] along these lines. I know how to do it, being cut out of the same cloth. This past week he was away and came back to a crisis with [a family where the father has a drug addiction]. Restrained by the Spirit, I did not go over, but prayed with [the wife] over the phone after giving counsel. It was hard not to feel guilty at first for not going to help her, but instead I sent Greg and Doris Lester [an older couple at NLPC]. They did a great job. Then Peter and Joshua [another elder] went, but Peter found grace not to be [further involved]. I really commended Peter for delegating that. He is seeing God's power in concentrating and he has been surprised at the effectiveness of others.

Then there was a family with huge problems, like a $10,000 series of debts and almost total disorganization. After urging by me, Peter found the grace to recruit two other believers with appropriate gifts to help and made only one call on the family himself. I was encouraged by this discipline on his part. Praise the Lord! We have both been impressed too by the willingness of others to help and the quality of help they give.

Peter and I spend time each Monday morning fellowshipping, not especially planning, but just sharing what Christ has been teaching us. It's very helpful and leads to some good decisions for life and ministry. I also spend some time with him each Thursday morning and write him letters rather often, encouraging him and also pointing out any weaknesses. I believe I sent you one of my recent letters. He certainly is a fine Christian.

For myself, I have been wrestling with the question of God's will for my life and ministry. It has been very profitable. I am also interested in interacting with you on what God wants me to do. I am equally concerned with God's will being made known to Rose Marie. She has been well received at PEF with this "first" women's seminar, led by her and Roseann [Jack's oldest daughter].

As I mentioned to you earlier, it has been liberating to have a solid day each week set aside for study and writing without interruptions. Some good writing appears to be coming as a gift of grace.

Several general conclusions have come to me, as I pray and meditate on God's will. Several of the issues have been raised over the past year during our staff meetings. Here are some that strike me:

1. *Concentrate.* I am convinced I am still trying to do too much.
2. *Block out sufficient time to do the job.* I constantly underestimate the time required to do major projects.
3. *Take time off* to get refreshed and recover energy and creativity.
4. *Plan my schedule* so as to recognize that Rose Marie also has a demanding ministry.
5. *Do the things—and only the things—I am called to do* and cannot delegate. I must remember that my life might be short and select my goals to get done crucial tasks in good order.
6. *Remember that I am aging,* and like it or not my health is not what it once was. To push myself as I did this past winter and spring is risky—if not to my physical health, at least to my sanity and spiritual health.

So as I chew on these issues and share my thoughts with you, I solicit your prayers and wisdom. I am strongly convinced that God will bless our working together at this time.

I also am moving toward some insights as to God's purpose in my life. One conclusion that I have come to is that writing and study should have more priority for me over the next two years. Rose Marie has the same burden. She hungers to get a firmer grip on Romans and Galatians and to get more material in written form.

A second conclusion that we have both come to is that we feel it is hard to get depth of study and quality writing done locally. I suspect you know what a difference it makes to go away.

A third conclusion concerns my job description. It has too many heavy areas of ministry on it. I do not mean simply what is written out, but what I actually do . . . [also] it is clear that WHM carries heavy emotional pressures for me.

A fourth conclusion concerns what areas I should hand over to the staff. Among those that I want to hand over are any heavy-duty local problems. I have had some success in this area this summer.

Though God has helped me to speak and act decisively and delegate, the conflict with Fred has been a burden. I feel that it takes years to plant a church, but only a few poorly expressed thoughts to lose one in a matter of minutes. But I must step back because it is not my calling, and I do trust your wisdom and the Holy Spirit's leading of you.

That leads me to a fifth conclusion. It is that I trust your leadership and believe that as you grow in experience and prayer you will fulfill your ministry fully through the power of the Spirit. Actually, my conviction is that too much leadership by me in local affairs will hinder your development. I do not mean that I plan to withdraw or not to give you my full support as a pastor. I shall certainly continue to do that as God gives grace to both of us to follow Christ. But I do believe that you need the opportunity to develop as a pastor with less—how shall I say it?—of my shadow on your path. I love you, Steve, and respect you greatly and believe that you will find grace daily and during the years ahead to penetrate to the core of life and ministry. You need freedom even to make your own mistakes—a thought that Bob [an executive friend who was working with the staff] has expressed as key to learning to lead. I urge you to get to know Christ better each day and to mature in expressions of His love. I expect to see you richly blessed by Him. Much of leadership is just loving Jesus and handing on that love.

In this light Rose Marie and I are going to submit a proposal for a sabbatical in 1986 from April 14 to June 14. You will notice that I said "Rose Marie and I." I have in mind our working jointly on a book on Galatians, but also using the sabbatical as a rest time, both physical, mental, and emotional. What we have in view is to tape our material on Galatians in December. I will give some of the lectures in Sunday school at her request. Then we shall take two months to study further and hopefully have the first draft of a manuscript. I am not putting the matter of the manuscript into the proposal, because the main purpose is to get the material thoroughly understood, digested, and organized. Too, writing may put too much pressure on us. We need a rest.

In the year that follows (1987), I want to organize my time so that I have about five months per year away from the church, not just to concentrate on WHM, but to give about one-fourth of my time per year to writing and study.

This summer I have been going over my files and various pieces of writing. It's awesome how much is about two-thirds to three-fourths completed and gathering dust. The material on abortion that you received was a further draft of some material on "Abortion and the Doctor" which I did about three or four years ago. Anyway this is a big help to my conscience, and after a bit more work I hope to send it to about ninety doctors and board members at Abington Hospital early in September. I need to get into the conflict.

Dear brother, I do feel seriously the need to speak directly and prophetically for our church in our time. I do not say this with pride if I know my own heart, but I do believe there are some things that desperately need to be said.

Again, let me assure you that I stand firmly behind you and your ministry, and do look forward to hearing all that God has taught you this summer. Paul Miller is all excited by what you were able to do on the leadership training before you left. And Jeff gave us a fine report at a recent 11:00 o'clock service on your lives and progress. We were all delighted.

We look forward to God's future with the thrill of a confident faith. I am sharing these thoughts with you first, to give you a chance to interact with me.

Most warmly in Christ,
Jack

Planning for the Future

To Jack's copastor who is coming back from his sabbatical. They are discussing planning issues that were left unresolved before he went away.

August, 1985

Dear Steve,

Welcome home to New Life! We were glad that you could get away, but you were also really missed by the rest of us.

[The churches I spoke at this summer] did a lot to deepen my appreciation for our New Life team . . . it impressed me that one of the problems in many churches is that pastors do not work hard on significant work. In other words, a good deal of old-fashioned wheel-spinning takes place. And I cannot imagine you or the rest of the staff doing these things.

[Many of the churches we visited were very small and they do have unique problems.] . . . A small church often has only a few people and the atmosphere tends to get heavy just from that. But it also gets heavy because of a desire to impose speedy control on people who come in. To show the mind-set, an elder from [a small church] asked me this question after I told him how many [from a nominal Christian background] had become Christians in our area: "Don't you have to be stricter— harder —on people with that background—to keep them in line?"

. . . I did tell him that many of them had an unusual godliness in life and seemed to respond with such enthusiasm for the gospel that we did not need to do much correcting. But how thankful I am that

127

we have a gospel freedom and joy at New Life—and that all of us have at least something of this in our lives and ministries.

Regarding your re-entry which you mentioned in your letter, let me say just enjoy yourself as much as you can. Don't try too hard, and let it all come naturally. We look forward to learning what God has taught you. On a more basic level, let me encourage you to have confidence that Christ by His Spirit is really with you, and you can rely on Him to give you grace to pursue your work aggressively without fear. I hope you are even willing to make a few mistakes, without feeling that this makes you a failure. Really, let me underscore that some failure just goes with ministry. What we want to do is to avoid repeating the same mistakes, and hopefully not to fall into disastrous errors of judgment. But risks we must take. That's why I really have appreciated your willingness to press issues before us on the "Big Picture" and on our job descriptions.

Here's how I think we should look at one another and our work. Each of us should make more decisions that might ordinarily be talked over with the rest. I think we do some time wasting, when we should make more on-the-spot decisions. How do you see that? In other words, we can waste each other's time on matters that can be decided individually. For example, I have been counseling briefly from time to time with [a couple struggling in their marriage], and I have made a number of decisions that ordinarily I would have handed over to a session committee or at least brought to the staff. But why do this? If I am wrong, then you can correct me, but if I am right then I have cleared away with very brief discussions a lot of road blocks and saved a good deal of time. Eventually the session needs to [make a final decision], but my hope is that my recommendation will make a committee and much staff time unnecessary. Not that there should not be some interaction. I believe that is needed, but only perhaps a little.

During the summer Peter and I also tried to disciple each other to avoid heavy counseling involvement where part of the work could be delegated. Specifically I urged him to delegate his work with several people and not to get drawn into "black hole" problems. Our fellowship on Monday morning, where we have just shared and shepherded one another, has been especially helpful. We try to keep immediate, heavy problems out of the discussion and discuss what we are learning from Scripture or bring up our own deeper needs. Somehow this time together seems to contribute toward our having more aggressiveness in ministry and more joy. I love it, it makes my week. Peter and I would both be most happy to have you join us.

Indeed, we long for that, after having a taste of what mutual shepherding fellowship can bring. Nothing like it! Except perhaps the quality of Bible study and prayer that Rose Marie and I have been having together. We have become so excited about the study of Romans that we are almost ready to take off—at least I am.

My fear is that in the fall we may lose our joy in Christ and become overabsorbed in work. I at least seemed to have fallen into this pit in the spring, and fear like the plague the thought of getting back into such a pattern. It eventually came to me that I was so busy with job descriptions, "Big Picture," and the residue of discipline problems from last November that I was getting emotionally and physically exhausted. Rose Marie thinks that during that time I seriously risked my health and that just now I am coming out of physical exhaustion. It also seems to me that we may have made two mistakes in handling the "Big Picture":

1. We did not give equal time to prayer, including waiting on God and asking others to pray for such momentous matters.
2. We did not allow a sufficiently lengthy period for considering such a weighty matter. Perhaps we should have allowed a full year to get the issues into focus.

My gut feeling is that if we make the wrong decision here we could undo a great deal of our last decade's work. This came to my mind as I saw what happened at [a church Rose Marie and Jack had visited]. The church, at one time, was headed in the direction of being the largest and strongest in the presbytery with influence in all directions. Then it subdivided and became just one more church. It is downright chilling to see how this church has declined.

To be sure, I do not want to vote against the Perimeter Church model or the Twin Mother Church model out of fear. I have really tried not to do that. But when I consider the balance of factors, I come out about where Larry [a fellow elder] does—favoring the larger church model. Several factors influence my thinking at this point:

1. Major organizational changes put heavy workloads on every one of the staff, and my sense of things is that we need to shift our orientation to more fellowship in the gospel, and let new organizational developments flow organically out of the working of God in our lives and minds as a fellowship of shepherds walking in joy.

2. Our lack of experience in developing another model. My idea is that we should first cultivate a stronger relationship with the Northeast New Life [a daughter church of NLPC] and Logan [a church plant in Philadelphia that NLPC was helping to support] and then move on from there with their cooperation. Too, I think the training program, with intern development, needs to get going before we plant more daughter churches.

3. Prayer is not yet the priority it should be in our lives as staff members. In visiting other churches, I came away with the conclusion that the source of God-centered growth is prayer alone and the accompanying power of the Holy Spirit. It appears to me that organic expansion of the church can occur

only as the elders and deacons are devoted to prayer continually as in Acts 1:13–14 and we mobilize the congregation to do the same. At this time I do not think we have yet broken enough of the busyness syndrome to get down to real business of aggressive church planting.

Let me add a note to this last thought. You mentioned that God had spoken to you on your sabbatical on your pride. He has really been doing the same to me over this past year, and He has become more insistent. I have been studying Romans 7, sensing that understanding it is the key to understanding Romans. Lately I have concluded that understanding chapter 5 is even more important for getting Romans understood. But anyway what has been hitting me is that indwelling sin in the believer is pretty radical stuff, and that my sin-sick soul is always being lifted up in one form or another with pride. I am thinking that much of my inward coldness and self-centeredness and unteachability is just arrogance, and yet the stuff is so strong that only the gospel and the Spirit through constant prayer can make me normal.

Take this matter of thankfulness. Paul, for instance, speaks of constantly thanking God for the brothers and sisters in the churches. Apparently thankfulness to God for these believers just flowed through him and out of his mouth. How convicting! I really had to repent for taking you brothers so much for granted. Of course, I was thankful for you, but not in the Pauline way. So in a new way I have sought to overflow with thankfulness for you. Steve, you mean an awful lot to me. Just thanks for being my faithful friend and brother in Christ. How much I appreciate all the loyalty you have shown first to Christ and then to me through all the years. It has been a gift of the Spirit to me. Your role at New Life has been absolutely crucial, and I do appreciate it very much.

Finally a few thoughts on job descriptions, my own and yours and Peter's. I am very open to interacting with you and others, but here is where my thinking has been heading after prayer.

Generally, I would like to move in the direction of you and Peter as being seen as the pastors at New Life Church, and myself as the missionary of the church. Under the title missionary of the church I would include the writing ministry and the training ministry. I am especially zealous to get space in my schedule to write on such topics as abortion and homosexuality and AIDS. I would really like to get out of heavy-duty counseling problems and lots of heavy planning sessions. I found that in the spring this was just too much for me. I also want to organize my time so that I have more blocks of it for working on specific projects. This is really improving, but it has a good ways to go.

It seems that my being more in the background as pastor will help you and Peter (and the ministry) in two ways: One, the congregation will become more accustomed to your pastoral leadership and less to mine. Second, you will both find it an opportunity to grow by the pressures of impossible tasks. For instance, I have noted how this summer Peter has grown through being given more responsibilities on his own. He has recruited forty people who have agreed to pray regularly for him and his ministry! And you can certainly see the results.

I have reason to believe that I am going in the right direction in my life and job description of my calling. I feel a strong pull of my heart toward a more prophetic ministry!

I also want to bring into sharp focus for you my limitations. Rose Marie was so distressed by the physical and emotional weakness that surfaced in the spring that she went to see my cardiologist about it. He told her four things concerning me: Physically I am still basically O.K. I'm getting older and will be having less strength. Emotionally I have a host of burdens to bear in the ministry which are very wearing. I have an extra unconscious burden which I will carry with me for the rest of my life—the knowledge that I could die any time from a heart attack. He says that the last burden is no small one. His advice is for me regularly to do something I enjoy—time detached from the ministry and church. . . .

I also need your prayers for an issue that my doctor touched on in his conversation with Rose Marie. He mentioned my fear of death—an unconscious one. At first I did not take that very seriously, but upon reflection it may be a bigger factor in my mind than I know. The human heart, including mine, is pretty deceitful. But looking back on all that I accepted on my plate in the spring and late winter, I think maybe I did have some kind of death wish—not so much the direct fear of death but a kind of desire to get it done and over with. At least I know that at one or two points death did begin to look attractive to me, a way of escaping from a ministry which just moved from one problem to another and one issue to another as though we as a staff were members of a Christian corporation not having much joy and fellowship together. Certainly that was my confused point of view, but it shows what a power sinful unbelief had become in my life. To some degree I think I am still working through this, and maybe it's something that will be a struggle for the rest of my life. At any rate Satan has his hand in it, and I ask for your prayers that Christ may deliver me from all the wiles of the powers of darkness. I choose life and Christ—but do pray that Christ will protect my mind from these attacks.

I have enclosed a proposed job description for your interaction. My idea is that if I were around about three months in the spring and about four months in the fall that would be enough to do the following:

1. take an aggressive part in the WHM leadership training,
2. work with interns,
3. do preaching series and Bible teaching, with Rose Marie also doing teaching.

Such a schedule would free me up for more writing time. For me this is crucial, at least for two years. It is now clear to me that writing is much more than just writing. One reason so many projects are three-fourths completed is simply lack of time for working things through and developing publishing outlets. Where we have followed through with intensive labor on writing projects, the results have been productive. P.E.F. now sells about 40,000 copies of the New Life booklet per year, and that without any real promotion.

I also wish to encourage you not to think of yourself as the person who must pick up the things I cannot do. That really is the responsibility of the Head of the church. What both of us must do is find His will for our lives. I want you to know that I am equally concerned about helping you with your job description and share your concern that you not lose your pastoral edge and preaching freshness through involvement in work as an "executive pastor." The heart of the matter is summarized in the accompanying Peanuts cartoon, with Snoopy as our pastoral model.

God bless you most richly in Jesus Christ. He must increase, but we must decrease.

Most affectionately in Him,

Jack

Church-Planting Basics

To a young man who is preparing to go to Ireland as a missionary.

February, 1986

Dear Randy,

Since you and I are both busy and I do want to get to you some of my thinking on your ministry in Ireland . . .

I want to set before you several things that you will want to make priorities for your ministry in Ireland. First, prayer. I believe God is calling you to devote yourself to prayer and also to study in Scripture its basis, its nature, and practice. I am persuaded nothing worth mentioning is going to happen in Ireland unless you set the pace in the area of prayer. Secondly, pastoring. Your primary task is to pastor the Irish Christians and even our team members under [the team leader's] oversight. I want to encourage you to reread my book *Evangelism and Your Church,* and I shall get you a copy of my new book *(Outgrowing the Ingrown Church)* as soon as I have copies made. You can also learn a great deal about pastoring from Richard who showed great zeal in pastoring you in Ireland. Third, communicating the gospel. You have gifts for communication and you should engage in a vigorous program of self-development. Your vision for writing a commentary is fine. But not now. Later I will share with you areas where I have worked and where I need to work. But I can mention four that are really important for you: simplicity, vividness, unity, and dramatic force in your preaching and teaching. What we must have in planting a church is not depth and complexity, but the basics brought home with love, tenderness, and clarity.

Finally, I am especially concerned that you develop your relationship with Lucy [Randy's wife] and with the team as a whole. Your relationship with her is the one that counts most of all. The relationship with his dear bride is the one which always reveals where the pastor really

135

is in his spiritual life and walk with the Lord. Richard mentioned to you and to me how concerned he was for your relationship to Lucy and your father, and I share that concern. Rose Marie has the same burden. We both feel that you and Lucy have some basic issues to work through . . . not that you should be perfect but as Richard says, "You ought to be enjoying each other, not just surviving together."

It is also supremely important that you and Lucy cultivate your relationship with the team, beginning with your team leader and his wife. I do have some concerns because of your experiences at [your previous church]. Some of the things you met there were not good team models at all, and my guess is that this background will make it difficult for you to have full trust of others, to think and work from within a team, and to develop a strong relationship with your team leader. . . .

I am encouraged by your progress reported to me by the WHM staff. Do pray for me to grow in humility. I think most human problems stem from pride as do mine. I love you both, dear friends in Christ. Do not fear the future, but trust Christ by His Spirit's power to field a team for Ireland full of grace.

Much love,
Jack

Learning to Listen

To the team leader of the missionaries in Uganda.

February, 1986

Dear Bill,

Here I am in chilly, rainy Dublin, thinking of you in sun-drenched Nairobi. Oh envy! Looking in the mirror, I can already see my East African suntan beginning to fade. I've been here five days and have seen watery blue sky only a couple of times for a brief period. You can believe when I mentioned the idea of a gathering of the whole WHM missionary clan in 1987, the immediate response from all was loud enthusiasm for meeting anywhere the sun shines. Switzerland? South of Spain? Nairobi—anywhere that the skies are not Irish all the day long. We all love Ireland, but we do agree it is a land of rust and rheumatism.

Please do accept my warm thanks for all the work you did for our recent meetings in Nairobi. We all want you to know that we felt your love to us, expressed in your personal warmth and your hard work of preparation for the team meetings and the evangelism in Kibera and Mukuruu. God has used the fiery trial of the evacuation from Uganda to mature you in the image of Christ's praise. The glory is His!

The crown of the whole thing was your obvious growth in your ability to listen. I know that could sound like a put-down compliment. But it is not at all. My belief is that comparatively few leaders in the church today are really sharp listeners. I know I have an ongoing struggle with listening, especially when issues are being considered that are very important to me. I get afraid that the wrong ideas will prevail. At such times I have an overpowering urge to talk rather than to ask questions and listen for answers from others. It seems supremely important that everyone be immediately brought to perfect clarity by my powers of illumination and persuasion.

Sometimes what makes this confusing for me is that the Lord has given me a measure of insight as a leader. I do have almost thirty years of experience in planting and growing churches. But my mistake is that I want to persuade *now* without first gathering in all the knowledge I need and do not see the importance of taking time to hear others, to learn from them, and to reveal my love with a sympathetic response to what they are thinking. Really, patient, attentive listening is another way of saying, "I love you and respect you." Not listening or half-listening is contrariwise, my saying, "I have a much higher view of my opinions than I have of yours." Expressed in that bold way, my not listening is exposed as egocentricity, perhaps even hardline pride.

Once [another elder] gently admonished me, "Jack, you are a born persuader as a leader. It's a good gift, but persuasion should *follow* listening and asking questions. Give balance to your leadership by delaying your persuading until you have had time to ask questions and to listen closely to the answers." I could agree with that in principle and did not have so much trouble applying it to meetings where the issues were not major. But when the concerns being considered seem foundational to me, it is hard for me to listen closely, or to refrain from breaking into someone's speaking. I feel a compelling need to get the problems and lines of thought into clear focus *now*. It's almost as though I try to act as the head of the church.

I know that may sound silly. Who after all is so stupid as to think he can replace Christ as the Lord over the church and its mission? Still, the history of the church has very few pages that are not blotted by the megalomania of church leaders. It is simply that we are prone to fall in love with our own authority as official leaders and unconsciously distance ourselves from Christ as the real Head of the church. We begin to try to control the church or the members of the team and end up in personality conflicts with brothers and sisters who either dislike our control or want to impose their own control on us. When this happens, we are inwardly swept by anxieties. For the irony of it all is that the more we try to control the work in our own name, the more the work and its problems control us. We begin by trying to own the work of God and end up with the ministry owning us. Perfecting the work becomes our bondage, and the bondage manifests itself by our losing the capacity to patiently listen to others and to be corrected by them.

Indeed when we get into this perfectionist frame, we can fall into some *very* nasty bondages in our leadership. We hate criticism; we get preoccupied with trivia and are willing to fight major battles over minor issues. We feel threatened when anyone disagrees with us or introduces an idea that is unfamiliar. I once knew of a church situation where a pastor and his associate gradually developed such a rotten relationship that more than once they beat on each other with their fists!

So I want you to join me in confessing our human depravity as leaders. Do not be surprised to find your corruption expressing itself in perfectionist self-will in your own leadership style. Expect to encounter in yourself defensiveness, dominance, and poor listening practices. But I also urge you to have much greater confidence in Christ's capacity to release you from such bondages. He is the crucified Head of the church, the only One who knows how to perfect it! Just to know that fact, to rest upon it, and to build upon it, is to be released from the bondages which duty imposes upon our spirits. You find His liberating grace through honest confession of sin and fresh release by surrendering the government of the church to its Head.

You will feel keenly your duty to hold the team in Uganda to the vision of reaching the Bakonjo and Bwambc people in the Ruwenzori Mountains. You will want to give your mind, heart, and will to getting each member to devote all his or her resources to implementing the plan for accomplishing this God-given vision. But never forget that it is really Christ who puts forth the executive for getting this work

139

done. Let His authority express itself through you, a loving shepherd who gently leads his fellow shepherds to a better knowledge of Christ.

This is His way, the way of release through harmonizing our wills with His.

Most cordially,
Jack

Trusting the Work to Others

To a missionary who is on his way to Ireland as a team leader.

March, 1986

Dear Mike,

By the time you receive this note I shall, God willing, be warming my toes in sunny Spain. I am committed to doing some of that, just taking it easy and developing a deeper relationship with Christ and my dearest Rose Marie in the sun. She's good fun, and a most gracious friend and deserves the best care I can give her. Do the same for Beth [Mike's wife] whenever you can. . . .

I guess the issue that I want to pose for you is your trusting God to take care of the work if you are not there. . . . A leader must be willing to trust the unfolding of the work to the Lordship of Christ and to believe that Christ has it in His control. I would also encourage you to have confidence in the wisdom that God has given to the sessions and the board. . . .

I am constantly in the struggle perhaps you are in, one where I am forced to trust the work to other people. The real test for me is this: would I rejoice if the team got a church started before I arrived on the scene? Would I feel left out if they succeeded or failed without me? And possibly in your case would you rejoice if the work had wonderful momentum before you stepped off the airplane? I think that might be hard to do. I know I would probably struggle with it— unless God gave me a bigger vision of the kingdom and His working which helped me transcend both my insecurities and my need to be seen as a success. But there is a freedom given by the Spirit when I submit myself to the moving of the kingdom and see myself and others as partners and stewards in God's success. In a nutshell, I must move by faith and not by fear, and certainly guard myself from feeling I need to prove myself or be in control.

For my money I know that you have the Holy Spirit and His gifts for ministry and trust Him to lead you to move with courage and wisdom in all things. I am behind you and for you all the way and think you have been moving in the right direction all along. . . . Mark 9:23: "All things are possible to him who believes." Philippians 4:13: "I can do all things through Christ who strengthens me."

We also believe that the Lord was with you at the missions conference and the fruit will be forthcoming for years to come. I look forward to seeing you in Ireland. . . . God bless. I love you in Jesus very much.

Most warmly,

Jack

Learning to Affirm Your Leader

To a missionary in Uganda. The team has recently gone through a hard time of sickness and a forced evacuation because of unrest in their area.

July, 1986

Dear Joe,

Greetings in the Lord Jesus Christ! What a series of adventures you have been through! It seems that our team has set a record—at least for us—of harrowing adventures, everything from evacuation to hepatitis—not to mention moving your families through Uganda and into position in East Africa. And add to that the problem Betsy had with her Rh factor and the pregnancy. So we are thrilled and delighted that you are in place at last, vehicles are there, and everyone seems to be in good health. And babies and mothers all are healthy.

This has certainly been a tale of satanic attack and Christ's deliverance in answer to many prayers. Praise Him for what He has done!

I am interested in knowing more about certain things, though, and you seem to be the one who can help me. First, do you have any idea how so many of you came down with hepatitis all at once? My concern here is to give guidance to other teams for the future—things to watch out for. But maybe it was just mysterious how it happened all at once—and just an attack conceived and directed by Satan. I'd like your input on this. Hepatitis is a problem in North Africa too. One of the macaronis [the name a missionary team in East Africa uses for itself] with Frontiers died from it, maybe about the time you all were coming down with it.

A second question. What about blood transfusions for team members and their families in cases of emergencies? We are reading horrible statistics about AIDS in Uganda and that it is often spread through blood transfusions. So—can we stockpile our own blood in case of emergencies? Are there other alternatives? Paul and I have a keen interest in doing everything in our power to protect all of you and your families.

A third question. Are the team members taking rest breaks and vacations? I am assuming that Bill and Debby must have about three months saved up. Am I right? I definitely do not count the time spent in Nairobi as vacation. Some of it they can take next spring when we have our WHM retreat in Europe—if we can pull it off. But in the meantime it is important that they get away for a week here and there, maybe for two weeks. The same is true for you and Cheryl, and for George and Betsy. I am really concerned about people getting worn down and becoming stale. This reflects my experience in Spain.

I am especially concerned for the Clarks. It has been an intense two-and-one-half years for them. I also want to encourage one- or two-day retreats for you men and the same for the women. It is so easy to get into a terrible rut and not know it. There is nothing more liberating than for a man to go away for a day all by himself. Steve [Jack's copastor at NLPC] did it last fall at my encouragement and he says that it was utterly transforming. He came back having stood in the presence of the Almighty. Nothing more cleansing and healing than that.

So I am encouraging you to take brotherly leadership in this crucial matter. I don't see it as an infringement of Bill's team leadership in any way. With your tact I am sure you can help him see the importance of this. Perhaps a good way to begin would be to encourage the three of you men to go away for a day of prayer and fasting, with the intention of developing a balanced schedule.

143

I will also be writing Bill about the importance of this.

I also want to let you and Cheryl know how pleased we are here at home over your recovery and your getting in place in Western Uganda. That is so wonderful. Your experience and maturity bring a great strength to our team there. . . .

There are also a few suggestions and thoughts on my mind how you can help Bill strengthen his team leadership. First, every team leader needs a great deal of affirming by his fellow workers. The tendency of the heart is to look at a strong leader like Bill and see more of the weaknesses than the strengths. Personally I think this is a serious mistake which we must always guard against. The truth is that most strong leaders also have strong weaknesses. It just seems to be part of the package. So do all you can to affirm Bill's strengths and use all your smarts to see how to make up for his weaknesses. I think Steve is a good example of this positive approach. He has done much to make up for my not inconsiderable weaknesses by supporting me in areas where I missed the boat and talking things over with me when I had major changes needing to be made.

Truly, I know you already do these things, and only want to encourage you to do more. You have the spirit that Paul commends in Philippians. My prayer is that you will cultivate it richly and by faith, with abounding joy in Christ. . . .

For me: pray for revival in my life and Rose Marie's. God did powerful things for us in Spain and Europe. We have come home and left the TV off, and this has given us extra time for work, prayer, and study—and other kinds of recreation. Not that we spent long hours before the tube, but watching news in the evening put splashes of violence, sensuous advertising, and general foolishness into our heads. We didn't need this mishmash of sensate values and violence bashing us every evening. It has been most helpful. So I envy your being in Uganda.

Pray also for the team in Morocco. They pray for you. They call themselves macaronis. Ask God to make them people of prayer and boldness in witness, to remove fears of men, and to grant them oneness as a team. . . . They do pray for you and want news from you—which, if you write, must be expressed without using words like missionaries, etc.

Warm greetings to Cheryl and all those great kids. Tell them that I told one or two of their jokes in my sermons. It went over big with the younger set.

Much love,
Jack

Love Makes Others Successful

To a young man who is a missionary in Ireland.

August, 1988

Dear Adam,

Many thanks for your recent card. The priest you met called me, but I didn't get the message because we were on vacation. In the meantime I dropped him a letter inviting him to call. So he called again, and I will get back to him. He said he definitely wants to get together.

Pray for him and for me.

I need prayer for strength and faith and love. And for Christ to deliver me from any submerged anxieties. For this is the time of year when my lymphoma symptoms began one year ago.

145

We are rejoicing with you over your forthcoming marriage. Praise God for the gift of a bride to you. He is very good.

God has wonderfully strengthened me and Rose Marie too. She had bodily weakness for about two months until about a month ago, and then she began to throw off her sinus infections. A definite answer to prayer.

Adam, thanks for your faithfulness. I believe it is going to be a special time with the coming of Bob and Steve [an elder and a pastor at NLPC who are coming to spend time with the team]. Bob has been undergoing a new yearning for repentance, and you can expect him to give some teaching on it. Steve is a great pastor and dear friend and will impart much wisdom.

A particular challenge I'd like to put before you. What does it mean to serve one another in love? Practically it means to labor to make others successful. Ask yourself: what can I do to make the other team members successful? What about choosing one to major on—perhaps Richard—and working with all intensity to make his work successful? Maybe this isn't practical at this time, but still I have found that it can really release the gifts of others and give direction to the ministry.

At New Life we need your prayers especially at this time, since we are facing a big financial crunch and a need to multiply leaders. But the outreach in Glenside has been great, many people promising to come through a telephone campaign. Would it work in Ireland? Talk to Steve about it.

You are in our hearts. Have much joy, work very hard, pray much, and take time to get away and refuel.

Much love,
Jack

Part 3

Persevering in Serving

Persevering through Spiritual Warfare

> *"Do not fear the devil as though he had sovereign power. Such fear is dangerously close to worship. Just move your whole trust to God alone; resist the devil by humbling the heart, and he will flee from you."*

This part of the book, "Persevering in Serving," has many letters from Jack that deal with the obstacles that Christian leaders face in ministry. The largest section is about conflict in the church, but it begins with letters on spiritual warfare because Jack thought that demonic forces play a role in many of the difficulties faced by the Christian leader.

Jack did not spend much time thinking about spiritual warfare in the early days of his ministry. But in the 1970s, as he started to share the gospel and his home with all kinds of people, he met young men and women who were active worshippers of Satan. One young woman who lived with his family shared with him that Satan had told her to kill him and Rose Marie, but that she had decided that she couldn't because "no two people have done more for me." This got Jack's attention, and he began to pray for protection against Satan's attacks.

It was not long after this that Jack had the experience that he describes in the third letter in this section where he felt that he was under a demonic attack. During this time he realized that God was speaking to him, once again, about his pride. He felt that God was telling him that if he did not deal with this sin in an even more radical way, Satan would have a foothold in his life. As he told this story to a discouraged missionary, he said that God's message was clear to him: "humble yourself, and the devil will have no power over you" (James 4:6–7). After this he spent many hours studying James and thinking through the connection between humility and withstanding Satan's attacks.

Studying the book of James helped to prepare Jack for the Satan worship he encountered in Africa. In Kampala, Uganda's capital city, he often preached in large outdoor markets. While Jack and the local Ugandan pastors shared the gospel with the crowds at the market, the witch doctor would set up shop right next to them. He saw how superstition and fear held the Ugandan people in bondage and that they had put their faith in amulets, potions, and the witch doctor's spells. In his marketplace preaching Jack encouraged them to rely instead on the one true God who would set them free from the witch doctor and his spells.

These letters, although they are addressed to American Christians, have essentially the same message as Jack preached in the Kampala marketplace. Jack's challenge to the American Christians was to see that their reliance on themselves, their technology, and their skills was essentially the same as the Ugandans' reliance on amulets and incantations. He argued that through these things they were seeking to control their world instead of relying exclusively on

Christ. In the long third letter in this section he points out that the result is often self-righteousness, pride, selfish ambition, and the conflicts that come when these things are present. The answer to this was Jack's usual—repentance for pride and self-reliance, faith put exclusively in Christ, and a life of prayer for the Spirit to change hard hearts. Jack took seriously the power of Satan, but he always saw him as a defeated enemy that had no lasting power in the life of a Christian who was totally dependent on his Savior, Jesus Christ.

Self-Reliance Reveals a Demonic Faith

To a missionary and his wife who had recently arrived in Uganda.

June, 1985

Dear Sam and Marian,

Greetings in the wondrous name of Jesus Christ. We rejoice with you, dear brother and sister, that we know Him together. We really do give Him thanks for raising you up and sending you to Fort Portal to spread the knowledge of His gospel in its fully gracious character.

Bill writes that you both are doing well in the language. That encourages me because language study can be intimidating, and often you get satanic suggestions that you are really never going to be able to learn it well enough to share the gospel. Please reject all such fiery doubts.

We have been praying for your safety and your language study, but most of all for you to make knowing Christ and loving one another your first priority. By now you know that just living in Africa takes about all you have in the way of time and energy. You also are learning an unwritten law of Uganda—which is that anything that should take only a week in our eyes ends up taking six months to a year to get accomplished. But there is an advantage in this slowdown which we hasty westerners can use for our profit. It is the value of taking time to love people. So you may have delays in getting the Suzuki and the container to Fort Portal, but you need never delay loving people in a selfless way.

Actually delays are great because they often reveal the power of indwelling sin. We are flying high, then comes a postponement of our hopes, and we end up with an irritable spirit which shows an alarming degree of self-independence and reliance on human capacities. What we fail to see is that reliance on people, their capabilities, their keeping their promises, is a demonic faith, a cooperation in heart with the powers of darkness. We join the enemy, Satan, when we fail to rely on the promises of God to move on our behalf. In brief, our impatience often has a Devilish, earthly side to it, which reveals that we have unconsciously forgotten that trusting Christ is more important than doing things for Christ.

I do not mean that we should be sluggish when God says,"March." But all too often we march when He wants us to wait and rest, and then do not march when He calls us to go forward with power.

This morning I had confident prayer that the Suzuki would become available soon. "I believe, Lord, but help me with my unbelief!"

Richard was here from Ireland for almost two weeks. It was a fine time, and the WHM board invited him to become our missionary. If all goes well, Ireland will become our new WHM mission field very soon.

I also want to thank you for your very high quality letters. We are both edified and inspired by them. Keep up the good work!

Much love,

Jack

Satan Is No Match for Jesus

To a young man who has spent a lot of time thinking about Satan. He has been feeling very oppressed by him.

July, 1988

Dear Gary,

Cordial greetings in Christ! I had mentioned my intention to write you a letter of encouragement. And here it is.

You may ask, what can encourage me? The work of Christ can and must. Believe, only believe! My great concern is to see you trust that Christ can help you. Hope in Him. Your back is to the wall. The army of Pharaoh is behind, the desert on both sides, and the Red Sea before you. Who can save? Only the angel of the covenant, the Son of God. I do not pretend to be a match for the devil, you are no match for him, but I must tell you that Satan is no match for my Jesus. No match at all. One word from Jesus and the whole host of hell must flee. Get, then, a vision from the Scriptures of what Christ can do to change and release those who are entrapped by the devil's lies, deceptions, and bondages.

He has certainly attacked your mind through the voices that speak to you. You have laid some bad foundations by shifting your life interests from the gospel to negative issues. You spent some lengthy time doing this. The negative chemistry has gone deep. But it appears to me that the devil has attacked you in a much more foundational way than this: somehow he has convinced you that there is little or no prospect for you to be delivered from his influence on your life and mind. He has made you think Jesus cannot really help you because your struggles, your weaknesses, your bondages are too much, too special, too unique. Well, you have listened to a lie. But once he has persuaded you of his strength and power, then he does hold your attention; then you virtually are compelled to do his will. For thinking about him all the time is virtually a form of worship.

But oh to get your heart back to the gospel! What power there is in this sweet message! Simply take John 3:16–17 and chew on these verses, say them, sing them, shout them, preach them to yourself— until your heart is filled with awareness of the marvel of the Father's love to you. Read Luther's commentary on Galatians, especially on chapter 2:19–21. Personalize it for yourself. Put your name in the place of the personal pronouns. Hold on to these promises. They are like great branches hanging out over the sea of self and sin. You must grab them and hold on, and the Savior will pull you to safety.

Then, form a mental picture of what you want to be a year from now. Dream some holy dreams. Reckon yourself dead to sin and alive to Christ. Expect Him to accomplish the dream, but dream it. Think of qualities you'd like to replace those that now trouble you. Name them to yourself, write them down, sing them, shout them. Preach more gospel to yourself. Make a fight for your life.

Finally, we are organizing a shepherding group. I want to ask you to meet with these brothers and have them pray for you, probably on a regular basis for a time. We also will likely want to have some special prayer and fasting for your deliverance through faith and prayer.

The King is on the march. Who dares stand against Him? He is our omnipotent intercessor. Who can condemn? He is the author of the gospel, and He sends His Spirit to apply His message to the fountains of life. Who then can remain unclean? Praise Jesus!

In His grace,

Jack

The Weapons of Spiritual Warfare: Humility and Prayer

To a missionary in Uganda who is discouraged by the many attacks on the missionaries and the work they are doing.

March, 1994

Dear Tom,

Hello from London! We are in the midst of an uncharacteristic heat wave, almost like the tropics. Yet we feel it came as an answer to prayer. Rose Marie prayed for warmer weather to dry up our dripping sinuses. Well, Jesus heard prayer. The London area has been the hottest spot around, with the rest of the U.K. remaining fairly cool. And our bodies have really responded well. We all came from Eastern Europe tired and needing refreshment, in body as well as soul, and the warm weather was a touch of His loving, healing majesty.

Isn't Jesus wonderful? Sometimes in love He is severe with us, but He knows how to bring us into safe harbors at just the right time. He lets the storm shake us up, so that we toss overboard our idols, and then we are free to sail into waters that are even more raging. But also He has those times where He guides us into a safe haven, and we rest in the quiet.

In my own life, He has sent me through much suffering in order to move me from self-confidence to Christ-confidence. I think He has been doing that with you and your precious family and with [the other missionaries]. You are in a place where the demands on you often seem unlimited and the powers of darkness rage against you with malignant intensity. Add to that the drying-up effect of language study, and you feel that you hardly have the energy to engage in spiritual warfare. And this sense of things is partly correct, for spiritual warfare does take strength! The Enemy seems vague and evanescent; then he suddenly strikes with terrible power; next, you fear that his forces are sovereign—or almost so. In an African setting, our ordinary resources fail us. We Americans are especially vulnerable because we are secularized and find it hard to take the devil and demons seriously, and we have a great deal of trust in ourselves and the technologies that have often become our power sources.

When all this fails, when rumors fly to the effect that the missionaries are headhunters, we experience isolation and inward aloneness that is deep. Who can combat this Satanic evil? Not us! Then a demon attacks Mary, and next a young woman who has just received Christ runs off into the bush shouting, under spiritual attack. To top it off, Ben [another missionary] has to be in Nairobi with health problems when it's all going on. Who can even understand all this, much less fight against it?

I would entreat you, dear brother, not to permit these things to move you from your foundation in Christ. But we must not pretend to be firm in our faith when events shake us, and the honesty of your letter shows that the Spirit has been leading you to confess need and weakness in a God-glorifying way. But in all this *do not* lose sight of the *goodness of God* and the *sovereign power of God*. Satan's aim is to get you to focus your attention on his strength and to conclude that his wickedness is sovereign. He cannot get you to praise him, but the devil still wants you to tremble a bit before his power and forget about the awesome goodness and majesty of the triune God. Resist him, firm in your faith; resist his attempts to fill your mind subtly with negative thoughts about the Father and His goodness and power. Resist Satan as he seeks to insinuate critical thoughts into your heart in respect to your team members, fellow Christians, leaders, and family. One sign of his disturbing work is a kind of negative irritability, an unholy impatience, with others. Especially watch out lest the devil draw you into selfish ambition and the conflicts that ambition and envy generate. I am especially burdened that our team leaders become sensitive to how much of this mess is in us. Study carefully James 3:1–18, especially verses 13–18, where earthly/demonic wisdom is contrasted to wisdom from above. The antidote to this mess is the humility that falls at the feet of the Father, pleading for grace. See James 4:6, and verses 7–12.

So what do we do when visible attacks threaten—rumors fly, our reputations suffer? We glory in Christ! We glory in Christ! We praise Him! We preach the gospel more fervently and we forsake all self-trust—all reliance on our education, gifts, and abilities—and rely on God alone. We refuse to be rattled, though at times we are, and must quickly repent of giving way to fear. *Do not fear* the devil as though he had sovereign power. Such fear is dangerously close to worship. *Just move your whole trust to God alone; resist the devil by humbling the heart, and he will flee from you* (Ps. 62; Heb. 11:6).

Let me open my own life to you on a most personal level. Many years ago, I experienced a direct demonic attack. It happened early one morning. I was sleeping and a dark cloud appeared at the bedroom door. It rushed at me with intent to destroy or possess. It struck my left side near my heart, and, though I was sleeping, I have no doubt that this was an attack of a demon that was real. Immediately I cried out to God for help, and He heard my cry. Again, I knew instantly from the Spirit what God wanted me to do. The message was: *Humble yourself, and the devil will have no power over you* (James 4:6–7).

I did. I humbled myself, and, at that moment, was completely delivered from this violent assault on my person. I had claimed the blood of Christ for cleansing from my pride and self-centeredness, and I was left astonished at the powerlessness of this messenger of Satan. To this day, I stand in awe of the gospel working in the life of the broken and contrite. Here I had humbled myself a little, and great power resulted. What was intended to destroy me became a whole new way of life. I had at least glimpsed the truth that demons are defeated enemies and simply no match for those who humbly rely on the gospel and God alone—and give up all reliance on our secularized Western selves.

Timothy Warner says that the bottom-line issue is always one of control. In his view, each of us has many wonderful potentialities within us. Our problem is that we want these potentialities to be realized under our own control and on our own terms, but God wants them to come to fruition by our deepening submission to His rule, His control. The demonic counterattack is to get us to think God's control is not good, really stifling or unpredictable. Satan and his cohorts hit here again and again, and the proud in heart are easily carried away with this deception.

Let's apply this to particular battles you face in Uganda, and that really all of us face increasingly:

1. Don't assume automatically that we are relying *exclusively* on God and His grace. Read Psalm 62 and Hebrews 11, esp. v. 6, and let the Scriptures do a job of unmasking our self-dependence and reliance on our instruments of "magic": education, finances, organization, etc.

2. Recruit others to pray for you in any demonic encounter. Could you get a group of about 50 people who would pray for you constantly and have special intercession at times of crisis? *I am thinking of people who would agree to pray for you 3 times a day.* Then seek to know your idols and confess them to several key people for prayer. Especially confess false trusts and hopes, any reliance on people rather than

Christ, etc. Base it all on the blood of Christ. I know you may be doing all this better than I am, but we cannot do enough work in this area.

3. Frequently humble yourself as you did during our recent time at Entebbe. That was great! But let the team and the Ugandan Christians see you as the chief repenter, the one who is quick to renounce idols. Confess hindering sins like pride, impatience, coldness, anger, lack of tenderness, love of preeminence, self-dependence, boasting, and misuse of the tongue. Perhaps you don't struggle with all of these nasties, but I do, and I suspect they are the sins that much afflict leaders like us. Please read Bonar's *Words to Winners of Souls* and Joe Church's *Quest for the Highest*. Pray for me that I would be more ready to confess and forsake publicly my own sins. I had a dreadful day in Spain just before we left for Poland and Russia, a day of dryness like death. On that day, God showed me what my flesh was really like, what I was without the Spirit. Terrible! Yet it drove me to cry out for grace and receive it. By the end of the day, the influence of Satan was also broken because he had tempted me to despair.

4. *Make the whole ministry center on private and corporate prayer.* Do not expect bigger victories in tough areas until corporate praying becomes *the complete center of the ministry.* The reason? It is in prayer together that we find grace to give up control to the Father, rely exclusively on the Spirit, and see the demons subdued. *It is here we get our life, vigor, zest, and authority for the battle.* Lesslie Newbigin said in *Honest Religion for Secular Man* that "Christian missionaries have been one of the most secularizing forces in the world." Without constant adoration, thanksgiving, intercession, and confession together, we are going to teach people to rely on our traditions, plans, technologies, and methods rather than on grace. Such converts will simply be switching their idols from the witchcraft stuff to the tools of modernism.

5. Therefore, our whole aim ought to be a model for new Christians of a lifestyle of constant renunciation of evil things and a

reckless self-giving of everything to Jesus Christ. Here is where we hit the demons hard!

6. A conclusion: assume that new converts are very likely to have divided hearts and are still trying to do what we do, i.e. retain control over their lives by their own technologies. In *this case* the power technique is witchcraft and its instruments! Therefore, prayerfully ask believers pointed questions about amulets—around the neck? under the shirt? in the shoes? over the door of the hut? on the wall? in the pockets? Then have them take the exposed tools of witchcraft and burn them publicly. Next, have prayer for the cleansing of the home from all demonic powers. I would also ask the Lord to rebuke all the demon powers over the family as a whole. Should you rebuke them directly? I do so in those cases where they don't immediately clear out. Usually praise, gospel preaching, and repentance will drive them away, but when they refuse to give up their oppression, then it seems to be that a rebuke and a command to leave are in order.

One word of caution: suppose the demons refuse to leave a person in spite of all this—what to do? Here it is important to give all your attention to the person's repentance—really the lack of it. In one instance demons would not give up their oppression of a woman though they had their hold over her virtually broken. So I asked her, "Do you want them to leave?" After a time of reflection, she admitted she did not really want them to leave her. I was horrified and reasoned with her about her eternal danger, but she then left us. She hated the bondage, but she wanted "their power." Ghastly!

So do not separate the fight against demons from bringing souls to repentance, especially for the sins that led to demonization.

What has been said has powerful application to places and persons where demonic power has been entrenched for long periods, re enforced by national or tribal group sins, and where *self-righteous pride and bitter envy have not been identified as sins.* The demonization is especially strong where deep sins have been commended as virtues. I want to apply this thought to rumors, slander, and gossip. Always look behind the verbal (or physical) attacks for the work of demons in the matters of group, family, tribal, denominational, or church conflicts. In these cases, look for self-righteousness in the group or individuals, really for any form of feeling superior to others, any attempt to rise above others. Western culture is rotten with this form of sin and the associated demonization. So is Ugandan society—tribal group, church, family have been demonized. A missionary in Holland told me that Amsterdam has had centuries of self-righteous encrustation leading to a divisiveness in mental outlook and critical speech. To deal with it in Bundibugyo, you should consider the following:

1. Take two days to fast and pray to rid yourself by grace of these things. Usually after about four hours of praying, I detect aspects and elements of self-exaltation, negative attitudes in myself that were concealed from me. Sin and self-deception go together.
2. Have group prayer (team and church leaders) for the same purpose of self-humbling and cleansing moving into reliance on God alone, repenting of all secularism too.
3. Then move into a period of praise, following the pattern of Jehoshaphat.
4. Next, look for ways outwardly to humble yourselves together, confessing sins, affirming one another, etc.
5. Come to one-mindedness as in Acts 1:13–14; 2:1, 42; 4:23–31, and then together claim Bundibugyo for Christ, rebuking the demon powers, or better, asking the Lord to rebuke them.
6. Finally, pray for wisdom to work along the line of James 1, especially the prayer for wisdom, but also get to the end of the chapter where it speaks of tongue control and care for the widows and orphans. Especially ask God to show you as Christians how to fight on a practical level the dark powers in this town. In Kampala, Amin brainwashed the people to think all whites, especially

160

from the United States, were CIA agents. You may be fighting this as the origin of your rumors in Bundibugyo.

This sounds almost silly (?), ridiculous, in its simplicity. But Rose Marie and I cast ourselves in a dependent role and smiled constantly in Kampala. We stayed away from riding in vehicles and simply walked the streets of Kampala smiling. We smiled till it hurt! I don't know exactly how you can apply this to Bundibugyo, but count on it: there must be people in the town who have bitter envy, and the dark powers are directed against you. You have vehicles, you look strong physically, you have houses, etc. Well, this is stuff for envy. Don't doubt it. How to overcome it? Seek particular wisdom. Reflect on how you appear to the people of this town and ask God to show you *ways to relate to them without visible strength—even to the point of seeming dependent on them.* One way to do this is to get to know key people in the town, make friends, honor them, etc. Now I realize you are probably doing ten times as much already as I am suggesting. But there is always more. For example, in Kampala I often prayed with people on my knees in the marketplaces. We went out of our way to pray for the sick and to have healing meetings for them. Rely on the Spirit!

When I was almost halfway through this letter, I was exhausted. It was spiritual warfare. I did not have time to write this letter. It took a long time. But more than that, there was an invisible barrier that the Spirit wanted me to push through. As I did, I became weaker in body and needed the rest of the day to recover. By evening, I felt a bit recovered but waited two days to resume. During these two days, lots of things seemed to go wrong. The next day, Rose Marie and I planned to go for a prayer walk through Southall. I locked us out of our house in Ealing by leaving the key inside. The morning was seemingly thrown away by my mistake. It was a strange blunder, because I am almost paranoid about keeping track of keys. Was Satan involved? I don't know. But we decided we would begin our prayer time on the street while waiting for help. We prayed then. We also prayed in the car. We prayed at breakfast. We prayed after breakfast. We prayed as we drove to Southall. We had several times of prayer in Southall, even though we were so late that we drove around rather than walking. I believe we also had more prayer in the evening. We included you and all the team in Uganda, and the churches, and Bundibugyo in these prayers.

Too often we don't pray for what seem to be good reasons for not praying. There are times, perhaps, when we should just rest, relax, or work rather than pray. But, also remember that we are all prone to be self-indulgent and not soldiers/sons pressing forward regardless of tiredness and feelings of apathy. So, let's fight for Bundibugyo and Southall together. Join us!

I would like your permission to use this letter with other missionaries, because I am deeply concerned that all of us as a mission should move from self-dependence and a rather casual approach to prayer to a full mobilization for battle. In other words, we all struggle with our many failures in prayer, and I believe I need to undergo big changes and deep repentance for my feeble prayer life.

Much love,
Jack Miller

Persevering through Conflict

What I long for is a love big enough to be disturbed by what people are doing, and strong enough and patient enough to carry them to the place where Christ wants them to be!

This next set of letters deals with conflicts between Christians. They involve many different leaders—pastors, missionaries, counselors, and elders—who were struggling with many different issues. Some issues were personal, others were ministry-related, and a few were doctrinal and theological. Often all three elements were mixed together. All of them were messy and heartbreaking. For anyone who has been in ministry it will come as no surprise that this is the largest section of letters in this book.

Because Jack was the pastor of a large church (NLPC) and later the director of World Harvest Mission, he often had to mediate in conflict situations. Many times he would come into an ongoing conflict and work to move both parties toward forgiveness and reconciliation. Jack was not someone who liked conflict. He confessed in one letter that, "It's often easy enough for me to be disturbed by where people are in their rebellion, but then in unbelief to drop the matter there by simply avoiding them." He knew that this was wrong and went on in the same letter to speak of his own need for repentance so that he could "love others the way Jesus loved me."

Repenting for his own sins was where Jack started as he entered into a conflict, and this was also the place where he asked others to begin. In letter after letter he challenged all participants in a conflict to examine their own hearts, look for the log in their own eyes, and then repent of their sins before they attempted to correct someone else's life. In a letter to a pastor who was counseling a missionary couple Jack says, "The time [I spent with all of you] was hard for me too, but it gave me an opportunity to do some good humbling of my heart and repent of many sins. . . . I was impressed by how many blind spots they had. That was frightening. But it was even more scary to think how many I may still have in my own life!"

Along with repentance, Jack encouraged those who were in a conflict to meditate on God's love for them. He knew that without knowing God's love, it is impossible to love others. The gospel, Jack taught, is all about reconciliation. Understanding this gospel will bring "the power to forgive and bless and serve others because we have been captured by God's own pardon and acceptance of us by free grace."

When Jack was involved personally in a dispute he often referred to the need for God's love to be expressed in the way the conflict was handled. Often he was more concerned with the way that things were said than with what was actually said. He reminded one counselor that Jesus was always humble and gentle in His dealing with others. This was the example that Jack counseled others to follow. He felt that many tough conflicts could be solved by the counselor beginning with humility and then speaking gently. Jack said to one counselor in a difficult situation, "I am not called to be an accuser of the brethren, but a gentle restorer of the erring."

Even though it was important to Jack to go into a conflict with humility and gentleness, he was also willing to speak into the lives of those who he thought were caught in sin. He did not shy away from saying hard things. He was especially concerned that the principles laid down by Jesus in Matthew 18 be followed. He thought many potential conflicts could be avoided or contained if this was done. To a pastor who had listened to charges against Jack from another pastor he said, "I have some question about the ethics of your listening to charges against us. Doesn't Matthew 18 enter in? Did you do the right thing in listening to charges against us—without insisting that the person see us first? I feel many problems can be avoided if we are pretty strict on this matter."

Jack also advised caution in associating with Christians who have a history of unresolved conflicts with others. In a letter to a pastor whose church had split he included a very helpful list of character qualities that lead to conflict. Then he went on to say that it is not these qualities themselves that lead to unresolved conflicts, but an unwillingness to see them and repent of them. It is this unwillingness that, he felt, should disqualify someone from leadership in the Christian church.

Finally, Jack knew that not all conflicts can be solved. What to do when there are irreconcilable differences? In the same letter where he discussed those who have a history of unresolved conflict, Jack said that sometimes the only thing that can be done is to "pray for those who are like this, show them love by deeds, and forgive them. . . . Pray with ardent hope, show love, be kind, and resign from trying to be the Holy Spirit. . . . Maybe the best definition of a leader is the man who knows how to wait. During the waiting he learns to lead by prayer. He deepens his love for people and his hold on the throne of grace."

Jack thought that any conflict situation was an opportunity to learn more about your own sins, more about the God who forgives sins in Jesus Christ, and more about how to attach yourself to Him through prayer. Because of that, although his sorrow often comes through in these letters, there is also a strong current of hope. He was full of hope because the gospel had changed his hard heart and because he had seen it change the hearts of many around him. It was Jesus Christ on whom Jack centered his hopes, not the people who followed Him, and it was the blood of Christ shed for sinners that filled him with faith even as he faced the hardest problems in the church. He wrote to a man who had asked him for forgiveness for something that happened thirty years before in his first pastorate, "Soon we shall all be face to face with the Lord, and none of us can have any hope other than the blood and righteousness of Christ freely shared for us sinners. May this hope bring great encouragement and comfort to your own heart."

The Gospel Is All about Reconciliation

This is a letter to a pastor with whom Jack has some the-ological differences. Carl's church has recently dismissed him because of doctrinal differences. Jack is concerned for reconciliation. He also wants to make his theological position clear because he believes they need to learn from one another.

December, 1981

Dear Carl,

We are resting up in Nairobi for a few days before we go on into Uganda, and I want to take this breather to write you. . . . You have both [Carl and his wife Susan] been very much in our prayers. Our love for both of you has deepened and strengthened as we have prayed for you and understood the burdens you have been bearing.

I am sorry that things have not worked out with your church. I believe that if I had been a more mature person with greater wisdom and courage, perhaps this could have been prevented. I am not positive on that point, but I can see that greater grace in my life might have made a difference. What strikes me, however, is the common failing we have all shared in. What is the gospel all about? It is the reconciliation of sinners to God through the blood of Christ and the reconciliation of men to one another as the fruit of that reconciliation to God. I believe that this is the priority which is on the heart of the Lord—and one that we sadly neglected in our relationship with one another. It must be greatly offensive to the Lord to see us defending the gospel in a manner that puts us at a distance from one another. . . . I fear that none of us have done all that well in living out [the gospel] as Christian brothers together. What has developed all too often is an adversary relationship among us, much like that in the court system. I am thinking of the tone, the pitting of position against position, the lack of mutual listening, and sometimes a breach of our covenant calling by bitterness and backbiting. . . . At the last day, "the only thing that counts is faith expressing itself by love." What does not count is "biting and devouring each other."

How shall we give an account of ourselves when we are suddenly brought before our all-holy Father and asked to explain our divisions and quarrels? I fear that we have acted hypocritically as brothers together in debating issues that we know little about as part of our own obedience. Who among us has been practicing [the gospel]? I do not mean that we have always been at each other's throats, but it seems clear to me that the kind of love which is produced by a living faith has been in mighty short supply. If it had not been, I believe these issues would have been resolved long ago. The whole matter makes me sick at heart. I see little honor for Christ in what has happened, and no victors, only mutual shamefacedness.

. . . I am your friend. I hold you in my heart with all good will and wish to be held in your heart with all good will. . . . [Jack goes on to discuss some of their theological differences.]

I have not tried to write a letter with legal care or perfect theological precision even if I were capable of doing that. But I now want to make an attempt to state the most serious problem that I have with your thinking. I am thinking of the up-front emphasis on covenant faithfulness or obedience. Like you I do not think anyone is

168

saved without obedience to Christ issuing from his faith. But the drumbeat of the new covenant is not covenant obedience. The accent is rather on the forgiveness of sins. In His inauguration of the new covenant in the giving of the Lord's Supper, Jesus does not say anything about obedience but rather: "This cup is the new covenant in my blood, which is shed for many for the forgiveness of sins."

In the new covenant, the heart of things consists in "redemption through his blood, the forgiveness of sins" (Eph. 1:7). The obedience which flows from this state and experience of forgiveness through Christ's atonement is not a kind of generalized or vague "lawkeeping" but a being "kind to one another, tenderhearted, forgiving one another, as God in Christ forgave you"(Eph. 4:32). Thus the covenant drumbeat of "forgiveness" carries right on through into a life of forgiveness and kindness. Our obedience is charged with the power to forgive and bless and serve others because we have been captured by God's own pardon and acceptance of us by free grace. . . . You cannot have the kind of family tenderness you seek if covenant obedience is the primary focus. Here I think you are putting the accent in the wrong place and in doing so have really undermined your fine emphasis on the covenant concept as a family relationship.

I am simply expressing my mind in a friendly and open way in the hope that we can come to oneness in these matters. It deeply grieves me that we have not been able to come to real oneness as a community on these matters. Above all, this is what our faith is all about. Covenant faithfulness must mean, among other things, the ability to get along with one another and to harmonize our understanding of doctrine by using insights from one another. I need yours, and I believe, you need mine. I would challenge you, in the name of our common Redeemer, to take up the task of expressing and realizing mutual forgiveness and reconciliation even at this late date. . . . We have done enough defending of ourselves. So what I am asking you to do is to take time to reflect on what I have said, and if in anything you find yourself in error, be willing to correct yourself by appropriate apology. More than once through these lengthy discussions and debates, I found it necessary to apologize to brothers, including you. Such willingness to correct ourselves publicly does not destroy us, but rather reveals that we have true self-knowledge, for there is none of us who does not in many ways sin against his brothers either by acts of commission or omission. And if we escape acts which are sinful we often have attitudes which dishonor Christ and alienate one another. . . .

We are all getting older. Life is slipping by quickly, and soon we shall all stand before Him who will ask us to give account according to our works done in the body. When that happens, it will be important for us all to say in our final vindication that we led a life of ongoing mutual kindness and forgiveness as a community of Christians. Even though you may feel wronged by others, it is still crucial for our standing under the Father's blessing that we work hard to have no personal alienation and continue to work for that oneness in spirit and doctrine which is so pleasing to the Spirit of unity. At a time of what must be unbearable burden bearing for you, I would yet encourage you to seek out others and be at peace with them. Shall we not "make *every effort* to keep the unity of the Spirit through the bond of peace"? Together we must hear the voice of the Spirit saying, "Be kind to one another, tenderhearted, forgiving each other, just as, in Christ, God forgave you."

Through prayer my affection for you and Susan has grown greatly, and I want to see our lives together full of Christ's reconciling Spirit. That means I am most ready to hear you point out sins and faults in me. I have found such correction given in the right spirit (and even in the wrong spirit) can bring into lives the power of the kingdom like nothing else. If such reconciliation comes more to the forefront, who knows what mighty works of God may follow? I think you will agree that sometimes we must all be humbled to the dust in order to be lifted up in praise and service.

Pray for me. My responsibilities in Uganda are very great. My weaknesses are even greater. But through prayer and the supply of the Spirit I know that Christ shall make me sufficient for these things.

Most cordially,

Jack

Dealing with Others' Sin Starts with Our Repentance

To a young man who is a member of NLPC. Rich is concerned because of the many sins he sees in people at NLPC. Jack writes to him from Uganda about learning how to deal with the sins we see in others.

January, 1983

Dear Rich,

Since I have been praying for you in Uganda, I thought I would drop you a note of encouragement and share with you a couple of my needs for your prayer.

In Uganda I prayed for you with some regularity and want to let you know that behind those prayers was real love and affection for you. In turn I am very thankful for your prayers. I really depended

171

entirely on such intercession. Otherwise I believe there were times I would have given up in the struggle against evil.

Sometimes in Uganda evil is so widespread that you bow before it as the prevailing wind, for your life and everyone else's too. Or again you can have an evil reaction to evil, trying to fight it with the weapons of human wrath or fleshly wisdom. At other times you are tempted to throw up your hands and become cynical. But by grace and through many prayers, I found the power to stand against much evil in my life and in the lives of others. As in the U.S., the love of money is a bigger thing than people recognize. God helped me turn from my own love of money and face even dear brothers with their problem with it.

One of the heavy costs of discipleship, I suspect, is not what my discipleship costs me, but what my discipleship has cost others in the way of pain. It is hard—very hard—to make a brother feel bad by telling him that you fear his feet are being entangled with the love of what money can bring. It breaks you down before the Lord because you know that inwardly we all are tempted by the attractiveness of material things, and that to tell another brother that he is in danger or has fallen is somehow humbling.

I found, of course, that my deepest love is for myself and my own will. It seems to me that the kingdom visited me with power by giving me a healthy despising of seeking my own ends and honor. At any rate God visited me with a much stronger love for the church here in Jenkintown and in Kampala. I have been able to pray with some heartbroken earnestness of spirit for revival in both places.

Something happened in Kampala that shook me to the roots. About a year and one-half ago, a young man who had been a government spy was converted. He had very little materially, yet God seemed to give him an open heart and hand. He lived in one room but shared it with less fortunate believers. He also shared his food. But about six months ago he began to become very greedy for money and was asked to move out of a Christian group home. Gradually I began to be afraid that he would go back to being a spy to get money and begin to inform on church leaders. My worst fears were realized. He attempted to blackmail one of the New Life team members in a most blatant way in order to get money. The case against the New Lifer was silly, but it is not so silly when you consider the paranoia of an African secret service. Of course, I doubt that anything evil could be done successfully, but what makes me sick at heart is the Judas spirit in a person who is a dear friend of mine. I love that young man in Jesus Christ but am deeply grieved by the evil of his sin. It has been a great burden to me and I ask for your prayers. It would be easy for me to become preoccupied with this man's evil.

But what God is doing is using evil in this man's character to get me to hate evil in myself and in others. I really despise what has been done, and I think I am learning from it to hate evil in all its forms, including that in myself.

As I take up my labors at New Life, I know there is much sin to be dealt with, but it seems that God is giving me great confidence in dealing with it and a hunger to see Him work holiness in all of us together. New Life is not like a typical OPC or Christian Reformed Church. As Donald McGavran said, "The OPC and RPCES have pursued the elite and the pure among Presbyterians. Their biggest problem is to get in contact with sinners." But that is not a New Life problem. We have many sinners, often intensely selfish ones. Our problem is to separate ourselves from our own self-centeredness so that we cannot endure it in others because we know the joy of a Christ-centered life.

To put it another way, I find I lack the courage to hang in there with self-centered rebels until God breaks down my own intense self-love. But there is a joy in that, really beyond description. It's the joy of being clean and loving another person enough to cause him or her pain to bring them out of their uncleanness.

I would ask you also to pray for the young blackmailer in Kampala. At first, I was so hurt and grieved that I stopped praying for him. I now regularly intercede for his soul. I hope this has not been a sin to death.

Before long, I would like to have that meeting with you, perhaps a breakfast together.

Most cordially,
Jack

Facing Unfair Criticism

To a young man who is leading a small group at NLPC.
In the last small group meeting he came under attack from
a group member. Jack writes to help him understand what
happened and to know what steps to take in dealing with
the problem.

March, 1983

Dear Edward,

This morning I heard that it was a bit rough on you during last Wednesday's [small group] time. Apparently you were "rebuked" by someone without any cause in you for the correction. I think I understand what happened and why. It's very easy for well-meaning Christians to think of harsh rebukes as proofs of sincerity. Some folks with a counterculture background even think of frontal assaults as sure evidence of caring—at least until the frontal assault is returned to them. When that happens it is easy to read the assault as a lack of love. The person who loves to rebuke others or feels it as a duty typically does not like to be corrected. That's what Luke 6:39ff is about.

How do we show love in such a situation? First, we can use the situation positively. How many times have we all hastily judged someone else without troubling to get all the facts? Actually we all do it instinctively. Our hearts are pretty evil. That's why in James 4 he moves on to judging as one of the chief ways we can express our lust and pride, and the giving up of judging as one of the chief ways we can humble ourselves before the true and only Judge, the Lord of hosts.

Next, we need to do some teaching on the subject. I think you should sit down with Al [the small-group co-leader] and together plan some teaching and sharing on the subject. Part of the practice of condemnatory judging comes from ignorance as to what Scripture says about it. I really mean that. There is not much teaching today against the sins of the tongue. Joe [an elder at NLPC who had gone on to become a missionary] had an excellent ministry on this subject when New Life was young. He made it his goal to get people to commit themselves not to speak evil of one another and in case of complaints to go privately to the person. Joe even had people make a covenant not to misuse their tongues and to concentrate on praise. A powerful passage on grumbling and complaining is Philippains 2:14ff. The first word ("grumbling" or "complaining") refers to complaints that are spoken, and the second word refers to "arguments" in the mind, unexpressed or only half-expressed.

The last thing I'd urge upon you to do is to pray as you have been. What we are involved in with complaining and grumbling is serious rebellion against the King Most High and His government of our affairs. Such rebellion invites the rule or at least influence of the powers of darkness. So it is no ordinary battle [that we must] fight, first in ourselves and then in others. I freely admit that the whole negative unbelieving attitude which goes with it all too readily controls or influences my own mind-set. Pray for me on this matter to be clean and I'll pray for you, and then let's pray for each person in the group on this matter, and then particularly remember those that have a special problem with it. Also pray for my writing this week. We'll be away. God bless you.

In Christ,

Jack

The Big Issue: How We Deal with the Issues

To a member at NLPC who had recently reconciled with another member of the church.

November, 1983

Dear Sam,

When you told me on Sunday that things had been worked through with you and Larry [a member of NLPC with whom Sam had disagreements] I was pleased. I had prayed that there would be a reconciliation between you and felt Christ's joy over this development.

I know that you both love the other. You are both intensely concerned people. That is a strength but sometimes our strengths work against us, and where the concern is so intense the emotions can become volatile without our hearts wanting that to happen.

I know I love you both and rejoice to see progress in your drawing near to one another for the glory of God. Christ is pleased by that kind of movement. Too, I'd like to see that same kind of drawing near in all our congregation. One thing that has really inspired me lately is the way children in the congregation have drawn near to me during these past months. I called Sally White on the telephone and she quite eagerly gave me a very full account of her bout with pneumonia, and I know that Debby Falls sees me as her own grandfather.

After our congregational meeting I was momentarily discouraged. I guess I came away concluding that many times the biggest issue is not the issues being discussed but the way we handle the issues and show concern for one another. It appears to me that is where the Head of the church has His concerns. So I resolved for myself to do more standing back, and then I asked God for grace not to take myself and the issues too seriously. I think sometimes after a few weeks we even have trouble remembering what the excitement was all about, so why get overly involved at the moment?

So I do want to make sure you and I have a right relationship. Your note after the meeting was appreciated by me—but do we need to talk more? Have I wronged you in any way that I need to straighten out? I was also thinking about your relationship with the other elders. It seemed to me that I felt a bit of tension and wondered if there was peace among us. Especially I'd like to encourage you to put on Christ's forgiveness where any of us may have given offense to you. All of us have many faults and sins and need much forgiving as well as your prayers. Do pray for us—we are not strong men but weak in ourselves.

Let us keep ourselves from idols like obedient children and not make an idol even out of the good things like the ministries, our

177

homes, our gifts, and even New Life Church. Philippians 2 and 3 are worth our meditation.

In Christ's love,
Jack

Begin by Setting an Example of Faith

To a couple in leadership at NLPC who are having a hard time getting along with another couple (the Smiths) that they are in ministry with. Jack is concerned because they have recently involved a pastor from another church in the conflict.

August, 1986

Dear Jim and Rachel,

Greetings in the Lord Jesus Christ! We come back from overseas with much joy over what God has been doing. . . . We thank God for the growth of the [missionaries there]. It gives promise of many good things to come.

The way I have seen God working this summer fills me with hope and joy. God has been changing me too, and I need a lot more changing, and I expect it to come.

[Jack goes on to discuss the problems that Jim and Rachel are having.] . . . But I do want to express my deep concern about Jim's

178

telephone call to Adam [another pastor] in which [the conflict with the Smiths was discussed at length]. Here are my problems with your handling of this matter:

1. Major issues like this communicated to me through another person are really open to misunderstanding. As a communication method it is just not good. I really don't know how to read it and will be tempted to react negatively to it, something I don't want to do.

2. It spreads stuff which very likely should not get spread. Adam [is a friend and a pastor] but he should not have to bear the weighty burden of pastoral knowledge and oversight which you seem to have put on him. This is for the session, and especially for me to deal with. . . .

3. Most important: Assuming Adam and I have understood what you were saying, my reply is that there is nothing that I heard that you cannot work through if you have the heart and faith to do so. Ministry cannot be done without faith, and if others need faith too, then start by setting them an example of faith. But the phone call did not seem to issue from faith but from fear. Please, dear Jim and Rachel, out of love, I entreat you to approach the Smiths with confidence. Expect the Spirit's working to unify you and accept the pain that it may take . . . take the time to learn how to love one another.

4. About the differences: Why can't you combine concern for repentance, etc., with concern for deep personal relationships? Why polarize over such matters? Why not enrich each other instead of react to each other?

5. In conclusion: Though in no way do I minimize the burden you feel, it seems to me that you have a duty. That duty is to make the ministry work. Run away from these relationships and you will likely keep running. At the very least whether you work with the Smiths or not, you do have a duty to form a solid friendship with them and to learn from one another.

You have my confidence and so does Lee [their counselor], so get in there with him and get the counseling moving. To do anything less is to give in to what seems to me to be a satanic attack on you and the ministry. But suppose your worst fears were true? That is no reason for not working through the issues. . . .

Finally, Jim and Rachel, I wish to counsel you boldly from the heart, with love. This comes from a dear friend who knows you both well. I have a gut feeling that both of you in your weaker moments gravitate toward problems rather than praise. Let me make it even stronger: sometimes I have wondered if you did not need an intense problem and the attendant anxiety to give your lives focus and direction. I see no reason why you cannot deal with this weakness, if I am right, with Lee's help. Grace is for us sinners, and we all have plenty of sin.

I commend to you, dear ones, the study of James 4. It has had a powerful influence on me lately. James 4 says it all. Practice it, and Philippians 3–4, and all will turn from tears to sunshine. Let God have the future, the plans and all; just walk in joy in the present. Expect great things from God.

Most warmly in Christ's love,

Jack

Jesus' Methods: Gentleness and Humility

To a missionary who is struggling with the death of his mother and conflict with another missionary.

September, 1986

Dear John,

Greetings in the Lord Jesus Christ! As I get back from vacation and read your two letters, my earnest prayer is that He will prove to be full of grace and peace for you. In the midst of struggle keep your mind stayed on Jesus. Actually I think that means discovering by faith that He is both sovereign in power and loving in heart toward you. I have interceded much for you and Liz and have great confidence that the Lord has been hearing my prayers.

I am so very thankful for you and Liz. You are dear friends who live in my heart, and I rejoice in Christ giving you to me as gifts for enriching my life. In tough circumstances, despair of your own strength and wisdom, but do not despair of Christ's commitment to you. He will be working mightily in your behalf. The things that have been so hard for both of you during these past two months will be used of the Holy Spirit to draw you to the Father in a new way. I believe that with my whole heart, and I believe in you, confident that the Holy Spirit will see you through a hard, hard time and bring you out on the other side.

The death of your mother must have been a tremendous wrench to both you and Liz, but especially for you, John. . . . Then add to it the problems that have surfaced in your relationships with Chris. Then the sense of flight and failure that you mentioned in your letter and on the phone, John. Whee! You know that no human being can deal with all of this. What counselor can help—except the Spirit? That is why Rose Marie and I have just prayed for you and prayed for you. In your sufferings I have suffered, perhaps far more than I could ever explain as the Holy Spirit knits my heart to yours in love.

I did so, perhaps with special effectiveness, because much of this began to unfold at a time when I was very weak. After I came back from P.E.F. [the annual Presbyterian Evangelism Fellowship

181

conference], I had a time of severe sickness, which lasted for about two weeks or more. Very humbling indeed. But I learned afresh the meaning of James 4:6, "God opposes the proud, but gives grace to the humble." So I humbled my heart with considerable zeal. As part of that humbling I gave myself in prayer for you. Is God speaking to all of us: "Not by might or power, but by my Spirit"? Fall afresh on us, Holy Spirit; mold us, remake us, and fill us till we shine with the joy of Christ!

It would be easy to say: it all works together for good. But it is not cheap and easy. The context of Romans 8:28 is one of suffering, especially the suffering of intense persecution for the faith. . . . But things do work together for good, for those who are willing to accept the suffering. For God uses the sufferings to chisel away at our pride, self-dependence, and self-boasting. His methods are sometimes fiery. He has a hot chisel, if you will. He must see in each of us a resistance to His will that is very intense and requires the strongest measures to change us into Christlikeness.

It is also important to know that pain by itself does not necessarily sanctify us. I am persuaded that pain sanctifies us only as we trust Him, surrender to His blows in faith, conscious that our Father is reliable and that He is our own dear Father. I trust that the Father is not my judge executing me, but the Master Sculptor. As the craftsman He has a pre-vision of me which is beautiful and clean and self-forgetting, as sweet and pure as the sunny day after rain.

So let's not run away from Him because the cost seems too great. Or because I am afraid He will put me on a mission field with someone who [doesn't think like me or even like me]. No, dear friends, always look to Christ and find your security in Him. Even the greatest ideas and the purest ideals and the best of friends are not Christ. They really cannot provide the love we need. He alone can raise Lazarus or each of us dead and disabled missionaries who are facing a dead and disabled world. Remember: He alone is the Author and Finisher of your faith. Not [anyone else] . . . He gives faith, He is the object of faith, and He is the goal of our faith. He is life from the dead. When the tomb was opened, the smell of Lazarus' sin and death came forth. The Lord must have felt like running away, since He hates evil in all its forms. But He stayed there. He does not run from us in our state of decay and smelliness. I tell you when Jesus deals with us He does not pretend that we are lovely and odorless, but it is in the midst of our smelly death that Jesus draws near with tears and power and love and calls the dead and rotting into new life. I tell you, Jesus is something.

I tell you with tears how much needless pain I have borne in my own life because I have been so slow to look to Him in believing prayer. Look to Jesus, fix your eyes on Him. I know of no one else who can help the heart in its deepest needs, who can comfort the soul, dry the tears, or even bring us to more sincere tears for our cleansing and healing.

In your present upheaval with Chris, I would call attention to Jesus' methods for bringing us to life. His methods spring from His gentle, humble character. He is "gentle and humble in heart." That is His own self-description in Matthew 11:29. Paul speaks also of the "meekness and gentleness of Christ" (2 Cor. 10:1). In Galatians 5:23 and 6:1, we learn that the Spirit of Jesus is working in us "gentleness" as a fruit of the Spirit and as a style for correcting an erring brother.

I am persuaded that these are the only methods that can plant churches around the world. The church has been torn with conflicts among leaders. It has been a scandal. Historically we who are followers of the gentle Christ have produced an awesome quantity of sour grapes, thorns, and thistles. And it is going on at the present time. Renewal, revival, and evangelism can go forward only as we humble our hearts and get grace to live in gentleness with one another.

So my feeling is that Christ is calling the team to join me in learning gentleness and humility and love. You might instinctively think that what has happened among you has ruined everything. But not necessarily. Is it possible that God is trying to stir up revival by a gentling of us? Is it possible that the only thing really ruined is human pride and self-confidence?

My temptation is to get on the plane right now and seek to help all of you work these matters through. But at present God has convinced me that my role is primarily to pray and wait on the Lord. It is His love which bids me wait. I am cheerfully—confidently— expecting Him to do a miracle in the relationship between you and Chris.

I say that without trying to make any judgment at all about all kinds of questions. I am just waiting here with the quietness and docility of faith. I am looking to Jesus. Join me!

That does not mean that I am unwilling to come. But I do think that it's only right for me to defer to you at this moment and give you the opportunity to look to Jesus for the answers to impossible problems. I do that for many reasons. One is that the glory will be Christ's, not mine, as the difficulty is worked out. Too, I am eager to see you learn how to walk in the Spirit in the midst of a problem that is impossible. This is your big opportunity to see things through by faith. Put away your fears. Find your security in Christ. Don't give way to anyone else's fears. Let Him be Lord of the situation. Love Chris with the love of Christ. Be an encourager before you are a corrector. Apologize quickly when you err or sin against others. Whenever you correct, do it with much tenderness, with the brokenness of a fellow mortal and sinner.

You will notice that many of the things mentioned to you on the phone I did not bring up here. But I will follow up with another letter. But somehow I just felt constrained to share with you heart to heart. I love you and Liz. I expect to see God do great things for you and through you.

> In Christ and His wonderful love,
> Jack

Learning to Restore Gently

To an elder at NLPC who is in a conflict situation with someone in the church whom he has been counseling. He has asked Jack for advice.

September, 1986

Dear Harry,

We certainly praise God for His blessings on our recent meeting. You also continue to be in our prayers, and we commit ourselves to pray even more earnestly for you as you struggle with your relationship with Jason [the person Harry is counseling].

Our new little garden behind the carriage house is in place, and looks lovely. Our "new" piano is tuned, and I am learning a bit of Spanish for relaxation. Jill's [Jack's daughter-in-law] dad is doing better and is out of the hospital.

For whatever it is worth I would like to offer a few suggestions regarding the counseling of Jason. Bear patiently with my thoughts. Probably you were doing these things a long time ago. First, in

185

circumstances of high emotional intensity, I assume almost automatically that there have been some miscommunications and misapprehensions which need to be taken seriously. So I pray for wisdom to see what things may be heating up the situation unnecessarily and confusing communication.

One of the things that almost always turns up is a feeling of *rejection* in the person being counseled in a conflict situation. The presence of this feeling may be warranted or unwarranted. But so long as it is there, it cripples communication. It just hinders the release of the Spirit to cleanse and heal the relationships.

This feeling of rejection is often concentrated around the belief that "I am not being listened to."

To overcome this feeling, I would suggest the following: more time in prayer with the person who feels left out; asking of questions that give the person opportunity to express the isolation; good, patient listening to put the fears of rejection to rest; and avoiding language and attitudes which foster any us vs. them relationships.

An example of how the Holy Spirit can work came up the other day in the conflict we are having with Robert [a leader of a ministry at New Life who is angry at the session]. Peter [one of Jack's copastors] was moderating the part of the session meeting involving this alienated brother. He asked me, "How do I handle it?" My answer? "Ask him what weaknesses he sees in us that he believes are hindering him and his ministry." Peter did this with an attitude of real love and gentleness. The brother was willing to point out failings that he saw in us. His criticisms actually were quite helpful and had a good deal of truth in them. So we apologized for our failures, and I said, quite frankly, that I saw myself as struggling in the area of sin he mentioned and needing his prayers.

Ergo, we all relaxed and were able to get down to the core of the difference and now are making excellent progress. Up to this point the whole thing was tangled in a ball of twine including differences in theology, personality, and culture. I don't say every aspect of it is solved, but the sinning against each other is gone, and the whole matter has come into focus and there is love prevailing among the brethren.

So my suggestion is that you might want to ask Jason to point out areas where he believes that you have failed him or sinned against him. Hold on to your hat. It might be a bit rough. . . .

Then as to the heart of the matter—the issue of submission to authority—I'd suggest that you begin this issue with acknowledgment of your own lacks here (obviously we all need to work on attitudes toward authority). Then go for broke in this area and dig into the intensity of his reaction to [authority in his life]. See what comes out. But don't forget to relate the authority issue to 1 Corinthians 13. People who love can submit. Frequently express your own love to him through the whole process of counseling.

Finally, in counseling where the counselor has become a main part of the issue, you need to see that you have been . . . what— outsmarted? Or at least outmaneuvered? I think so. It has happened to me before, and I always felt I was beaten before I started. How to avoid this? Obviously, express regrets wherever you have failed and express love frequently and do much to call attention to Christ as the Lord of counseling—not you. At the same time watch out for what I have often detected in myself: the assertion of my strong will coming out of a desire to dominate someone that I really don't respect. Anytime I sense that the love of Christ has left the counseling room, I have taken over with my imperial dominance and react inwardly to the counselee.

I especially try to get in my head a positive view of the counselee, the person as Christ is going to remake him or her according to His grace. This positive image of the person as remade by Christ in the future is really important for praying. It's almost impossible to pray effectively for a person if in fact you have no positive image of what Christ is going to do.

What I do to defuse the relationship is to make it as low-key as I can, especially avoiding anything that may be accusatory in tone. I am not called to be an accuser of the brethren, but a gentle restorer of the erring. Remember: Jason is an intense person, and so am I. I think perhaps each of you is also in your own way. So don't let your intensity conflict with his intensity. Too much intensity binds up the expression of love by making everyone self-aware. So relax a bit. Wherever you can, affirm him. . . . And don't lose your sense of humor while counseling, though it would be foolish to use lightness in a serious matter. Especially avoid trying to bear the burden of the thing as though you had to be the Holy Spirit changing another person.

It is with joy that I look forward to seeing Christ really change all of us.

Much love in Jesus,
Jack

Following Matthew 18

To a pastor from a nearby church. He had recently met with a group that was angry at Jack and others at NLPC, and then he wrote to Jack about the things that were said in the meeting.

December, 1986

Dear Tom,

Warm greetings in Christ! We are fresh back from Ireland, and full of joy over what Christ has done there. It is such a blessing to see the new little group struggle to its feet. We saw the Word go forth with weakness from us but with the Spirit's power carrying it home to hearts. Now we wait for the results.

It was also most heartening to see Richard and John [missionaries in Ireland who had just started to work together] get to know each other, and especially to learn to pray together. This is something that grew while we were there but it needs much strengthening. . . .

Regarding [our brothers from another church]: I know you wrote your concerns with the best of intentions and with a deep love for them. I share that love and do pray for them. They will always have my heart. I am deeply thankful for them and have no resentment of any kind against them. And I do not feel like I have great wisdom, but I do not wish to be diverted from the ministry God has given me.

But, yes, I did find it very upsetting to read. Therefore I am answering it as promptly as possible to get it off my mind. But this new disclosure from them left me hurt and discouraged. But after prayer it is good for me to open up my heart and mind to you.

[Jack goes over some charges that have been made against him and others at NLPC. They involve issues that happened many years before this letter.]

It disappoints me that whatever matters bother them they did not approach me on them during those days. . . . It could be argued, though, that it was my fault, that I was unapproachable or intimidating as a person. What can I say to answer that? I am genuinely sorry if it is true, but I don't know that it is. How do you handle something like that? . . .

189

And I do not see how we can avoid their feeling that we have somehow betrayed them no matter how much time we have spent trying to talk through philosophy or personal issues. I can understand their disappointment, but do not think that feeling and what seems to be the suspicion it carries will depart easily.

The biblical root of the matter is that it is any brother's duty to view another as innocent until there is evidence that he is guilty. In this case it seems backwards. Somehow we are guilty and must prove ourselves innocent. This leads to my question for you: Can brothers work together closely if there is no trust? And—how would a phone call help that trust? . . . and how can I untangle problems that go back so long . . . ?

. . . I have some question about the ethics of your listening to charges against us. Doesn't Matthew 18 enter in? Did you do the right thing in listening to charges against us—without insisting that the person see us first? I feel many problems can be avoided if we are pretty strict on this matter.

But here is what you can do for me. You can encourage them to call me and assure them of my love and willingness to listen to any criticisms of us. It seems the right order for them to call me, not for me to call them. I don't say this out of stubbornness or unwillingness to be corrected. My concern is for them to act in love in a biblical way. To talk to you about it is not biblical.

Again, I am grieved by this whole matter, very deeply, but I also forgive you and them from the bottom of my heart. But with this letter I now put it out of my mind. I suggest you do the same. Sometimes the world is a most imperfect place. It will take a while before you and I perfect it, and that includes the church. So keep your perspective. Be willing to wait as you work. Watch your emotions and your heart. Give them to Christ and not to problems. Let's keep praising Him and get our own work done.

190

I am looking forward to seeing you soon. We will be again, Lord willing, in Spain before that, working on a new book. Have you received the book yet, *Outgrowing the Ingrown Church*? Donald McGavran wrote me that it is an excellent book, probably because I mentioned him in it? No, I hope not. The new book, *Come Back, Barbara*, is at Zondervan, but they won't let us know for a couple of months what they will do about it. . . .

Rose Marie and I grew in Christ and our unity with one another while in Ireland. Boy, the devil is active there, like in the U.S., but he got outfoxed this time. Christ used the hard things to bring us closer to Him and one another. The last Wednesday I was there I spoke on "Coping with Depression." The place was packed out—especially with depressed people. It was something. Several sitting up close to me could hardly hold up their heads they were so down in spirit. One woman told me afterwards that this was the first time she had been out of bed for weeks; she had been so down. Anyway, my talk was really a bit more academic in its design, and so when it began there was a struggle to get going, to get these people in focus. Then I lost my place in my notes. I was drowning. But suddenly I gave them my own personal testimony how Christ liberated me from despair. The place woke up and my whole being turned into a joyous declaration of the liberating power of justifying grace. Some of the depressed people began to laugh at my jokes and humor, and a good group came back for follow-up the next night. Jesus was there with saving power in spite of my foolishness. I would be very surprised if several people did not come to Christ as a result. It ended up so thrilling to see Jesus work in such a hard place.

In Him and His grace,
Jack

Christ Breaks Us Down Together

To a pastor who is in conflict with his session. He is being counseled by a pastor whom his session had asked to help. But now there is conflict in that relationship also. Jack has been asked by both parties and the session to step in and help resolve the conflict.

January, 1987

Dear Frank,

Warm greetings in the Lord Jesus Christ. It was good to be with you all day Monday. I love you very much and have you in my heart, and I was pleased to renew fellowship with you. I do know, though, it was a time which was not easy for any of us. . . .

My prayer is that this letter will be received by you in faith. I want you to be supremely confident of the Father's love for you and be strongly reassured that I love you with all my heart. My concern is that God give you grace to pray, to meditate, and talk over these things with Rob [Frank's counselor]. My hope is that powerful changes will occur in all of us as a result, and revival will spread in all directions as the Spirit works new things in our hearts. Will you now trust Him to be your Friend and Comforter as you read on? Don't let Satan interpret this letter to you as one more rejection. My view is that it will help make you a mature believer who is filled with joy, peace, and contentment. If you have those qualities you are ready for whatever God calls you to do. . . .

Let me begin by a personal word. I do sorrow with all of you. There did seem to be so much sorrow in both of you—and fear and

192

hopelessness as you observed each other. I love you both so much that if it were possible, I would have carried your sorrows on my shoulders and in my heart. In a way I did, but I did not have the power to carry them *away* from either of you. That is not my work nor is it in my power. Rather, it is the sweet role of the miracle worker, the Holy Spirit. And lately I have tried to resign from the proud attempt to be the Holy Spirit in another person's life. To the degree that I have received grace to do this, my joy has greatly increased. What a burden it is to try to be the Holy Spirit and what massive egocentricity on my part when I try it. May the Father in heaven deliver us all from this trap!

Naturally it was my preference to stay longer and fellowship with you and with my dear brother in the faith, Rob. I also had more things to say to you and him, but you know that was not possible. . . . After listening to you for four hours, I needed more time to digest what you said. All that you said deserved more of a response from me than the couple of hours I could give you, but at the meeting we had to choose between letting you get it all said and my having an opportunity to reply fully. So please don't think my response to you was complete when I finally began to speak in the afternoon. I believe my opting to give you the full time was of the Holy Spirit. Actually I would have liked to ask you many more questions to improve my understanding of you. But there was no time for that if I was to give you even a brief reply while with you.

But it is now my obligation to impart to you more formal and definite conclusions. I am here trying to speak both as a dear friend and as an elder in the church. Since I certainly lack wisdom, your prayers for me are coveted and your corrections of any misunderstandings that I have are welcomed, indeed, solicited. I am intent on listening to you at all times.

To begin with, let me say once more that in numerous ways you have shown growth [in the last few months]. I do believe that the primacy of faith, the power of the gospel and the Spirit, and the wonder of adoption have captured your mind and had a good effect on your life. Things in you that have concerned me seem to have changed for the better. As Rob mentioned to me, you have grown. . . .

The credit for that goes to Christ. As well, the church and its session should be honored for the way they have given themselves to you and helped you grow. I see that as remarkable, a gift to you from the Holy Spirit. It seemed to me that one of the deepest problems in the situation was your failure to see what a wonderful expenditure of love has been shown you by the church and its leaders. I can hardly get over how much they have given you in the way of energy and time and help as leaders.

What puzzled me was that you did not even mention this care from Rob or the session during our time together. Put plainly, I know of very few churches or pastors who would have done anything like this for you, and for you not to be visibly grateful for it struck me as one of the strangest things I have met in my whole ministry. You showed signs of active rebellion in your relationship to Rob, but even more alarming was that you seemed unaware of your lack of gratitude and love.

At no point during the hours you spoke was there much evidence of heartfelt appreciation for the amazing self-giving to you by this brother. What struck me as equally remarkable was the way he bore so patiently with your lack of thankfulness to him. So far as I can recall he bore with you in a most Christlike manner: he said little or nothing about the absence of your thankfulness for what he had given you of his heart's blood and tears.

How can the Holy Spirit be released for revival and missions if you are completely ignorant of His method of working—which is through constant thanksgiving for others? Beloved brother, how do you explain your apparent lack of gratitude to Rob? It left me not just puzzled but *dumbfounded.*

194

There is a second area which left me amazed. As you criticized Rob, it seemed to me that you had very low level awareness of the pain he was going through at that very moment and the frustration you had caused him (and others) in the past by your defensiveness. What you were aware of was your own intense hurt. I am not doubting that hurt; it was clearly deep. But as I grieve with you over your wounds, I also grieve that you seemed so unaware that you were doing to Rob on the spot what you said he had been doing to you. Your old wounds were leading to new wounds for others. You were so concerned about yourself that you hardly seemed to see or think of them as people at all. That was pretty cold, was it not?

What I feared I was hearing was something like this: "I have been wounded and therefore I have a right to wound. Indeed, that is the way I will be healed."

My plea is for you by faith to move away from a self-centered view of others and yourself.

See all that has been taking place more broadly, less personally, and without defenses. Please be in heart what you really are: a son of God and brother to Rob.

So love as a son, think as a son, see these painful events as an exposing of all of our sins together by the Spirit of sonship as part of revival in the church and its world mission of the mid-1980's. See Rob in a new light. He is a brother authority introduced to you by Christ. Christ is at work in him and through him; the King is on the move! We easily forget the moving of the kingdom in situations of conflict and think secularly, carnally, and not spiritually about such matters. Christ is not abandoning us, but breaking us down together. . . . You need to learn from Rob and to expect Rob to learn from you.

Perhaps I felt the absence of this kingdom point of view in both of you as we talked and often wondered if either of you saw how serious was this vacuum of faith. Forgive me if I am wrong here. But

195

was there a kind of a frozen hopelessness in both of you? Am I wrong? Were either of you seeing the other with confident faith in Christ and His power to change? Or were you together looking at problems as though God and Christ did not exist or at least had no saving power?

This fact really troubled me. Hopefully this is not said from a proud stance on my part. My being there was timely because about two weeks before someone attacked me personally. What made it so hard was that I had poured much love on the attacker. My first reaction was to get terribly upset and then sit in the muck of my own self-pity. It all seemed so threatening and out of control. I did penance off and on for three or four days. But God helped me to repent of my *weakness* of faith and to have my eyes opened a bit to the sovereignty of Christ over the people involved. So I repented and forgave the person who wronged me and am now filled with love for him. A gift of sheer grace! In the whole thing, my weakness was so powerfully exposed because my upset and sorrow revealed that my first reaction was self-centered and atheistic. I was acting as though God did not exist or have control over the circumstances.

But what the devil meant for my destruction brought glory to Christ through a speedy, humbling repentance on my part. Joy was restored. I cannot describe the joy I found through renewed faith in the cleansing blood. I actually feel so desperately weak in such conflicts that I urge people who support me in prayer to constantly pray this for me—that I might get the revival point of view. That means a confident trust that nothing happens that is independent of my God of grace, the movement of His all-conquering kingdom. I also want to seek only the welfare of the one who has wronged me. In that process let God be true, but every man a liar. Let no one worry about his own vindication but only about the honor of God!

Frank, [I have already mentioned to you] my concern that you seemed to be so motivated by fear in conflict with authority figures like Rob. But, I was unprepared to see so much fear, flight, and fight in you when the heat is on. Honestly, how could you who have been taught to contain conflicts, go through proper channels, and follow Matthew 18, go to Lee [another pastor in a nearby town] the way you did? You did not tell us that you were going to anyone else with your difficulties.

You really hurt Rob by that, greatly disappointed me, and left me wondering how you could work through any conflicts in the church without spreading them endlessly. In the mercy of God, Lee is a mature person who quickly got in touch with Rob and it turned out well. But again is this the way of the obedient son, one with a quiet spirit?

Again, Frank, forgive me, but did I understand your comments on 2 Corinthians 7? Were you saying that the text teaches our duty to vindicate ourselves? If so, is that interpretation really in the text? Does it say a word about our duty to justify ourselves in a defensive way? Doesn't it really mean precisely the opposite—humble yourself, repent? Isn't Paul commending the Corinthians for clearing themselves of sin by repentance for self-centered ways? Isn't Paul actually praising them for vindicating God by changing themselves, by clearing the record of their evil by repentance and amendment of their evil ways? Dear, dear friend in the Lord, nothing scares me so much as seeing someone using the Bible to justify distancing oneself from the brethren and adopting a stance of "them vs. us."

My entreaty, my heart-felt plea with tears, is that you listen to Rob in a new way. Please listen for Jesus' sake. . . . Rob has acknowledged that he has not been approaching you with enough confident faith and love. He has apologized to you. If there are more ways he has failed you, tell him. But do make sure you have forgiven him. Put on forgiveness as a lifestyle. Do it constantly and add to it blessing of others and making friends, not enemies. Then go forward to make a friend of Rob, love him, seek him out, help him, treat him as a brother—not a foe.

I now need to tell you what seems to me to be the root of the matter. How do we explain your growth in Christ and your love for the lost, etc., in the light of the self-centeredness and the lack of self-knowledge that I have described above? How can these contrary qualities co-exist in the same person? Is it possible that my evaluation is in error?

The answer seems to lie in your confusion about your calling as pastor. . . . It's hard for me to escape the conclusion that you are getting your identity from pastoring, and this identity is being substituted for a personal knowledge of Christ and a love for people. You cannot even see the self-centeredness because you are on a ministry pedestal. . . . Because of this confused self-identification it is hard for you to engage in wholehearted repentance.

Instead, it is much more natural for you to judge others for insensitivity to you and your calling. For this reason, your repentances tend to be partial and elastic. All too quickly you bounce back to where you were before and lose ground. Compounding the problem for you is the difficulty you have had in loving authority figures and people who are your peers—a lack of love which is manifested when conflict arises, when the authority figures threaten your security on your pedestal and seek to enter your life fully and talk about the roots of the problem.

Because I love you I tell you these things. Hard as it is for you to hear these concerns, my confidence is that Christ will use this forthrightness to bring you release from bondage. There is not a single thing that I have found in you and mentioned in this letter that has not been in me. Indeed, one of the best things about my visit was my opportunity to see how many things were yet in me that cried out for speedy repentance. So I did some prompt repenting while listening to you. I recalled how often I am dreadfully egocentric and so insensitive to Jesus' love when I am that way. So I am only asking you to join me in revival and repentance. Be a son of God with me.

[Jack then makes specific suggestions of things in Frank's life which he needs to work on and change.]

It is all said in faith, hear it in faith, act in faith. The results will be glory for Christ.

> Much love in Jesus,
> Jack

Self-Dependence Is Our Biggest Blind Spot

To a pastor (Mike) who is counseling a missionary couple (the Parsons) who have returned from the mission field because of interpersonal conflicts with other missionaries. Jack has recently met with Mike and the Parsons to assess how things are going. The Parsons are very unhappy with the counseling they have received from Mike.

January, 1987

Dear Mike,

Greetings in Christ Jesus! My many thanks to you and your dear wife for your gracious hospitality shown to me. I rejoiced in your kindness and love. That was a wonderful dinner we had with you. . . . My good appetite showed how much I appreciated it, but let me say again that the food was delicious.

199

It is also with joy that I think of your faithfulness to all of us and your willingness to resume the counseling with the Parsons. Your labor is a sacrifice of praise to Christ. Thanks so very much! I believe that God has given you a tremendous ministry and rejoice to hear of all the good things that you are doing by His grace. . . .

Remember it is not finally up to you or me to make the Parsons ready [to go back to the mission field]. I think it is important for all of us to remember they are in the hands of God, and what they are is what they are. We would see your work as successful even if you said they do not appear to you ready to go anywhere for missionary outreach. We still put our shared wisdom before the executive committee and Board and see what the evidence happens to be. So there is an objective side here to the whole thing—which can help keep you and me from feeling we need to be the Holy Spirit with them.

The time [I spent with all of you] was hard for me too, but it gave me an opportunity to do some good humbling of my heart and repent of many sins. As I listened to the Parsons, I was impressed by how many blind spots they had. That was frightening. But it was even more scary to think how many I may still have in my own life! Here are dear folks who love the Lord and yet are unable to see how some of their deep-seated attitudes are Christ-resistant. I sense that is true of me. So I groaned inwardly and cried out for mercy not just for them, but for me and you. How many blind spots we all have! So the pain was used to make the time very helpful to me. Humbling myself kept my focus off the intensity of the conflict and helped me focus on the joy of knowing Christ who is such a beautiful Savior. Mike, isn't it wonderful just to know that Jesus loves you? . . .

Well, do I have any counsel for you? Not much really, maybe a little offered in the spirit of brotherly openness and sympathy. I guess my prevailing thought is that God's work begins when ours comes to its end. Sometimes His presence is not felt with power through our methods however useful they may be, especially when we are confident we have the right approach and insights. God has a way of wanting to be God and refusing to get too involved where we have our own wisdom and strength. Then when we run out of wisdom and strength, He is suddenly present, a lesson I find myself relearning practically every day that I am in my right mind. (On my crazy days I am not ready to learn much!)

I think He wants our confidence to be exclusively in Him, and when we lose our self-confidence then He moves in to show what He can do. Perhaps self-dependence—and forgetting the strength to be found in Christ-dependence—is always our biggest blind spot. There is also presumption and pride that go with self-reliance. So let's not lose our trust in God and the power of His gospel and the spirit of praise which goes with its proclamation (Rom. 15:13; 1 Cor. 1:18, 22–25; Gal. 6:14).

This was my one primary concern in listening to you. I was concerned that you both seemed weakened somewhat in confidence in Christ, slow to hope, and removed from praise.

Certainly this was understandable. You were taking a beating, and who can ignore the pain that was felt by you? You did so very well in the fire. Forgive me if you think I am trivializing what you went through Thursday morning. Still, let's not forget that God's plan is bigger than the pain. In the pain God calls us not to linger long over it, but to exercise a childlike simplicity or trust and devote ourselves to an intensity of thanksgiving that gives us a God-centered joy and freedom in the gospel.

It is not possible certainly just to sit down and will praise. Praise grows out of God-given perception of reality, a seeing that God is infinitely good and infinitely good to me in Jesus Christ in every circumstance. To have that kind of praise, you need to take time, to wait upon the Lord in prayer and meditate upon His greatness and grace and the might of His kingdom. I would urge upon you the importance of taking at least one day a month to wait on the Lord in prayer, claim the promises, seek His wisdom, and deepen self-knowledge of blind spots and firm up your repentance.

In brief, I would like to see you abound in thanksgiving because of these trials and count them "pure joy" (James 1:2–4). My wish is to join you especially in praising Christ because He has worked to give you a self-forgetting love for the Parsons that came to you as a gift of the Holy Spirit. I do not mean to suggest that you do not love them now. You do. But probably you know what I mean. When we have been fully exposed to another's ingratitude and intensively criticized by a fellow believer and friend, the lamps of love seem to go out by night. And they need to be relit by Jesus as He kindles forgiveness in our hearts and enables us to see them from the standpoint of Christ's love to us.

I trust this is not self-centered to ask you this, but would you be willing to read the chapter on the divine glory in my new book? I know how busy you are. Still, to develop the life of praise is the heart of all effective Christian living and working. So I'd make bold to urge you to read the chapter in *Outgrowing the Ingrown Church* which is concerned with the divine glory as the motivating power for going with the gospel. Let me know what you think of it. Perhaps I am out of balance, putting too much emphasis on thanksgiving and praise and possibly doing it in a superficial way. Still, it seems to me that one sign of real repentance is joy and praise, and without joy and praise one is simply indulging in worldly sorrow, not in biblical repentance. Remember: repentance is always a tear in the eye of faith, an eye fixed on a crucified Lord. In that vision of Christ dying (Isa. 53) my pains are virtually reduced to nothing. I mean that, and, I think, my life has not been without some pain.

You have been in my prayers, very much so. Counseling in the best of circumstances is such sensitive, impossible work. It just needs the touch of Jesus' hand on it. That's why as I get older I try to listen more in my counseling sessions. I said "try" because I often fail and talk way too much. But when I listen more, it seems to make the counselee more teachable and less likely to feel I am trying to impose my will upon him or her. I also think the Spirit may be released in a new way when work is done with less haste and pressure. It seems to me that the Spirit would really bless your relationship with the Parsons if you could strengthen your patient listening to them. I do not mean that you have not listened to them or that you need to agree with what is said. Obviously you have done an excellent job discerning their spirits. But we can all grow in listening skills: to hear them with a quiet spirit where possible and with deliberateness and respond to what they say both with directness in confronting them and yet with the gentleness of Christ (Gal. 6:1–2). . . .

[Jack goes on to discuss how humility in the life of the church leader brings the gentleness of Christ. He also talks about the danger that comes when church leaders think too highly of themselves or even other church leaders.]

I also mention this because of my own experience in our church here. I have been here a long time. It is very easy for me to get exalted in the eyes of others—and perhaps even easier to get exalted in my own eyes. Or even to feel forgotten and overlooked when younger men take over many of my responsibilities. But to give in to these temptations is almost to set yourself up for fleshly conflict. I try to flee man-centered exaltation of myself or others like running away from a dread and disfiguring disease. . . .

May living exclusively for the glory of Christ bring you much joy. There is no one so wonderful as Jesus. WHM and yours truly stand forever in your debt for the patience, love, and care you have shown the Parsons. Praise Him for the grace He has given you.

Much love,
Jack Miller

We All Have Blind Spots

To a missionary who has theological differences with the board at WHM.

January, 1987

Dear George,

For some time I have wanted to write you a thank-you letter for your work of service on [the mission field] and also encourage us all to draw closer together in the bonds of Christ's love. I believe I am speaking not only for myself but for our whole board at WHM when I say how much we appreciate the intense and self-sacrificial love you have shown on the mission field. We have the same appreciation and thankfulness for the outpouring of life by Martha, your gracious and joyous wife. We want her to know that her presence and her joy in the church there have been such an encouragement to all of us.

Probably none of us here can fully appreciate the depths of suffering that you have both gone through in your battle for Christ and the gospel on the mission field. But we have some idea of the cost you have paid and want you to know that we love you for yourself and also for your persevering faithfulness to the Lord Jesus Christ.

It appears to me that there has been fruit upon your preaching and witnessing seen in conversions of unbelievers to Christ, in your powerful and effective praying, and in your lives together as a couple. My heart still feels the joy of our shared ministry. . . . What a working of God was often with us as we witnessed together.

It also seems to me you have grown a good deal and learned much as a Christian man and evangelist. What really stands out in my mind is your gift of faith which has grown strong in you and has been a personal inspiration to me. George, I just love to see your faith in action, your simple trust in the living power of Jesus, and your willingness to walk on water right in the midst of the storm. This demonstration of your faith has meant a lot to me. It has been a personal inspiration to me and a learning experience. I gladly sit at your feet and learn as your pupil. I really mean this. I love you much, my dear brother. Keep this faith and love strong, keep it growing, and keep going with the gospel. Don't ever let Satan blow out the flame of your love to Jesus and your spiritual confidence!

We have also been praying for you. . . . Our burden is to see you in just the place God wants you to be with our hearty blessing. We also are concerned that the fruit of your labors [the fellowship of believers] be shepherded in a good way in the days ahead. I know you share our concern for this shepherding to take place. As a board, we do not know the best way for this to be done, but our concern is that healthy spiritual life and healthy biblical teaching prevail in the fellowship, bringing the members to a deeper knowledge of our Lord Jesus Christ.

Again, I wish to apologize to you for our many failures and sins in not doing more to support you in this ministry. . . . As much as we appreciate your heroic efforts, we can hardly have felt and understood the depth of your spiritual warfare there.

I could wish that we had done much more also to build a strong friendship with you. . . . Any impression we gave of not being willing to listen to you is regretted by me. Please forgive me and any others of us for any of the ways that we may have failed you.

It seemed wise also for me to entreat you with all gentleness in Christ to consider something that occurred to me as I read your letter. First, when I read it I did not feel very much loved by you. We both know how easy it is to misread a letter. You cannot see the smile on the face or the tear in the eye. Still, I really did feel that I was not loved. Was I mistaken? Please forgive me if I am wrong in this matter because in the past I have felt your love to me. . . . But after reading your letter, I felt hurt and somehow left out of your affections. Correct me, please, if my sinful heart has misinterpreted your intention. I am so prone to be wrong and really hope that I am wrong here. It would be my greatest pleasure to apologize.

Secondly, I wondered if you had forgiven us for what you believed was wrong with us and our approach to [this theological issue]. I mean things perhaps like feeling we did not listen to you, were incapable of understanding, and were unteachable. . . . My question is, have you fully forgiven us for what you see as our blind spots? The reason I ask this is your bringing up again issues in your letter that I thought were considerably worked through between us. I don't say that you have not forgiven us, but the apparently sharp edge in part of your letter led me to wonder if you had forgiven me and the other board members.

Third, it occurred to me that you may believe that our repentances and apologies are insufficient or insincere and we are still not listening to you. I am not saying that I know this is so, but if it is so my heart says, "Dear George, please come and tell us about it as your brothers in Christ. Let us know face to face and heart to heart if you believe that we have sin in us that is not repented of and perhaps sins committed against you. Let us preserve the sweet unity of the Spirit of Jesus in our midst." We love you, George, and promise to hear you out if your heart says we are sinning in some way.

My final heart burden: This question is one for your conscience in relationship to us as elders and brothers in Christ. It is simply this: Are you really doing everything in your power to cultivate oneness of faith with us? Is it possible that you may be sinning against us by viewing us as "them over there," maybe even "the enemy" or those who are "out to get you." Please don't misunderstand my questionings. My idea is not to suggest I know the answer and am accusing you. I really don't know the answer. But my heart felt sad after thinking a good deal about your letter. I thought, "We must have hurt him more than we ever knew."

I felt like someone at a distance from you, a person "over there" and far from your heart. For me it is related closely to the first question I raised, "Does George love Jack Miller [and the rest of the leadership at WHM]?" I believe you do love us, but I have trouble finding it in your letter. Dear brother for whom Jesus died, comfort my spirit by telling me that you love me and you love the other brothers too. I want to be reassured that you believe that Jesus also died for me and the rest of the board. Again, if this feeling of mine that I may not be loved is a sinful response to your letter, please forgive me. I am most willing to be corrected.

But I am appealing for you to be honest with us and meet with us to discuss ways that we may have sinned against you or failed you—if this is how you see us. George, we all have thousands of blind spots. You could do us a favor by pointing them out in the gentleness and tender love of Jesus Christ (Gal. 6:1–3; 2 Cor. 10:1). Who knows how God might use our mutual repentance to trigger off revival in the church of God! Perhaps the heavenly Father's concern is not the "issues" or the "differences" but how we handle them together. [And whether or not we handle those differences] with mutual respect and love.

George, I love you with my heart. My heart is wide open to you. Assure me that your heart is wide open to me and to your brothers at WHM. We respect you for your dedication to Christ as a Christian brother and honor you for your labors [on the field]. Thank you for all the blood, sweat, toil, and tears, for unrelenting warfare carried on day and night.

In Christ, God's Son,
Jack Miller

Learning to Discern Who Will Cause Conflict

To a former student at Westminster Theological Seminary who is now a pastor. The church he is pastoring was involved in a church split. He tried but failed to bring one faction back to the church.

January, 1987

Dear Jason,

Greetings in the grace of our Lord Jesus Christ! Who can express the surpassing wonder of the love of Christ to sinners like me!

It was with much joy that I heard your voice on the phone. The communication was so clear it sounded like you were next door. Well, your sounding so close reminded me how I miss you. . . . Out my study window the snow looks like it is almost a foot deep and getting deeper. The daylight will sign off early tonight. It's four o'clock and already you can feel the night brooding in the wings, ready to close off the day. But it could not be more lovely out my study window, with the leafless tree branches covered with snow.

We certainly praise God for your faithfulness and your devotion to our Lord and Savior. He is a good Master, even though my own service to Him leaves so much to be desired. I am so glad for the free and absolute forgiveness of sins by the Father because of His reconciling love revealed on a blood-stained cross. I need His righteousness to cover over my best deeds as well as my worst. . . .

Concerning [the former members of your church] that you mentioned in your recent letter, I would like to indicate something of my own thoughts about the issue. . . . Here you have a heart of love for them and you know of their love for the gospel. It would have been wonderful if they had come and the power of Christ had been manifested in unity. You are broken in heart that you cannot be more one with them. But . . . you as the pastor also have broader responsibilities, both to God and the work He has begun. So like me you need to understand people, and be able to face the facts about where they are and yet do it without harshness. A leader must not be either naively idealistic or cynically uncaring. He must be a humble man with twenty-twenty vision.

First, he must distinguish between loving people with all his heart and having open eyes to see when believers have sins that might be destructive of fellowship and ministry. The pastor must not play a game of hearts pretend, as though wishing could make people what they really are not. How many times I have had to struggle with getting clear sight of people because my heart wanted them to be different. Sometimes I am so eager to see a missionary candidate or an elder candidate as sweet and lovable that I will create a myth in my own mind that shades the reality.

But people are what they are, not what we fervently wish them to be. And to close our eyes to what they are will not change the facts. That is only failed leadership. I know whereof I speak, having erred in the area of wishful thinking so many times.

Secondly, my counsel is always to be cautious about working closely with believers who have a history of conflicts which have *not* been resolved. I do not say never work with folks who have had conflicts. Obviously we all have had our struggles with other people. But do be *very* careful about giving power positions or roles of influence to leaders who have behind them a record of *unreconciled* conflicts. Believe me, in one hasty day or hour you can undo years of your own hard work. In the first church I served in California, a distinguished-looking man became an elder, based on very little knowledge of his life and character. It took me at least two years to repair the damage he was able to do in about a month.

Be wise as a serpent and harmless as a dove. When in doubt, don't take unnecessary risks. Instead wait—wait on the Lord for wisdom and trust Him to reveal to you what people are.

Third, there are qualities that can be discerned in immature leaders. I mean persons who are habitually unable to work through conflicts to resolution. In general I have found they have—

    a. A desire to get their own way at all costs and/or be prominent
    b. An inability to admit and correct sins in themselves
    c. A strong trend toward blaming others and self-righteous gossiping
    d. A failure to practice deep and ongoing forgiveness
    e. An unwillingness to listen

Actually these are failings in all of us. I know I struggle with each of these weaknesses. But here is the key: the immature or neophyte leader cannot *admit* that he has any root problems in these areas. That is, there is no vigorous struggle with root sins, just insecure defensiveness.

Wherever you are working as a leader, you can save yourself and others a great deal of pain if you are willing to claim God's grace for struggling with these qualities in yourself to the degree that you still have them. Rely exclusively on the help of the Spirit. Let me encourage you in this matter as you have encouraged me by your example. I am glorifying God for your growth in humility, your honesty, and your vigorous repudiation of self-defense. I treasure what I have seen in you, dear brother, and make myself your pupil. Your willingness to be searched by God in these matters is proof to me of your calling as a leader and indeed of the reality of your being in Christ.

You also need to remember that you will have great trouble with persons who have these negative features and do not yet know it. For instance, I have worked with one missionary candidate for two years and only last week did he begin to show signs of seeing some of these things in himself. Another promising potential leader at New Life has had a number of these negative qualities. We elders have watched and waited to see what God would do with him for about eight years, and only now is the brother beginning to leave behind his immaturities.

Even for myself, that paragon of all virtues, it took me about fifteen years of school teaching and pastoral ministry before I even saw what a sinner I was. That's a long time, and leaves me humbled. But God is willing to wait. We cannot rush His kingdom.

Sometimes all you can do is pray for those who are like this, show them love by deeds, and forgive them. At the same time do not despair of brothers who have these qualities. It took God a long time even to convince me that these features were in me, and if He has done something to release me from my blind spots, how much more will He do the same for others. So pray with ardent hope, show love, be kind, and resign from trying to be the Holy Spirit. He gave us once the East African revival and the great revivals of the past in the U.S. and Europe. Just devote yourself to prayer and wait for the Holy Spirit to work.

Maybe the best definition of the leader is the man who knows how to wait. During the waiting he learns to lead by prayer. He deepens his love for people and his hold on the throne of grace. He becomes the man in touch with God and the man who understands people. Matthew Arnold says that he sees things clear and whole. I like that. . . .

I also learned to trust the Spirit to protect the work, and by grace my fears were put away. Do you remember how we were studying Spurgeon and the Psalms the last time we were with you? Well, I think you were on Psalms 3 and 4. They were a wonderful

211

deliverance for me, especially Psalm 3. God delivers, God mysteriously revealed Himself to *me* as *my* God of deliverance. . . . I do not think I have ever known a time with more power in my prayers. The answers keep flooding in. Amazing love! Keep up your courage. It is with delight I look forward to seeing you soon.

In His covenant faithfulness,
Jack Miller

Knowing the Love of Christ Brings Perseverance

To a missionary on the field. He and Jack are involved in counseling the Stevensons, a couple who have left the mission field because of problems in their marriage.

February, 1987

Dear Todd,

Greetings from Lake Guerrero, Mexico! You may wonder what I am doing in Mexico at a fishing camp. Well, so do I. Actually, I'm very glad I'm here with Rose Marie about 150 miles south of Brownsville, Texas. To the north, a snowstorm is sweeping the U.S. from northern Texas to Pennsylvania, and we don't miss it at all. The hardest thing we have put up with is today's dip in the thermometer to 60 degrees. And I can live with that. We came down to hold a conference in Harlingen, Texas, and ended up traveling to Mexico for a three-day trip. Thanks, Todd, for your recent letter and the encouragement it brought.

We have been praying for you and Jane through all the changes and are comforted to hear that Christ is strengthening you in the midst of trials. I have found there is nothing like testings of the soul to drive me to Christ and break my pride. Samuel Rutherford says, "Pride rots in winter." Lately, Rose Marie and I have gone through a good deal of "winter," indicating that we must have much need of humbling to rot away our proud self-dependence. Since we left you in December, I have been sick twice, with long sieges of sinusitis and bronchitis. [A tough counseling situation] left me really bone weary, and I began to come down with sinusitis. Very humbling. Still, God's grace abounds in weakness; obviously His hand worked powerfully in all our lives. . . . [Jack discusses the counseling he has been doing with the Stevensons, a missionary couple. Todd is also involved in the counseling.]

During this month of struggle, I was doing much preaching and teaching and sensed that the Lord was pleased to anoint me with His wisdom and insight. I think my sense of humor and joy often overflowed as I preached and taught. Rose Marie on her part has grown remarkably. She has an evident new freedom in the Spirit. On the way to Texas, we were snowed in at the Philadelphia airport, and she used the time to win friends and hand out New Life booklets to the people stranded with us. I felt beat out and so joined her only half-heartedly. That night I repented, and on the airplane the next day, I was used of God to lead a businessman to Christ. His life had been remarkably prepared for hearing about Jesus.

[Jack explains more to Todd about how he counseled the Stevensons.] On my part my heart was also convicted and much humbled. I also need to become much more teachable and open to correction. I did not find many blots in them that are not also in me in worse form. I especially have begun to hunger for a new knowledge of

213

Christ through the Scriptures. Out of that trial my mind seems much more in tune with the mind of Christ revealed in the written Word, and I have done a good deal of saturation reading in God's holy Word. I too am getting glimmers of new light and a deepening love for Jesus.

Todd, please cultivate a knowledge of Jesus Christ's love for you (2 Cor. 5:14–15; Rom. 5:1–6). Then cultivate your love for Him. He is infinitely worthy of our love, just as we are infinitely unworthy of His love. Do, then, spend much time thinking about His love. It is the only thing that enabled me to break through the crust of my own strength and sufficiency and reach out with patient love as I counseled them. It's often easy enough for me to be disturbed by where people are in their rebellion, but then in unbelief to drop the matter there by simply avoiding them. How I admire [the other pastors involved] for refusing to do that! What I long for is a love big enough to be disturbed by what people are doing, and strong enough and patient enough to carry them to the place where Christ wants them to be! I pray that kind of love will become habitual and prevailing in me—not just occasional and flickering in its faintness.

God change me in the depths of my being! Fill me with Your holy presence until Your will is my chief delight. I want to be a man willing to endure the pain of snatching sinners out of the fire. Cleanse me of any unholy fire in my own heart! Teach me how to love others the way Jesus loves me!

It was disappointing to hear that the Sunday afternoon service faded over the holidays and did not recover. But obviously you cannot push a string when the Holy Spirit is not pulling it. Is it possible that you need to gently ask those who say "Don't count on me" some searching questions? When New Life first began, we were besieged by this kind of problem. What I often discovered in undependable Christians was a mix of unbelieving anxieties, a hurting conscience, and a powerful self-centered pride. Worship was difficult for them because the fruit of all this was a discouraged unforgiving spirit.

You could begin by asking them questions about the depth of their forgiveness of the brothers and sisters at [the last church that they attended]. I especially think that a strong pride can lead people to suppress their feelings about others, and to have a bad conscience because of constant condemnation of self and people from the past. You could also ask about forgiveness of parents and other authority figures like their former pastor [the church had split].

A helpful way for you to go might be to share with them your own struggles with forgiving your parents. I found doing this extremely helpful in working with the Stevensons. First, it was honest. I have had to learn to forgive habitually the people in my primary relationships. Secondly, it gets the log out of your own eye before you look for specks in others. Thirdly, it gets you down from your own pedestal so the Spirit can help you grow together. It makes you much more gentle too; I become less of an attack person and more of a brother weeping with a brother. . . .

Todd, I never did get to complete this letter, but will send on this long fragment. I'm very encouraged by what you are doing. I'm praising God for you and Jane.

In Christ's love,
Jack Miller

Jesus Is More Concerned with Our Followership than Our Leadership

To a missionary who is having some struggles on the mission field. He is home on furlough, and Jack has suggested that he take some more time off from missionary work.

March, 1987

Dear Ben,

Greetings in the holy name of Jesus! I am most pleased that you are going to be coming to pray with us [the board at WHM]. It is my conviction that God mightily works when brothers come together to bless one another. We look forward to blessing you with both our hearts and our prayers. We also need your blessing upon us. Indeed, how much we need it! I am persuaded that there is much gold of God's wisdom in James 3, with its teaching that we should not use our tongues to bless God and curse one another, but by implication that we should bless one another while we bless God. We are very much for you, and want to assure you that we feel the trial that you are going through. You are definitely in my prayers and the prayers of others here at WHM with a heart of deep concern.

It might also be of help to you for me to explain how I see things just as a friend who loves you. I wish to assure you that there was no intention on my part to open old wounds by our recent communication to you. My ultimate burden was for your sake, to help you to make a decision about the mission field and for you not to keep things suspended too long. It appeared to me that it was important for you to move forward in the light of your own expressed desires to do so. To delay a decision too long could prove to be hurtful to you, to Sheryl [Ben's wife], and the work on the field. It was not meant to be a long-term evaluation of what you should eventually do or an attempt to decide for you what is your calling from God. Actually I thought you would probably agree with us, that your calling is not primarily pastoral but evangelistic. It was my impression that you saw yourself as more of an evangelist than a pastor. I know that has been my own view of your gifts. Am I missing something here?

My impression is that you also need some time to work through to a fuller understanding of your life calling, your ministry direction, and your theology without the pressure of heavy-duty missionary responsibilities. My concern is also that you make sure that your identity is in Christ, not in being a missionary. Bear with my saying so, but my idea is that you are showing stresses that often characterize missionaries working in a cross-cultural setting. Many of the things you do and say sound so familiar to me. Forgive me for putting it so plainly, but you seem to me to have some of the symptoms of "missionary paranoia." Even the most mature missionaries can and do suffer from this as they undergo spiritual warfare in a demanding and different environment. Typically, they completely identify with the culture which they have entered, sense alienation from their own culture, suspect the home office is made up of neophytes, and feel completely isolated and misunderstood. They then tend to see the leaders at home as unenlightened, indeed, so insensitive to reality that they need waking up by rebukes, sometimes severe ones. The person undergoing this stress often seems to those at home to be marked by lack of respect for them because they are being viewed as outsiders who just don't understand. . . .

It is against this background that I felt you should not now seek to go back to the mission field. There are some heavy-duty issues to be worked through. Is this ministry your calling or is it something else? It also seemed to me that because of the intensity and the drain of your ministry over the past several years you should go very slow about even going on to a different mission field. You have paid a high price for your service to Christ and to us, and it takes time to regain focus and strength. In other words, I am appealing for you to have a little patience with yourself and take some time to think through things in a much less demanding situation.

How blessed it is just to be a follower of Jesus! Really, isn't being a good follower the very heart of being a leader? And isn't our leadership often lacking just because we have weakened in followership? I know that is my own experience repeatedly. I get overly concerned over how to be a better leader, but Jesus is concerned about making me a better, more humble follower. Would it not be a breakthrough for you to submit more to our leadership? I need constantly to accept from Him the disclosure of my own sins and weaknesses, and usually this begins by listening to what my brothers say about me that is critical. My sins—they are vast, vast, my dear brother. Of late the Lord has been breaking my heart over the uncountable multitude of shortcomings in myself. He has especially exposed my pride and defensiveness to my own heart. It's ghastly stuff!

I also am burdened for a few things that appear to me to be shortcomings in your life and ministry. Would you be willing to consider that there may be some blind spots in you as well as in me and the rest of the board? Could you consider that some of these sin patterns might be deep-rooted in you, just as they are in us? One of my biggest concerns is [that you seem] to assume that any criticism of you is unbelief directed against God. Could this also be called "pride"—pride which makes it very difficult to listen to another person's point of view? To put yourself in another person's shoes? To listen carefully and weigh objectively what is said about you? I think this humble listening is part of the maturity of a leader, and my impression is that you have definite weaknesses in this area. It seems to me that anyone who cannot listen patiently and understandingly to personal criticism is going to cause confusion in the church of God. A pastor must be a good listener, and, dear, dear brother, you do have a way to go in this area.

All I can ask you to do is consider these things before the Lord. If my insights are inaccurate, discount them. But I do think that you must agree that I have some knowledge of leaders in general and of

218

you in particular. You do seem to me to adopt an adversarial approach to the brethren when criticism is offered of you. I and the rest of the board have been troubled by this in you. You do need to take into account that we feel sinned against in this matter. It comes out repeatedly in your letters, the stance of "I" vs. "them."

Let me explain a bit more how it comes across to me. First, it takes the form of putting a negative construction on whatever we communicate to you. Granted that in the past we have had a history of insensitivity in failing to build bridges with you. I am very sorry about that. We may still have our own ongoing insensitivities. But I am concerned by how you instinctively react to us as "them." If you feel you need to keep on rebuking us . . . fine. But are you willing to consider that this kind of charge may not be from the Spirit but from the flesh? I am not saying we may not need help, but is this the way to help us, the Spirit's way? Is it the way of godly spiritual warfare? Is it possible that right here you need to approach us pastorally—as a brother talking to brothers, not as an enlightened one dealing with walkers in semi-darkness or worse? Can you be sure the Holy Spirit is not speaking to you through us? Are we always the big sinners and are you alone the small sinner? I can certainly accept that I am a much worse sinner than you. Still, I'd like to believe that the Spirit brings revival by convicting us *together* of our sins, so that no one is really a small sinner.

In writing this lengthy letter to you, I do not wish to suggest that I am not defensive as a person. I am. I believe all the other board members would say the same thing about themselves. We are defensive. We constantly struggle with our ugly pride. But right here is my concern for you. I'd like to see more struggle on your part with these issues—really more spiritual insight into your own weaknesses. Man, Ben, we are all so weak and foolish; none of us really knows how to practice spiritual warfare without constant brokenness before the Lord. None of us really leads well in the church of God unless we constantly learn from each other. So be ready to teach us, but I entreat you, be a bit ready to learn from us too.

Above all, let's be humble servants together, not kings fighting one another. Let's not use [any of our differences] to escape the realities of our oneness in Jesus. Ben, you are our brother, first, last, and always, very dear to us. You have the Spirit and so do we. Let's promote revival by our gentle love for each other. I love you and count you most precious in Christ.

Let grace abound,
Jack Miller

Soon We Shall All Meet the Lord

To an elderly gentleman who had worked with Jack in ministry while we were in California. He had been critical of Jack, and apparently thirty years later that was bothering his conscience.

July, 1987

Dear Edward,

Your recent letter was very encouraging to me. I was very glad to hear from you. If my memory does not fail me, it has been almost thirty years since I saw you to talk to you in any full way.

I am very sorry to hear that Emma is suffering from Alzheimer's disease. This must be a very hard experience for you to go through, but what a comfort you must find in the knowledge that Jesus is watching over her.

I mentioned that your letter was encouraging to me and I really mean that. In it you ask me to forgive you for any way that you have hurt me in my work in [California], etc. I forgive you fully and freely for any hurt that you may have done to me or my ministry, and I do so gladly. In this life I believe repentance is a gift of grace and that this grace has been given to you from God. I also want to assure you that through the years I have harbored no bitterness towards you and have only wished you well. Soon we shall all be face to face with the Lord, and none of us can have any hope other than the blood and righteousness of Christ freely shared for us sinners. May this hope bring great encouragement and comfort to your own heart.

On my part I would also like to say that there are a number of things that I learned from you during our time of association—things I needed to change. Also for anything that I may have done in sinning against you, I ask you to forgive me. I need a lot of forgiving also.

I received your letter as a renewal of our friendship. May God richly bless you and fill you with hope.

Most cordially in Christ,
Jack Miller

Avoiding Those with a History of Conflicts

To a pastor who is involved in a conflict with another Christian group.

July, 1988

Dear Greg,

Warm greetings in Christ! We rejoice that you are serving Christ and thank God very much for you and Louise. You are a gift of the Lord to us and the church of God because of your faith and love wrought by the Holy Spirit. We also feel for you in the sicknesses you have endured and other suffering for the sake of Christ. May it seem light to you because your hearts are set on His glory and not your own or any glory of man. God alone is glorious and worthy of our praise.

My prayer is that you also may abound in wisdom through much waiting upon God. There is certainly no other place where we may find it, because we are all so prone to weakness, error, and sin. Yet the blood of the Son of God avails to cleanse us and wipe away the mists that obscure our vision. Oh, Jesus, be our wisdom in this dark world! Remember how easily we go astray and guide us into wisdom that goes into the deepest part of the soul. How much I lack wisdom; therefore I offer these thoughts with the understanding that your wisdom may be greater than mine.

But at least you can evaluate my thoughts in the light of the Scripture. I want to attempt to give counsel respecting your relationship with those brothers who are dear to you but obviously estranged. . . . The general principle that I try to follow is to keep a distance from ministries that have a history of conflicts that do not seem to get resolved.

Harvie Conn says that in Korea he simply stayed away from churches and presbyteries that had intense and entangled personality conflicts. At the time that seemed to me to be severe, even maybe too severe, but through the years I have come to respect that judgment.

Of course, where and how you apply that principle may be difficult to know.

In general, I have come to see that it is difficult for conflicts to get untangled where issues of money or personal power or both are involved. . . .

[I wish that you could reconcile with them.] At the same time I am neither the Holy Spirit nor the Lord of history. Therefore I must submit to the will of God. It also appears to me that God is all-wise. . . . Therefore I urge you not to be discouraged, but to walk wisely and in love. Forgive, bless, and show love whenever it is consistent with holy wisdom that God will give you. . . .

May the grace of the Lord Jesus Christ abound in your lives and ministry!

In His great love,
Jack Miller

Persevering through Change

Ordinarily don't move into a new thing until you have made things happen where you are (by grace). That is, you need to have solid evidence of effective leadership on one level before going to another.

The five letters in this section contain some thoughts from Jack on how a Christian should make major life decisions. Not surprisingly, they do not offer a secular cost/benefit analysis. Instead Jack laid down some general principles that focus on the heart.

In counseling those who were thinking about going into ministry, Jack thought that it was especially important to not be controlled by fear—specifically fear of suffering. He wrote to a young woman who was considering going on the mission field but who was full of fear: "What you discover is that there is no permanent joy in Christ apart from a willingness to deny ourselves, take up our cross, and follow Him. That is, your life cannot have any power in it or even salvation if you refuse to be like a grain of wheat that must fall to the ground and die in order to bring forth much fruit." When the issue of fear was dealt with, Jack believed that the specifics of God's will (which church, ministry, or mission field) would become clear.

He was also concerned that Christians, before they make life-altering decisions, be humbled by God. This is one reason that he thought it was important for those in ministry to stay in one place for a long time. Jack once asked a group of Christian leaders why they should make it a priority to stay in one place. They replied with the usual answers—getting to know people over a long period of time, continuity of leadership, and the ability to see your plans worked out over a period of years. Jack replied that those were all good things, but the most important reason was that over the long run you were more likely to notice your own sins, repent of them, and learn to rely on God for everything. He reiterates this advice in the first letter of this section where he gives some guidelines to a young leader who wants to move to a different ministry. Jack points out to him that when a leader moves on too quickly, "people just don't get to know him, and he moves on before he gets humbled by seeing how impossible ministry is."

Finally, as you read this section of letters, you will notice that Jack does not seem to think the most important issue is where someone ministers. Instead, his emphasis is on how the ministry is accomplished. He emphasizes that knowing Christ is more important than doing things for Christ, and "that the process of reaching the goals is at least as important as the goals themselves." What is that process? Jack goes on to say, "In that process we are called by the Spirit to walk in intimacy with Christ, to enjoy Him and His people." It is only through that day-by-day fellowship with Jesus that Jack believed ministry could be accomplished and major life decisions could be made.

Stay in One Place Until You've Been Humbled

To a pastor who has written Jack and asked him for advice about whether he should leave his church.

April, 1980

Dear Jim,

Just a few thoughts to share: I'd like to begin by affirming the obvious working of grace in your life through the Word. I praise God for it and your growth in love through the gospel. I'm convinced that God has also given you a faithful heart.

But here are some guidelines for launching out on a ministry which I see as crucial:

1. Ordinarily don't move into a new thing until you have made *things happen where you are* (by grace). That is, you need to have solid evidence of effective leadership on one level before going to another.

2. This leadership effectiveness includes: (a) the grace *to express love to others* in a public manner, (b) willingness and determination to shepherd by *being a servant,* (c) *courage* to act in humility to disciple others in the face of resistance, and (d) *ability to command respect* by maturity of life so that others feel they are being led in a Christlike direction.

226

3. The best way this kind of development takes place is by staying under one set of leaders to give them enough time to know you so that the obvious impossibilities of (2) in your own strength can be pointed out and the young leader broken before the Lord to abandon pride and move into Jesus' love. But usually this doesn't come very soon if a man moves about too much. People just don't get to know him, and he moves on before he gets humbled by seeing how impossible ministry is. It's one thing to see things happen with others leading; it is another to see them happen to you and through you, and that takes time and sweat.

With much love,
Jack Miller

For Life to Go Anywhere It Must Have a Death in It

To a young woman who has been thinking about becoming a missionary. She is dealing with her own fears and the fears of others about security issues, especially in Africa.

April, 1983

Dear Catherine,

I was sorry that I didn't get to see you yesterday. I hope this brief letter may be of help instead. Rose Marie told me that you were concerned about the safety in Uganda for the small children of [our missionaries there], and that you also had a need to know how to relate to the fears that others might have. It appears to me that you have come to the first test that we were talking about a few days back. Remember? I asked how you thought you would do in an upsetting situation, one that might or might not have danger in it but would appear to be threatening. I think this is pretty close to what I had in mind. That is, what has happened to rattle things is that you have been faced by the doubts and anxieties of others and felt the power of these doubts and anxieties. This is the biggest problem in Uganda. It is the fear that is so strong that it becomes like a practical atheism, a mind-set and attitude which in its manifestation in Uganda leads people sometimes to spread rumors like crazy and which is out of touch with the divine sovereignty. It is in me in a very deep way. The only thing is that I have, bit by bit, started fighting it in myself. I now see it in myself as a kind of demon-inspired paranoia which entirely departs from awareness of the Father's all-powerful supervising love.

There are three things that I find I need to do to cure it. First, I need to get the facts about the actual dangers in any situation. In this case, Uganda. Usually the fears are much worse than the facts. In Uganda there are risks. You could get killed there. But the facts happen to be that not a single Protestant missionary has been killed over a three-year period or more. Missionaries from most of the denominations represented in that country have returned, and new ones have come, some with families of children. There are enough European and American children now in Kampala to have at least one school for them. The fact happens to be that rumors fueled by fear pass quickly to Nairobi and the BBC, and the dangers are sensationalized by the Kenya press in an incredible way, and I have heard tales over BBC that were just incredibly false, too. So what you should do is to call the Hudsons [missionaries who were getting ready to go to Uganda] and get the straight stuff from them. I do not see how anyone could get better firsthand knowledge. If you still have concerns, call the Uganda desk at the State Department.

Secondly, it is of even greater importance that you understand your own call in the light of God's calling of all believers to the privilege to suffer the way Jesus did. It is given to us—a gift from God—not only to believe in Jesus but to suffer with Him. What a privilege! See these passages: 2 Timothy 1:7–9; Luke 14:25–27; Philippians 1:29–30; Mark 8:34–38; and Romans 8:31–39. Also soak yourself in the book of Revelation. It's loaded with glory for those who are faithful to death and give themselves to witness-martyrdom for dear Jesus' sake. But with that you need to settle in a straightforward way what is your own calling. You are bound to have many fears and perplexities until you face that question more squarely. I do not think you can get that without some serious prayer and fasting and getting others to pray for you. Take a time in which you ask others to pray for you for God's will to be made known. Out of that praying you should come to a conviction that God has a particular will for you and that [might mean becoming a missionary in Uganda or doing some other type of ministry]. But do not hang in between. Once you have prayed, God will give you a desire to do His will if in your praying you have surrendered to His will. It's pretty simple once we have given all to God and learned to will His will. He does not want you to do something that you know is not your calling and therefore you cannot will it with your whole heart. Get wholeheartedness into yourself with all your getting and renounce all doubts about God's loving capacity to introduce you to His will.

Third, see such a waiting time as an opportunity to help others learn what God is teaching you. Guidance can only come as we believers function as a community of faith, living by prayer (see Acts

13:1ff). Help your friends to see the danger of living out of fear and not out of the promises. Introduce them to the promises of God. Open up the Scriptures which give us the full picture of the glory of suffering for Christ. What you discover is that there is no permanent joy in Christ apart from a willingness to deny ourselves, take up our cross, and follow Him. That is, your life cannot have power in it or even salvation if you refuse to be like a grain of wheat that must fall to the ground and die in order to bring forth much fruit. God calls you to greatness, Catherine, but greatness means fruitfulness, and fruitfulness comes as we die to self and our fears and rise from the dead.

I do not presume to know whether you should go to Uganda or not. Only God can finally show you that, but you must believe that He can and will reveal His design for your life to you. But your life must have a death in it if it is to go anywhere. The greatest thing hindering revival at New Life is the way we tend to run away from our own death. The cross can be evaded only so long. Then if we keep away from it we begin to create our own deaths, and we die thousands of times over, killed and rekilled by our anxieties.

I rejoice that the Spirit of grace will teach you those things. Don't mind at all a late winter spiritually. After all, as Samuel Rutherford said, "Pride rots in winter." But after pride rots, the Spirit will bring eternal summer to the heart. May Jesus breathe summer time into your soul!

You are in all our prayers. We shall gladly submit what the Lord pilots you into as His work.

Thankful in Christ,
Jack

How Does a Knowledge of God's Love Give Direction?

To a young woman who wants to know how faith can be practical as she is facing a decision that will change her whole life.

February, 1985

Dear Debbie,

Well, we are back from Uganda, all in one piece and with much reason to praise the Lord. The mission is registered definitely and officially; so this clears the way for visas, work permits, and other things. But I do think the best part of our trip was seeing Tom's [a missionary in Uganda] growth in wisdom and grace. He is a very gifted fellow, but he needed a crisis to bring him to the place of usefulness and soberness.

He told us, "I was doing ministry in all directions. Then finally in October I knew I had to give full time to language study. When I did this, it became a crisis for me to say no to many things I loved to do. But the process of saying no exposed how much selfish ambition there was in me and humbled my heart. It was very liberating, a real breakthrough."

As a result of this humbling Tom has made excellent progress in the language and has quickly matured. . . .

So it is with joy that we return and thank you for your prayers on our behalf. Truly faith born in prayer is "the victory that overcomes the world" (1 John 5:4). In talking with your dad, he mentioned you

231

could use a word of encouragement at this time, and I am happy to be able to urge upon you the knowledge you already have—which is that God loves you and you can know and trust in that love. The faith which issues from that love has the power to overcome the world.

But how can such faith become practical when we live on the firing line? I remember the concerns you shared with me in our last full conversation. How then does a believing knowledge of God's love help in the choice of life direction?

I think here is the problem. At the time the Spirit of God sheds abroad the love of God in our hearts, we begin life as a new adventure but an adventure with dangers and risks. The adventure consists in a new power to love people, the capacity to see Jesus Christ's interest in the lives of other people and to pursue that interest in the face of churchly indifference. We experience the freedom and joy of self-forgetting as we pursue His concerns in the lives of others. We delight in making ourselves available for others for Christ's sake.

The danger in all of this may be that we are not really so much committed to Jesus Christ but to those things which seem to liberate and fulfill us. When that happens, we may be inclined to dissipate our lives in directions that are not controlled by the Word and the Spirit. I go through that all the time. Actually the struggle Tom went through happens to me almost weekly. I don't make a big deal of it because it's pretty commonplace in my life. But I do need to learn to say no to my will, ambitions, and desires in a total way frequently.

In other words, devotion to Jesus Christ is not the same thing as my heedlessly throwing away my life. Devotion to Christ, rather, is infantry work, slogging through the mud and wet, digging in and holding the ground when under attack, and, above all, sticking to the basics of His revealed will.

I am not sure any of this can be applied to your life decisions. I hope it is helpful. But if it is not, bear patiently with a sincere effort, misguided though it may be. But at any rate I believe it is valuable for me to encourage you to seek God's will above all and accept that doing His will may cost you personal pain, it may even bring pain to others. Perhaps this last is the most difficult to bear.

Pray for me. So much of my ministry has in it a dying to my desire to please people. I can only do this by faith born out of believing prayer, yours and mine. Thanks much. We do have you in our hearts and pray for you.

Most cordially in Christ,
Jack Miller

The Process of Reaching Our Goals Is as Important as the Goals

To a young couple who have left full-time Christian ministry.

March, 1987

Dear Charles and Phoebe,

Warm greetings in the grace of our Lord Jesus Christ! You are very dear to me, friends much treasured in my heart. I am writing to you on an airline flight from Baton Rouge to Nashville on my way home to Philadelphia. I began to think about you and pray for you and decided to write you a letter letting you know that you are still much in my heart. I just gave a New Life booklet to a young woman sitting next to me. She is reading it with some care. That also made me think of your faithfulness in witness and leads me to urge you to continue faithfully in sharing the gospel with others.

I believe that this could be especially important for you at a time when you do not have any official calling to witness. I think there is something ineffably sweet about witnessing when the compulsion to do it springs not from duty but from delight in Jesus' goodness, from awareness of His faithful love. For me it is so easy unconsciously to become a professional Christian and do my service to Christ as a must rather than as a sonship delight. I hate that in myself and reject it as no longer part of the new Jack Miller being created anew in Christ.

I like to look forward to my ultimate destination—being like Christ without any admixture of sin. What a day that will be—when by grace I will be made fully pure in heart and with my own eyes see Jesus face to face! Oh, what a glory I will know then when I come at last to rest in His welcoming embrace! Don't you long for that day? Yesterday in Baton Rouge the sky was incredibly blue, the sun blazing with healthy warmth, and the green fringes of spring spreading through all the trees and shrubs. A new-minted day like one of the first days of creation. A small picture of the glory of the new world, with all the dark clouds of sin and the smog of human lust blown away by the King!

One thing that I'd especially like to commend to you is the priority of just walking with Him now in preparation for that event. In our world today we often give ourselves to visible goals. There is nothing wrong with that. We need goals and goals that are defined. However, there is a danger in this goal-seeking. We must remember that the process of reaching the goals is at least as important as the goals themselves. In that process we are called by the Spirit to walk in intimacy with Christ, to enjoy Him and His people. I think this fellowship also includes enjoying the common things of life—really seeing the world like the simple thing of a human friendship, a good relationship with a parent, and even something as ordinary as enjoying a ballgame. I think it also includes building a good relationship with your children.

These things are not secondary matters, but they are as important as winning the lost. Don't lose your heart for the lost, but in your fellowship with Christ, grow in your daily humility and you will become more effective in winning the lost. There is a beautiful harmony here. When our lives are empty of self and pride, we are freed to be ourselves. We are not under an iron law of duty, but acting and thinking and feeling as we were meant to by our Creator. In the enjoyment of that wholeness, we become attractive to sinners.

It would be easy for you to unconsciously look upon this as a time of permanent winter—life without a future and no clearly defined purpose. But remember what Samuel Rutherford once said, "Pride rots in winter." I know God has sent me a good deal of winter to rot my pride, but I don't regret any of that because the rotting of pride leads into a new springtime of usefulness. Likely you will be having all kinds of adjustments. I congratulate you on the birth of your new child. . . . Each child is a wonderful gift from God. But you will also find that a growing family can be draining. When you have small children, you may often feel you are simply full-time parents and nothing more. Charles also may be tempted to think of his job as a dead end with no future—and in his heart to think that real life is somewhere else. Let me encourage you to think of this as real life and [in that life] Christ is training you in the knowledge of God. For it's in the harassments of daily life that I learn about myself and how weak I am and how much I need God. And it is only when I know that I am weak that I can know God and His strength.

This is also a unique opportunity for each of you to begin to work on your family relationships with each other and with both sets of parents. From what you have told me, working with your parents is going to be a long haul. But as the Chinese say, the journey of a thousand miles begins with a single step, and you can begin to take small steps in reaching out to them. Keep on doing it even when they are not very responsive to your kindness and love. . . .

Please pray for me and Rose Marie as we go to Ireland and then Spain to work on a new book. God bless.

In His grace and love,
Jack

Criteria for Deciding Whether to Stay or Leave a Church

To a pastor who is wondering how to decide if he should leave his present church and go to another church that has called him.

June, 1995

Dear Eric,

Thank you for your warm gracious letter.

Your sensitivity to the will of our God encourages me. So does your honesty in wanting the best from Him through grace. May He fulfill your heart's desire!

You asked me to pray for your praying. I am happy to do that. It seems to me that God is speaking in this matter to others as well. I know He is speaking to me. Pray for my praying as I pray for yours.

On the one hand, I am encouraged by the Lord's helping me with my praying. As I have recovered physically and emotionally from the stroke—and from the New Era collapse [a charity that was allegedly giving matching funds to many Christian organizations had turned out to be fraudulent]—my heart has been enlarged to resume praying widely for missionaries, pastors, and churches. But, on the other hand, I want to pray with more faith and bolder claiming of the promises. Here I feel a tough battle looms. God hears my prayers in wonderful ways. But the Spirit within stirs me, leaving me much dissatisfied by my praying. He makes me aware that I need to pray with more authority than I do at present, especially in my private prayers and in praying with Rose Marie. The Spirit also seems to be giving me a conviction that stronger praying must be tied to bolder action—that is, putting feet on my prayers. Not only praying for the lost but getting out there and witnessing to them; not only praying for grace to come to Christian leaders but confronting them more directly with a broken and contrite heart; not only praying that I will love my family around me but acting to love them.

I have been praying for you and will do so with increasing effectiveness as God searches me out. Tell me what you learn and I'll tell you what I learn.

Concerning your staying with your present congregation or moving on—this certainly is a matter for prayer. Ultimately only God can show you. But my thought is that there is nothing wrong with going to a new congregation if a larger door is being opened to you and you have been faithful in the present church. I believe you have been faithful where you are. Perhaps you need to be bolder and more vulnerable. I don't mean to suggest at all that you have been timid. But when God teaches us great truths Satan is always there throwing cold water on us. I think he may have been throwing lots of cold water on you. So maybe you should combine more plain speaking with the gentleness that God has given you. Your gentleness has been apparent to Rose Marie and me, and with that spirit you probably need to take the Scriptures to some elders and question them about their brokenness before the Word of God. Don't accuse of course, but good questions can stir the conscience.

That's the way of the Lord in the opening chapters of Genesis. Too, I am thinking that you could use the brokenness passages in the Psalms (34, 51), Isaiah, and James 4:6–10. I'm praying for you to do this with fear of God and freedom from fear of people and human opinions.

If you have done this many times already, just forget about this advice. But pray that I may follow my own counsel. It's much easier to give advice than practice it! . . .

You mentioned advantages and disadvantages to your going to another church, including just the overarching fact that it seems to be a more positive situation all around. Well, my feeling is that if God calls you to this new church, there is absolutely nothing wrong with having a church setting that will help your family and where the opportunity for gospel proclamation is enlarged. One way to decide this issue (if you should be called by this church) is to make sure that the new congregation as a whole is solidly behind your coming as the new pastor. If the church is really for you and what you represent, then the case for going seems strong.

There is one issue you raised in your letter that does warrant further discussion. It has to do with your concern that you seem to be required to be on the scene if the programs are to work in the present congregation. Without the pastor programs seem to drift. . . . Everyone struggles with this, but there are ways to work on it. One way is to spend time teaching people to pray. Prayer breaks dependence on other people and increases dependence on God alone. Think about it carefully each day. Ask yourself, how can I help my brothers and sisters learn to pray? Pray with them constantly. Then, speak plainly. Teach the people of God that anyone who takes prayer lightly is a dangerous Christian: indeed, one of the marks of apostasy is resistance to prayer. God protect us from hearts that do not pray.

July, 1995

Once more I'm back to your letter. My apologies for not getting it answered sooner. I have been caught up in witnessing, calling people, writing letters, praying, resting, speaking, and repenting. Good times. The speaking has strengthened me in an unusual way both physically and mentally. Christ uses gospel preaching to strengthen my whole being. However, I have come to the place that I am saner about resting and doing it more often with Rose Marie's encouragement.

I also think that the devil may have been using some of the critical brethren to discourage you. It's very easy to let the spirit slip into a self-accusatory mode when you are criticized. Too, you see how slowly the work goes and Satan insinuates that you are a failed pastor. At such times it is important to claim scriptural promises as a basis for rejection of his attacks. Of course, we find that sometimes his charges are true, but even then the blood of Christ cleanses from all sin as we daringly confess our sins. I am praying that Christ Jesus will give you a childlike spirit, courage, and strong hope, and that when you are discouraged you will throw caution to the winds and witness boldly to some non-Christian. We all need non-Christian friends to keep us sane. Often they have a certain worldly wisdom that keeps us from getting our egos too deeply involved in our ministries.

So my conclusion is: feel free to go to the new church if there is evidence the call is from God. Do so with hope and joy. But don't leave your present church with a defeated spirit. Witness, pray, admonish, teach, love, cry, laugh till you pack up your car and go. If God leads you to stay, become bolder and more broken and more confrontational.

I'd also encourage you to do more thinking about the glorious appearing of our great God and Savior Jesus Christ. Think about Judgment Day. Clear thinking about that Day can do a lot to clear the head and the heart of the fear of people. I can get unconsciously bogged down by awareness of what people think, worried about my reputation, my success and failures, and forget about the only One who can evaluate me, and that is the Lamb on the throne. Lately I have been witnessing to congregations and people about the Judgment Day. It's surprising in a secularized age how many people really wake up when you call them to that great Final Accounting. It has a way of affecting me positively, because it will all come out in the wash there when we all fall on our faces before the Great White Throne. What force such awareness gives to the glad tidings of free justification by faith alone. Here I can know that Christ has taken my "doom" upon himself ("doom" is the language of Last Judgment used in Rom. 8:1). "There is therefore no more doom for those in Christ Jesus"!

Then pray that these truths would not be mere words to me. Jesus, grip our hearts with the great news that justification reaches to the Great White Throne! I need courage and love and wisdom and great endurance as never before. . . .

Tomorrow we start our High Leigh conference. Again, I will start it with a call to the Last Judgment and justification. May God grant grace to those who come to receive the gospel of hope against the background of holy white light coming with such blinding radiance from the Great White Throne. Glory, glory, glory! Walk, dear brother, in the glory!

Safe under the blood of the Lamb,
Jack

Part 4

Encouragement

Encouragement for Sinners

I refuse to see myself as a lemon made by an evolutionary production line, but as a sinner. You tinker endlessly with lemons, but with a sinner you have sure hope. Why? Because sinners can repent, whereas lemons can only be tinkered with; they are beyond repair.

Early in the 1970s Jack was speaking at a local church. He was finishing up a three-part series on the gospel, and he told the congregation that "the gospel can change anyone." As he was speaking, the pastor of the church stood up and publicly disagreed with Jack. The pastor said to Jack (and his own church members) that there are those whom only "medical experts" can help. His point was that the gospel is great for emotionally healthy people, but it cannot change those with the deepest problems. Jack said that at first he was taken aback by what the pastor said, but as he reflected, he wondered if he himself really believed in the power of the gospel to change anyone with any set of problems.

Because of this pastor's challenge, Jack and Rose Marie decided to open their home to some of the troubled people that they had met. Jack had seen the Holy Spirit apply the gospel to his own hard and proud heart, and he shared how God had changed him with those who came to live with them. Their houseguests included the suicidal, the depressed, the anxious, the angry, some who were in and out of mental hospitals, and others who were drug addicts. Many of these became hopeful, thankful worshippers of God. They found that the gospel can and does change the most deeply troubled hearts.

Jack's faith in the power of the Holy Spirit to change anyone was strengthened throughout this time, and as his ministry continued, he saw all kinds of people (including his own family!) change. His core belief that humans are not unfixable lemons but sinners that can repent and change comes through clearly in this set of letters. No matter whom Jack was speaking to or writing to his viewpoint was the same: the gospel had changed him, therefore it could change anyone. Because he believed this, he was full of hope for everyone he spoke with.

In these letters Jack challenged the recipients to join him in repenting of unbelief, and then to put their faith in the power of the Holy Spirit to come into their hearts and teach them to live by faith. Jack did not believe that anyone was a "special case." Although he knew that people came with different sets of problems, he believed and taught that all were sinners who needed to repent and turn to Christ in faith. In a letter to a counselor who was working with Mike, a severely depressed man, Jack says that while a psychiatrist could help Mike uncover the nature of his problem, he could not give Mike real hope. Jack goes on to say that Mike's deepest need is for "a foundation of faith, the inward experience and sure conviction that his sins are forgiven and that he is not an orphan but in loving partnership with God his Father."

Jack believed that this foundation of faith was nothing more or less than having a vital ongoing relationship with Jesus Christ. In each letter in this section Jack returns to the necessity of knowing Jesus, trusting in Jesus, and then depending totally on Him for everything. To a young woman who was concerned with whether she was repenting properly or even a Christian he said, "Christ calls us to abandon trust in our own strength and righteousness. We do not have the strength to improve ourselves morally or the righteousness with which to justify ourselves. 'At the right time when we were without strength, Christ died for the ungodly.' Faulty, blind, degraded, we can do nothing but depend on Christ alone to give us assurance of salvation. So repentance and faith entail coming down from our thrones of self-dependence and pride and simply giving ourselves in surrender to Christ."

It was this dependence on Christ alone that Jack knew could change the human heart. Whomever he was writing to—the depressed, the confused, those caught in flagrant sin, the self-righteous, those whom others had sinned against—his message was the same: depend on Christ and His Spirit to change you and those around you. His faith in God's power to change those with the deepest problems, and his and Rose Marie's willingness to put feet on that faith by reaching out to all kinds of people, were rewarded by God with the privilege of watching many lives begin and continue a life of faith.

Don't Seek Repentance or Faith as Such; Seek Christ

To a woman who is not sure whether she is a Christian. She has written Jack and asked him how she can tell if her repentance has been real.

Dear Elise,

Thank you for your recent letter concerning your desire to know whether you have had a God-centered repentance. So set aside any fears that I might be unwilling to take time to help you. Perhaps I can help you if you will recognize that all I can do is be a small finger pointing to a large Christ. But if you trust yourself to Him be confident He is not only willing to help you but has the power to help you.

What do you need to know? First, repentance and faith are not like a sidewalk that you must travel on to get to the house of salvation. They are the door or, perhaps better, God's ways for being near Him. When you turn to Christ, you don't have a repentance apart from Christ you just have Christ. Therefore don't seek repentance or faith as such but seek Christ. When you have Christ you have repentance and faith. Beware of seeking an experience of repentance; just seek an experience of Christ.

The Devil can be pretty tricky. He doesn't mind you thinking much about repentance and faith if you do not think about Jesus Christ. He wants you to worry a great deal about whether you have truly repented. Examining yourself is fine—if you relate it to the cross and Christ's love for you. But the point of my little book is that any sorrow for sin apart from Christ is not going to help you. So don't even seek sorrow for sin or to see whether your repentance is genuine. Seek Christ, and relate to Christ as a loving Savior and Lord who wants to invite you to know Him.

You raise the question whether or not you are saved, and rightly suggest that maybe what counts for you right now is not that question so much as getting to know Christ. You are definitely on target. Get to know Christ and you will be sure of your relationship to Him.

But how do you get to know Christ? Keep two things in view: first, you cannot know Him unless you are sure He loves you and died personally for Elise's sins, your sins. To give you faith that redeems you, Jesus gives you a promise. He promises to save you. The gospel is not only a fact, but a promise that Christ who died for sins and rose again lives to welcome you. That is the whole point of John 3:16 and the many promises in the Gospel of John. You trust God and His Son because God loves you and gave His Son for you (fact) and then commits Himself by way of promise to receive you (John 1:12). It's sometimes cheapened by evangelical Christians but it's breathtaking in its simplicity and awesome wonder. God loves you very much.

Secondly, Christ calls us to abandon trust in our own strength and righteousness. We do not have the strength to improve ourselves morally or the righteousness with which to justify ourselves. "At the right time when we were without strength, Christ died for the ungodly." Faulty, blind, degraded, we can do nothing but depend on Christ alone to give us assurance of salvation. So repentance and faith entail coming down from our thrones of self-dependence and pride and simply giving ourselves in surrender to Christ.

Still, the devil may say to you: "You do not yet have sufficient conviction of sin to come to Christ." Tell the devil to get away from you. Do you have a sense of shame over your sins? I think you do. That is a conviction of sin, not a feeling depressed or whatever. If you are ashamed of living a life independently of God, then the Holy Spirit has already convicted you of sin. Simply claim Christ as your Lord and Savior. Base your simple prayer of acceptance on His promise. Claim John 3:16–17.

Back to the question whether you are already saved. Don't spend much time on this one, but spend your time getting to Christ. Speak to Him simply in prayer and ask Him to show Himself to you. He loves to reveal Himself to people. Then make sure you are cultivating a forgiving spirit toward others. Bitterness, condemnation of others, will rob a genuine believer of his or her fellowship with Jesus, and raise questions about assurance. Jesus does expect you to see what a forgiveness you have received and then to forgive others and keep on forgiving others. Put on forgiveness as your whole new life.

I would especially commend to you the study of Romans 10 to see how faith works. I would like to hear from you again.

Most cordially,
Jack Miller

People Who Have Been Forgiven by Jesus Forgive Others

To Rose Marie's elderly mother who lived with them. She struggled with schizophrenia and paranoid delusions, but this did not stop Jack from telling her the truths of the gospel again and again. Toward the end of her life she did acknowledge her need for a Savior and was able to admit that she too had sins. Jack wrote this letter because she was very angry with someone who was helping with her care.

August, 1986

Dear Mother,

I originally wrote this letter to you while I was in Temple Hospital waiting to undergo tests for my heart condition. You will be glad to know that the tests were mostly encouraging and I am more and more able to return to normal life. My cardiologist has given me excellent care, and so has Rose Marie. She has shown me many kindnesses, borne many burdens, and devoted herself to me with all her heart—something I certainly don't deserve.

I thank you for your concern. I appreciate your loving interest in my welfare and your desire to see me restored to health. I do think the best gift you could have given me is already given—that of Rose Marie for a wife. You know Rose Marie is not only a talented person, but she brings something special to me and to our whole household. It is the gift of *a strong faith, a confident trust.*

So I thank you for the training you gave her and the hope you provided for her. I also want to explain to you how you can have the same confident faith.

Her faith is in Jesus.

It's very simple having confident faith in Him.

But it has a hard part too. It is humbling to believe in Him. It is difficult for us to admit we have things in us and problems we cannot solve ourselves. Our pride keeps us from seeing how much we need

247

Him. But once we see our need of Him we trust our lives to Him as Lord and Savior from sin. Such a trust is a surrender. It especially means we give up trusting in our own righteous deeds and good character and church attendance to save us, instead, we trust in Him alone. We put ourselves entirely in His hands.

But we trust Him only if we know some important things about Him. We can trust only a person we know.

First, He wants you to know that He loves you and died to save you from your sins. You can know that about Him.

Secondly, He wants you to know that He is alive from the dead and is a person at God's right hand. As a living person He can hear your prayers, present His righteousness instead of your unrighteousness to God, and make you His own child and give you a new heart.

So two things you need to know: 1. Jesus loves you and died to save you; and 2. He is alive to receive you as His own child.

But you also must know you have a need. The Bible says we need Jesus. But why? Why do you need Jesus?

The reason is that we are all sinners. The Bible says, "All have sinned and fall short of the glory of God." It says, "There is none righteous, no, not one."

How do we sin?

We all break God's laws every day and we also have a sinful nature inherited from Adam and Eve. Because we have this sin-nature in us, each of us wants his or her own way. Wanting our own way and not God's is our biggest sin. We want to control our own lives and be like little kings and queens in our hearts, having our own way in things that matter to us.

The Bible says that we should "love the Lord thy God with all thy heart, and with all thy soul, and with all thy strength." But we love ourselves much more than God and show it by spending all our time thinking about ourselves and not about Him and loving Him.

Not to love God with the whole of the heart is a great sin we have all committed every day.

We also sin against God by complaining and not being thankful to God. The Bible says that complaining and unthankfulness are very great evils in every human heart. We all have sinned terribly against God by our bitter complaints against people and our forgetting to be constantly thankful to our Maker.

That is why we have a need for Jesus to save us from our sins. We have many of them. A day is coming when each of us will die and eventually be raised from the dead when Jesus returns to make a new world. I was close to death in Uganda when I had the heart attack, and it made me take seriously the resurrection of the just and the unjust. I think you are aware that you too may soon stand before Jesus, the Lord. You have had ninety-three years, and I hope you have many more, but you should get yourself ready to meet the Lord. I want you to rise at the resurrection with the just, with a wonderful new body, and go to heaven.

One way you can tell you are going to rise with the just and not rise to condemnation is by a forgiving spirit. People who have been forgiven by Jesus forgive others. It's that simple. People who do not forgive will not be forgiven by Jesus.

That is why I am deeply concerned that you have not yet forgiven Joel [a caregiver with whom she had conflict]. You believe that he has wronged you. Without my saying anything about the truth or falsity of that, you still must forgive him. God commands it. The Bible says, "Forgive or you will not be forgiven."

You have told me you were not ready to forgive Joel. I agree. You are not able of yourself to forgive him. You feel it is right to condemn him in your heart. But you see only God has that right. God only is Judge. Therefore your refusal to forgive is a grievous sin against God, a taking of His work as Judge.

That is why you need to have Jesus as your Savior and Lord. Admit that you have sinned as I have. Ask God to give you a different attitude, but with that ask Jesus to save you from your sins. Trust in His blood shed on the cross to pay for all your sins. Receive Him into your heart and then you will have a forgiving spirit. God will not condemn you; you will be under the forgiveness of God, His own dear child.

Mother, Jesus loves you very much and so do I. Come to this Jesus. His death was a frightful price to pay for our transgressions. He suffered all the agony of our condemnation. By His wounds we are healed.

There is great joy in knowing Jesus has forgiven all your sins and removed them from you as far as the east is from the west. I am asking Him to open your heart to such love, such heavenly mercy, and make Jesus yours by faith.

Again, we all love you very much. We have you in our hearts. We also want you to be with us in heaven forever.

In the Savior's love,
Your son, Jack

We Are Not Lemons, We Are Sinners

To a counselor who is working with a church member who has been struggling with depression and recently been referred to a psychiatrist for further evaluation.

April, 1987

Dear Bill,

This morning I prayed for Mike and decided that it might be a good idea for me to share some of my thoughts about him with you. I want to assure you that it appears to me that you did the right thing by having him put himself under the care of your psychiatrist friend. . . . So let me assure you I do not feel that our pastoral work is being preempted by you or him. But I do have some suggestions for you and the psychiatrist. . . . I have a fairly good knowledge of Mike and think I see a pattern in his life which goes something like this:

1. First level—he has many surface worries and tends to be overly conscientious in work habits and keeps endlessly and restlessly busy working. At times he has been a real workaholic, one of the most intense I've seen.

2. Second level—he has many underlying fears which fuel the surface worries. My guess is that he has fears about almost everything: the way he appears to people, his lack of ministry or job success (in his own eyes), his relationships with his family, and finally his acceptance with God. It would be hard having so many fears not to be angry with people, circumstances, and God. I think he must be, though outwardly he appears quite controlled.

3. Third level—he is locked into unbelief and ignorance both of God's holiness and love. He may have a surface belief that his sins are forgiven, but it doesn't control the core of his being and supply him with the confidence that his sins really are forgiven. I use the phrase "locked in" advisedly. I mean by it that he has a mind-set which is now controlled by a completely negative evaluation of himself and his future. I believe it is likely that he really sees himself as a piece of junk, or at least as an orphan alone in a merciless universe.

It is obvious that this picture is grim, mostly shadows. But it may be even darker yet. Suppose one's life is filled with this kind of haunting insecurity and nagging guilt. It's easy to want to find emotional relief and comfort in bodily pleasures, and for men this often means sexual fantasies, etc., which can confirm him in his judgment that he is worthless.

How does he break out of this? The psychiatrist certainly can bring to the surface many core elements in his difficulties. I do not doubt that this can be very helpful, but even if the course of treatment is relatively successful, you are still left with a person who has lost hope or who has a measure of hope floating on a sea of dark anxiety, and sooner or later it is going to sink again unless the matter is treated in a more foundational manner.

How can this be done? Mike needs a foundation of faith, the inward experience and sure conviction that his sins are forgiven and that he is not an orphan but in loving partnership with God his Father. He needs to know that God loves him unconditionally.

But that still does not fully answer the question how this comes to his inner life. Do you go in and preach to him? Not really, that might simply deepen his guilt. But he does need to know that there is solid hope for him in the Lord and in his salvation. In essence, he needs to discover God's grace and how God gives objective peace as a free gift through faith. [Then he needs to discover] how this can touch the central insecurities of his life.

So what I believe he needs, within a context of affirmation, is the knowledge that we love him unconditionally, that we accept him as he is, and that we ourselves have gone through similar dark conflicts and eventually emerged on the other side by God's grace.

Inherently Mike's problem is that in his unbelief he sees himself as a special case. He just thinks insecurity, and the key to his thinking is found in his whole mind-set which even plans as though he were an orphan. To replace this mind-set is entirely possible. I do it almost every day in my own life. But what I do is different in one crucial way: I reject this negativistic thinking as unbelief and claim my relationship with God as my Father through faith in Jesus Christ.

I go to the Gospels and read and read until I find myself full of the knowledge of Jesus Christ. I read Hebrews 11, which tells how the people of faith passed through many dark times. Though they have my weaknesses, they also show me how faith can triumph. Personally I do not see anyone as a special case with special problems. I am a human being just as Mike is, and we are all subject to the same frailties and dark nights. So I know what I am talking about. I have been where he is, not perhaps with all the clinical intensity but I have been close enough to know where he is and what is the way out.

Let me put it another way. As Christians we all believe in the forgiveness of sins. Whenever we confess them to God through Christ, we know that they are released from having power over us and the guilt is removed through His atoning sacrifice. But often this does not really control where we live on a practical level. What we are saying is just words, good words, yes, but words nonetheless which have no reference to where we really live and believe. But it does not have to be this way. I can begin to build my life on the platform of God's forgiving grace. I can make the central core of my life the knowledge that Christ died for me and thus removed my guilt and with that accepted me permanently as His son.

Let me illustrate. Suppose I discover myself in the pit of despair. What do I do? Or suppose I am just beginning to slide into it. Obviously you meet this struggle all the time in the Book of Psalms. What I do is simply to admit that I am doing it, that I am slipping. I then face up to any anger within me that I may feel toward people and forgive them. I remember what Jesus Christ suffered in paying for my sins and then ask Him for grace to forgive others the way He forgave me. Then I repent of my unbelief. That's the big deal for me. I refuse to see myself as a lemon made by an evolutionary production line but as a sinner. You tinker endlessly with lemons, but with a sinner you have sure hope. Why? Because sinners can repent, whereas lemons can only be tinkered with; they are beyond repair.

Central to this repentance is my recognition that I am God's own child and He has a perfect plan for my life; everything that happens to me is part of that plan. I am not talking Pollyanna stuff. Evil is evil. But seen from the point of view of faith, every experience deepens my knowledge of my need and weakness and of God's capacity to help me. So I need to see that my rotten motives are really rotten. Grace is not cheap; it deals with really rotten people as we all are. But grace is also the power of God for cleansing the poison out of the fountains so that the streams of life can run clean.

In a word, I am saying that, at bottom, Mike's problem is one of unbelief, and as such it is capable of being solved by repentance toward God, for it is God who is being rejected by him in all his fears. After all, is not unbelief simply aversion to God and what we assume He is doing with our lives? But at the cross and the empty tomb God proves that His plan for us is good all the way, that His purpose is to make us anew the sons and daughters of His own household of faith. I believe that in his inward being Mike also has a faith which has been suppressed by nagging guilt and haunting worries. But through faith I know he will come through all of this.

I do again thank you and the psychiatrist for your persistence with Mike. You are most welcome to share this letter with the psychiatrist or even with Mike. He knows that I love him. He is in our prayers.

Cordially yours,
Jack Miller

Loving the Unlovable

To a young mother who has been struggling with how to love her husband's dysfunctional sister. Jack is writing this soon after finishing chemotherapy for lymphoma.

August, 1988

Dear Christine,

Thank you for your gracious letter and the openness of heart that is found in it. It was no burden at all to read it, and I read it twice to get aboard all that you were saying.

Many thanks to you and Ed for your love and your prayers for me. Believe me, this has been the toughest time of my life. Many times I feared I would cave in, and came close to it. Once I almost pulled the IV needles out of my arm I was so sick of it all. The urge was terrible, but the Lord delivered me from it through prayer of many people—including you and Ed. Thanks again for your prayers. It means so much to me to know that you have helped me this way, and it has been powerful. Not just the physical healing, but the recovery mentally, emotionally, and spiritually has been a remarkable gift of God. To Him be all the glory! . . .

You might say that God teaches well, but since we learn slowly many lessons can get through to each of us only when the truth is etched on our souls through our experiences of pain. That's how God gave the book *Come Back, Barbara*, to me and to Barbara as well. Without the pain a lot of Bible teaching would have remained just words for me, but the pain broke my self-centered pride and opened my eyes to see how grace works. Naturally, my spirit wishes that all of

255

this could be learned once and for all, and the suffering could be over and done with. But I think that if the suffering were taken away from me, I would soon forget the most vivid lessons God has taught me.

Therefore I am always being forced back to the cross as the place where I find grace—and wisdom too.

Wisdom? That is rare stuff. When I first read your letter and for the next two days I had no idea what to say about the problem with Ed's sister Joyce. Finally, I told the Lord of wisdom that I despaired of having an answer and implored Him to help me in my ignorance. My hope is that He has now given me some wisdom on the matter. If you think it is wisdom after you hear it, then we shall know that it is from the heavenly Father and not from me. If it seems to be from me, just ignore it.

But here goes. Your first obligation is to Ed and to your children rather than to his sister. I don't mean that you should be overly protective of them, but it probably is a good thing that you have not contacted her as you usually do. With Ed away so much of the time you have all the load you can carry without trying to help his sister with her very intense problems. So your conscience should be reassured that you did the right thing in not seeking a quick reconciliation with Joyce.

Too, you may need some time to ask hard questions about your relationship with Joyce. Remember: Barb was a manipulator, doing a lot of negative stuff to get attention, and as long as we gave the attention she did not change. She really needed to try life by herself for a while outside of the company of Christians so that she could get—what shall I say?—a stomach full.

But how do you love her? I think you need to let go of her. I don't mean to reject her. You should always welcome her into your heart. Still, Jesus did not chase the rich young ruler down the street when he turned away from Jesus, and you should not chase Joyce either. But how do you let go of Joyce with your emotions when you also want to pursue her with love?

1. Don't chase after her as though you could do the work of Christ for Him or be Joyce's mother and father. She can never see Christ if you do that. You probably are not helping her; in fact, you might be acting as an enabler, a sustainer, of her sinful patterns, providing a cushion so that she does not need to face up to reality.

2. Instead, pray more for her and ask God for wisdom which you don't have—and I know I don't have—to understand how you should relate to her. Also recruit others to pray with you for her and your relationship with her. Above all, pray for her with faith. Cultivate in your mind a vision of Joyce changed into the image of Christ.

3. Accept the fact that the pursuit of Joyce may be a long road. She's a manipulator and you don't rid yourself of deep-seated wrong attitudes overnight, and it sounds as though she has a big problem with self-pity. So it's likely you shouldn't rush into anything. Prepare yourself to wait, maybe even years.

4. Establish the fact firmly in your own mind that she is a threat to your children. I don't mean physically, but a mocker is a threat to children and their faith. You can find the book of Proverbs full of warnings about not falling in with such persons. So if what you say is accurate, and I believe it is, then you cannot minimize the destructive influence she could have on your family by long-term exposure to her. Therefore any acceptance of Joyce back into your family must be on your terms, not hers. Specifically, she should not be welcomed back into the family as an equal or regular visitor until she shows some willingness to struggle with her sins. That's a pretty hard line, but all my instincts go in this direction.

5. Try to develop some alternative strategies for seeing Joyce with Ed present but without the children. Instead of having her into your home, why not take her out to lunch as a couple? Even this, of

course, may need to wait, since it may be impractical until Ed is more on the scene. You might want to do some experimenting. How would she respond if you sent her a copy of *Come Back, Barbara*—and wrote her a testimony of how the book has influenced you? . . .

6. At some point you need to face her with her mockery and excuse-making—gently but clearly, with tears of hope but with a clear statement of your view of her sin. Only prayer can show you when this can be done. It needs to be done with a spirit of entreaty and kindness and much love, but you must not run away from the conflict. Love is willing to fight with all calmness and perseverance, and you will need to be ready to take some punishment when you face her with her sin.

Bear with these thoughts, since they are offered with the realization that you may need far more wisdom than I can offer. . . .

Finally, about this business of praying. Well, it's an opportunity right now to learn about it in the midst of your suffering. First, praying and honest, open living go together. That is, you can't pray well if you manipulate people or let them manipulate you. Now, I don't mean you take manipulators by the throat. We are all tempted to do that. But fight the temptation to give in to someone else's game-playing. For we all do our manipulating, and to give in to manipulation is to play a game too. But we must entreat manipulators to repent with us. I am repenting, and inviting my friend to do the same. Don't ask people to repent when you have not first done it. The Spirit is grieved when we do that, and when He is grieving we lose His support in prayer. So guard your conscience for effective praying.

Secondly, praying should include, among other things, a love offensive with:

1. Constantly forgiving, not suppressing angry feelings
2. Constantly blessing
3. Doing deeds of love where this is possible

So make sure that in prayer you are seeking wisdom from the Father as to how to do these things. He will give it abundantly.

Finally, praying should include the claiming of a promise in agreement, where possible, with other Christians. An example of such a promise is found in Matthew 18:19–20. You might get together weekly with a friend or two and claim this promise for say three months as you pray for their needs and for Joyce. See what God will do. He's quite impressive, is our Father. Don't underestimate His love.

Well, I see I have written a letter almost as long as yours. I'll call mine a novelette!

Much love to you and Ed in Christ,
Jack Miller

The Central Conflict: Belief or Unbelief

To a young man who is struggling in his relationship with his girlfriend and with how the elders at NLPC have tried to shepherd him through his struggle.

October, 1988

Dear Steve,

Warm greetings in the name of Christ!

Since I was away the previous Sunday and you were away this past Sunday, I did not get an opportunity to see you. My hope is that

259

you were able to meet with George [a NLPC elder] for prayer. He is a brother who prays with real faith. I will also be contacting [a few other elders] to pray for you. I also have prayed for you. All these brothers will be praying for you with deep concern for you.

Were you able to get the sermon tape of Peter's [one of Jack's copastors at NLPC] that I recommended? One of the brothers in the church told me that particular sermon was a great help to him. He said, "I've just been full of myself and my problems, but what a relief to see that being full of myself can be cured by grace, because Christ had resisted temptation for me!" He went on to say how liberating it was to know that a spotless Christ has atoned for his sins of self-preoccupation and had defeated Satan's accusations against his conscience. He had fear and trembling knowing his weaknesses, but this brother had been taught by God that Jesus lives in us by His Spirit and can enable us to take a stand against evil.

When I am weak in myself, then I am strong in grace. It has taken me a lifetime to get a little knowledge of myself, and what I have has all come the hard way. When I come to the end of myself, then and often only then I want and receive grace to understand myself and people. I wish I had a heart that did not constantly need all the hard spots in it to be crushed by steam-roller experiences.

But let me recall our conversation of a few weeks ago when you showed up at my study. Thanks for coming and sticking it out! Thanks too for forgiving me and the other elders for our many failings as shepherds. We always need lots of forgiveness and also your prayers. Our failure to help you at least proves one thing: we do not have the power to deliver you. No human being does.

Only Christ, only Christ, only Christ delivers.

It must also have been very difficult to wrestle with all the questions you and I were asking together. Believe me, I stress "together." Just remember that all of us elders are weak and sinful; we are, with Paul, "chief of sinners." Anyway, do you remember how you and I differed in our evaluation of you? It makes me smile to think about it. You saw yourself as too trusting, and I saw you as overly suspicious of people.

I didn't mean to single you out as having a problem that we as leaders don't also have. All I was doing was talking out of my experience of my own foolish way of doing things. I do not instinctively seek out people who may tell me what I do not want to hear about myself. We all have a frightening tendency to avoid and draw back from people of wisdom who really know us—at least to draw back when they may tell us something that threatens our image of our inner self as righteous.

So I am praying for myself—and for you—that we will not be afraid or suspicious of wise people. My plea for you is that you will seek out and listen to others. . . . [Here Jack mentions a few people that he would like Steve to talk with.]

I'd also like to share with you a few thoughts in this letter about God's method of healing the life and the conscience. In your recent telephone call you mentioned you simply could not pray, calling God "father." That must break your heart! Earlier I believe you spoke of your need to deal with the guilt which has clouded your life since you committed a particular sin. I believe you also mentioned that you struggled with thinking negatively about other people and judging them. Is it possible that this negative chemistry relates to your inability to pray? Negativism kills praying or at least converts praying into a form of penance which is powerless with God.

Usually our negativism is rooted in our feeling superior to people and rejecting the government of God over our lives. This self-righteous pride leads us into deep disappointment with everyone, and how can we pray when we really don't like God's form of government and the way other sinners have treated us?

261

I think it's important that you know we all struggle with these humbling issues: burdens of guilt and a tendency to feel condemned and then to condemn and fight others in our hearts.

The Devil also gets involved. He is a hard-hitter and refuses to quit at the sound of the bell. He is a relentless accuser of the brethren, and wants us to accuse ourselves as hopeless cases and to do the same for others. Then we are inwardly condemned and inwardly condemning.

In your life the struggle also seems to me to take the form of fight and flight. Would you agree? Think about it. I have found the same thing in myself. A tendency to fight people or problems and then run away from them by seeking some quick form of relief or comfort—or just distancing myself from people. Another form of flight is just going from one counselor to another—or rejecting all spiritual guidance.

It appears to me that you have a fundamental choice: will you approach these struggles with belief or with unbelief?

This is the central conflict for you. Belief or unbelief. Life or death. Which will it be?

Allied to that conflict is the struggle on your part to be honest. I believe I sense in you a desire for integrity. Well, the two battles go together. Where there is faith in Christ and the atoning power of His blood, there is the courage to be honest and to confess and forsake sins. Particular sins. Do you think perhaps that your inability to pray indicates that your conscience is troubled by something you may have suppressed?

Believe me, you didn't invent all this. I have learned this about myself: Where unbelief has been allowed to take over, then the name of the game is insincerity and self-deception.

I would commend to you a careful and constant reading of James 4 and Isaiah 53. The former passage deals with God and our evil desires; the latter passage presents the work of Christ which gives us the security to face up to the evil of our hearts without being destroyed by it.

Steve, we elders are so very concerned for you. Please heed our loving admonition. Get a heart for the gospel and the holiness which comes from the gospel. Then reckon—think, consider, know, yes, believe, that you are dead to sin and alive in Christ. Then present your members as weapons of your true and only Lord, to be used in His war with evil! Hate sin for His dear sake!

Pray that Christ will show you the Father and His love. Join that prayer with honesty in the following: no blame-shifting or excuse-making or defending yourself in your heart and with your tongue.

Go constantly to Christ; look to Christ, rely on Christ, think Christ; and as you do this, the blood of the Son of God will cleanse you of these sins. Be very specific in your confession of sins and claim a great promise like Isaiah 1:18. I know big sinners like me need big promises like this one! Actually, seeking out giant promises will lead to a giant faith!

Jesus loves you, and so do we who are your spiritual shepherds. Expect great things from Christ.

Much love in the Savior,
Jack Miller, on behalf of the elders

Fear and Egocentricity Go Together

To a woman who Jack and Rose Marie met on the mission field. She struggles with paralyzing fear and angry outbursts.

November, 1988

Dear Mary,

Tomorrow we leave for home with hearts that are both glad and sad. It makes us happy to be returning to our dear family and church, but we are sorry to leave so many fine friends here. We have learned to love this country and pray for Christ to do a mighty work here.

Rose Marie and I have tender hearts toward you and the pains which you have undergone in your life. We are especially burdened to see Christ deliver you from your fears. Fear is a terrible master, and the devil uses it to blind us to the love of God in Christ and the goodness of God's sovereign rule.

But you know, there is an even more powerful cause of our enslavements. It is our unconscious pride. Let me explain.

When I was sick with cancer, sometimes things would go wrong, complications or bodily weaknesses breaking down my peace of mind. Fear would seem to get an iron grip on my emotions. It was very, very hard.

But I did learn something. It is that fear is rooted in our need to be in control of our lives. And sickness and death are such a threat to us because they threaten to undo our pretensions to be sovereign over our own lives.

Once I saw this truth I told my heavenly Father that my fears were deep and that they were rooted in my ego-centered pride. God loves the truth, Mary; there is no point in trying to hide the deep sins of our heart from Him. He knows it all anyway, but He does want us to acknowledge our sins and to fall from our thrones onto our faces before Him.

Mary, I marvel how God should love me so much that He would send His Son to atone for my sins and to dethrone me. But I have learned there is no security, only fear and dread on a shaky throne of pride.

How does this relate to your fear and disappointments? Please know that—

1. You can't run away from your fears. You must ask the Father to help you identify them and hand them over to Him.
2. You must ask God to give you the Spirit to understand yourself and how your fears are rooted in egocentric pride.
3. Then humble your heart and repent of your proud spirit, grieve over it, hate it, and despise it.
4. Then claim the blood of Christ as the sole basis for cleansing, relying on the promise of 1 John 1:7–2:2.

It appears to me that you will have trouble understanding the connection between ungovernable fears and egocentricity. This insight can only be understood by faith. By faith you need to see how any attempt by us to run our lives without humble submission to God puts us in a position of having to control the uncontrollable. Who really can control his or her own life?—the people in it?—the events, joyous and painful, that occur?—the deep disappointments when others do not meet our expectations?

Indeed, you can end up hating God for not being the guarantor of our own idea of our rights and prerogatives.

But, Mary, you must by faith recognize the painful and liberating truth that you are not God, but a creature made in God's image, a person with dignity, but nonetheless a very, very small being compared to the infinite Majesty of the Most High. I know that when God revealed Himself to me, I was stunned to discover that He was the all-glorious one and that I was the most egocentric person who had ever lived. What helped me see this shocking truth about myself? It was His waking me up to the knowledge that my whole life was exclusively centered on my own glory, my own needs, and my own will.

It hurts me to have to say this, and I speak with all love in Christ. But it appears to me that you suffer from my evil self-centeredness, and evil egomania that is a betrayal of God and a denial of your humble creaturehood. Can you pray and ask God the Father to show you if I am right? Pray, Mary, for an honest heart.

With all tenderness in Christ, let me also point out how your self-centeredness manifests itself. When you were with us on Sunday and we had just finished hearing a message on repentance and personal sanity, you called your son-in-law a "swine." I was shocked, and so was everyone else. Your tone also seemed so bitter that I wondered whether you really had heard anything of the ministry of the Word and Spirit.

In company you are also so preoccupied with yourself and your own problems that you can give offence to people without knowing you are doing so. You have an opinion on everything, and you quickly express it without any regard for the feelings of others. For example, you put Nate [Mary's husband] down, interrupt him, and seem to assume he has no feelings at all.

I also believe that you talk down to people from a standpoint of superiority, and I have also seen you attack them or at least show a condemnatory attitude toward others. You feel condemned and you condemn others. From all I can see, you cannot forgive yourself and you do not seem to have forgiven your father and your son-in-law.

Dear friend, none of us are born innocent and all need forgiveness. We are all desperately wicked sinners and need so much mercy that we should be ready to extend it to others. "Father, grant such mercy to me that I may show it to everyone else."

I cannot save you, Rose Marie cannot save you, Nate cannot save you. But Jesus—Oh, that is another matter! He is ready to save poor sinners and how I pray He will show you your deepest need—to know the power of His blood and righteousness to save you from the hell of your own anger and bitterness.

Rose Marie and I are praying for you to meet with Jesus. We know that He is the omnipotent Son of God having a powerful salvation. Ask Him to open your eyes to see it and appropriate it as the poor beggar takes hold of bread. Eat of Jesus and you will live. You are in our hearts and I speak out of great compassion.

Grace flows downhill. It runs down from the heights of God to the humble at the foot of the mountain. Grace also takes away fear and reveals the mighty, tender, compassionate securities of God. As you humble yourself, you will find fears fading away like the morning mists. Believe, only believe.

Much love,
Jack Miller

Knowing the Gospel Means We Can Face Our Sins

To a young woman who struggles with alcoholism and sexual sins.

April, 1989

Dear Sharon,

Most cordial greetings to you in Christ! I am writing from Kenya! Here we have been ministering, preaching, and writing. Rose Marie is just back from Uganda, where she spoke several times and met with the missionary women in Ft. Portal. I am working on a book for non-Christians; she is working on an autobiography.

It has taken me a long time, but at last I am getting off a long overdue letter to you. My apologies for the long delay. I could think of a number of excuses, but I think the main reason is my not being sure what to say. Now I realize that may sound strange. Usually I have much to say! But my heart burden has been to help you, and my mind has not been clear as to how. Now I think it is clearer to me what the Lord wants me to share with you. I think it came to me as I was helping Rose Marie work on her book.

In it she makes the point that it is important to know your family roots and the sin patterns you have inherited. Actually the book could help you more than I can. But anyway she says that sin patterns get repeated from generation to generation, taking different forms but always reflecting inherited attitudes of pride, independence, self-deception, lust, love of control, etc.

Her next point is that people really can't stand to look closely at themselves and these patterns unless they understand justification by faith and union with Christ. According to her, it's pretty easy to say, "God, be merciful to me, the sinner," and be thinking only of external actions while ignoring the darkness of the human heart. But if you want to look more deeply, begin by studying the gospel of the cross, know the meaning of Christ's atonement for you personally, and you will be able to take the deeper look.

This deeper look can then lead to a more thoroughgoing repentance and a hearty confidence through the Spirit that I am not an orphan, but a living son of the heavenly Father through faith.

Take a specific sin like anger. You and I know its visible consequences. Everyone is shamed by how our anger has maimed others. But then take the deeper look. Why am I angry? What fuels it? Why do I forgive people, but later on end up taking it all back?

These are burning questions.

They also have a wonderfully simple answer in Scripture. In James 3 and 4, God says that we are angry because we are proud. We have pride in our own sinful nature, but we also have had models of pride in our family background. We have deeply ingrained attitudes of superiority inherited from a dark past. Our sinful nature responds to these inherited attitudes with enthusiasm. We have seen in our models attitudes of superiority, contempt for others, and patterns of pride coming to expression in bitterness or rage.

How do we overcome the pride? Our ancestors probably did not; how then can we expect to do so? Actually it's impossible. But that's where grace begins. When the Spirit works a healthy self-disgust, a hatred of my sins in my heart, then I pray honestly without a secret intention to remain unchanged.

Honesty, humble integrity, that's what moves God to run to our cry.

You see, we often pray and see little fruit because we are praying one thing but in our heart we have other plans.

Take the person addicted to drugs. He cannot get off them for the simple reason he does not want to get off them. The day he wants to get off them he does. But until he really wants to be changed he always has a secret intention in the heart not to go off the drugs. The rest is all talk.

So my suggestion is that you study James 3 and 4 closely and take a close look at your inner life, and at the same time study Galatians 2 and 3 to see the beauty of the love of God in the gospel.

Put it together by faith. Or better, let the Holy Spirit put it together for you as you cry out for divine intervention to work deeply in your life.

Please don't think I am speaking to you as an outsider. As a nonsinner. No, the reason I understand you is that God has given me some understanding of my own vile heart.

Do you remember the time you came to my home for prayer meeting several years ago and you and I sat on the couch? I questioned you about your inner life—but you were not listening. At least that was my impression. I believe I said that you did not know yourself very well. I tried to do it in love. Maybe it was done with some frustration too. Well, the reason I knew what your inner life was like came from a knowledge of my own desperately evil heart!

Let me be even more forthright. I think it is a lifelong process getting to know yourself. Paul said that when you get to know yourself you confess that you and every man are liars (Rom. 3). Now I am ashamed to confess how many deep lies there are in my heart. How is it now with you? Have you brought your innermost deceptions into the light? Are there still secrets in your heart?

Think once again of your visit to our home. As I sat on the couch with you I thought that lying was as natural to you as breathing. Do you remember how many times I asked you if you really meant what you were saying?

Now I understand that you believe that God has worked in your life, and the church has accepted your repentance. Praise God for that! I rejoice in it. But have you taken that close inner look at the roots of it all—the proud, independent unbelieving heart, a deceiving heart?

That's scary for me. To do that.

When I do that I know the engine does not need just a tuneup but a complete reworking.

I think such an inward look is possible if you know the power in the blood of Christ. It is the sole basis of God's justification of the ungodly. What a wonderful thing for God to do for us! Complete forgiveness.

Such a teaching cuts the root of our sin. Self-centered pride is the root, and to rest on free justification kills our pride. Why? because in our justification we must accept that nothing of righteousness comes from us, could come from us, and we are forced to acknowledge the shame of our sin. Only mercy and love can save us, and these come from God to the ungodly (Rom. 5:5–6).

But there is even more. We are always properly concerned to get sin out of ourselves. At least we should be. But we need something more foundational. We need to have the Lord transfer us out of sin. To bring us into a kingdom of righteousness, to kill us and resurrect us under a new lordship. We are not justified in our sin. No, justification carries along with it a death to sin and a resurrection to righteousness.

What do you have to do to get this? Nothing. Just come undone and rest on what Jesus has done! Look, the gospel is a mighty power. See the Lamb. One look at Him takes away a universe of sin from the human heart. [The last page of this letter is lost.]

In Christ,
Jack Miller

Encouragement for Sufferers

God's appointments sometimes are our disappointments, and when that happens it is hard to trust in God. The feeling we have is: "Well, what is He going to do next to rob me of my hopes and values?" But I think that getting to know God does not come out of skill in being able to evaluate my experiences. Instead, it must come from my understanding God Himself as He is revealed as a Father of all love in the self-giving of His Son. I want to ask you to focus your faith on that love for you.

Can God be trusted in the shattering experiences of our lives? Jack's answer to the men and women that he wrote to in this section was a resounding yes. These letters were written to those who were suffering through a variety of hard circumstances. Jack wrote to them all from the standpoint of a fellow sufferer. He had grieved the untimely deaths of his father and his brother; he had survived a heart attack, cancer, and a stroke; he had prayed and loved one of his daughters through a long period of rebellion; and he was still dealing with the pressures that came with ministry. So, in these letters, Jack was sharing the insights that God had given to him through his suffering.

What were some of those insights? First, Jack counseled that in dealing with hard circumstances the place to begin was not with the painful experience, but with the love of God. He wrote to a woman who had been deeply hurt by those to whom she was min-

272

istering, "Getting to know God does not come out of skill in being able to evaluate my experiences. Instead, it must come from my understanding God Himself as He is revealed as a Father of all love in the self-giving of His Son. . . . Get to that center, and then the experiences will be seen in a new light. Start with the experiences, though, and you will never find the center in God."

One of Jack's favorite verses was 1 John 4:16: "We know and rely on the love God has for us." Jack often reminded himself and others that the love of God, as expressed in Jesus' death on the cross, can be relied on even when life seems to be falling apart. The God who would give up His only Son so that His enemies might become His friends can be trusted even in the most confusing of times. Jack knew how easy it is to despair in hard circumstances or to have all of your thought life consumed by them, but he constantly encouraged those who were suffering to meditate on the love of God. He wrote to one man whose wife had left him, "See yourself as a new person. Hurt and wounded, yes, but not controlled by that hurt, but controlled by your Savior in whom you live and move and have your being. I don't have any great counseling formulas, only Jesus. Only Jesus."

Secondly, as Jack reiterated in many of these letters, in order to experience the love of God there must be a submission to the will of God. In one letter he wrote about an experience he had on Lake Victoria when he was caught in a storm and the motor of the boat failed. He said about this time, "The whole thing seemed senseless, going from bad to worse, without prayers being answered. . . . My last comfort was the sound of the Johnson outboard motor. I asked God to keep it going, and hardly asked for it when off it went. We were adrift. . . . There was just God, seemingly battering us. . . . There was a kind of message in it. . . . It was simply that God was still a God of infinite love and compassion, but not according to my ideas, but to His."

Jack went on to say that accepting God's will for him, even if it meant drowning in Lake Victoria, allowed him to get to know

God in a deeper way as his Father. It was this getting to know God as his loving Father and Jesus as his Brother and Savior that was most important to Jack. As he applied this to himself, in the midst of his struggles, he also applied it to those to whom he was writing.

Finally, another important theme in Jack's thinking about suffering was how temporary this world is. The legacy of Jack's losses early in life and his many life-threatening illnesses was what he called "a dark heritage of fears." Especially after recovering from cancer, Jack was full of fear. The way that God helped him, he said in a letter to a man who had AIDS, was through meditating on Psalm 84 and the truth that we are on a pilgrimage, finding our home now in God, and headed to our heavenly home to be with Him forever. He wrote in this letter, "God is my home. What does that mean? . . . It means that as I lose my other 'homes' in this world I find that God is there to receive me. But I would add, God is there as I want Him for myself as my God. . . . Bring together my yearning heart and a God who alone can satisfy that heart. That is true home comfort for the life."

Jack was received by his God on April 8, 1996. It was then that he saw clearly those things that he believed by faith. He would be pleased if these letters are used by God to point others to his faithful Savior, Jesus, and the "true home comfort" that can be found only in knowing Him.

Where Do We Seek Comfort?

To the wife of a pastor who has been asked to resign from his church. The family must now relocate, and this has been particularly hard for the children to accept.

August, 1982

Dear Pam,

This Saturday morning I have been praying for you and for your family. I want to be able to pray effectively for you, and I think I can pray most effectively if I share with you what I have been asking from God. The first thing I have been asking is that all of you may have unity, and oneness as a family in discovering God's purpose in what has happened. But I think that a great hindrance in discovering and following God's will is our difficulty in believing that His will is good—and good for me. We need to learn to love God's will if we are to be mature believers, but we can hardly love His will if inside ourselves we have not been persuaded that His will is for our good and is itself a good will.

I was in a very shattering experience in Uganda a few months ago, lost in the dark in a small boat during a storm on Lake Victoria. The whole thing seemed senseless, going from bad to worse, without prayers being answered. In the blackness and the rain and the utter misery of the cold, my last comfort was the sound of the Johnson outboard

275

motor. I asked God to keep it going, and hardly asked for it when off it went. We were adrift, very literally powerless, directionless, and exposed to who knows what, including pirates who prowl the seas of the lake. There was just God, seemingly battering us. I don't know how to interpret it all, but I do know that as the water sloshed over my feet, there was a kind of message in it, one that I didn't like. It was simply that God was still a God of infinite love and compassion, but not according to my ideas, but to His; and I had to see that I was not in any way in the same league with Him. Only as I submitted my proud heart to His bigness and majesty and will could I really experience His love.

I don't know if any of that makes sense to you, but it comes down to God's insistence that He is God and only in my accepting that can I know Him. What this has led me to see is a second thing. It is the necessity of stopping, being patient, waiting, listening to God, right in the circumstances that overwhelm, right where I am tempted to feel left out and hurt. There I meet His grace as He meets me in silence. I need the silence; I need the time without easy answers that I may see that God's Fatherhood is not something simply for me to use, but a love of heart to heart and the willingness to walk with Him no matter what is happening.

I hope this makes sense. Life is inescapably a way of pain. The only question finally is where we seek our comfort. If we seek our comfort in the Father of our Lord Jesus Christ, then we will know joy and fulfillment beyond anything we have ever imagined. In the darkness a plan will begin to emerge. The plan must not be rushed, but it will come. It is much too early for me to presume to suggest what I believe it may be for your family, but be sure it is there, waiting to be discerned through a time of learning to wait and listen to His teaching voice.

In my own life its whole strength lies in that God has kindly imparted a confident knowledge of His Fatherhood. I may have a better knowledge of the Father than do other people. But would you believe that this knowledge really began with the death of my own father? He was killed in a hunting accident when I was two years old. A senseless hunting accident. A piece of foolishness. Yet I am not bitter, and am grateful to God for the perfection of the plan.

The emptiness, the dark nights when I was afraid as a small child to go to bed for fear I too might disappear, led me by God's grace to seek God as Father, to know what Fatherhood meant, to give up self-pity and self-awareness and walk in the confident knowledge of my heavenly Father's love. Many people have been helped, converted, built up, through God's revealing Himself right in the empty place at the center of my miserable life as a God who is awesomely wonderful (John 3:16). I love my Father in heaven and trust one day to see my earthly father and to join him in praising God for the marvel of a plan that is sound beyond ordinary human understanding.

I know that an earthly mind cannot grasp heavenly dealings, and my prayer is that you will together be given a mind that understands heavenly dealings. You are dear to me. Pray for me too; my life is lived in the storm, and your prayers are very important to my growth in submission to God's will. I want you to pray that I will delight in His will as Christ did. "I delight to do thy will, O my God."

Let's not lose touch.

Cordially in Christ,
Jack Miller

Letting Go of the Earthly

To a missionary in Uganda. Jack is sharing how God met him during a time of discouragement.

June, 1985

Dear Bill,

Greetings in Christ, dear brother! We give much thanks for you and your labor of faith in Uganda. It is a joy to think of you and your love to Christ and our being one in Christ's mission to the lost. It is very precious to all of us here.

On our part we have worked our way through a severe trial of faith as leaders and as a church with the matters that broke open in a tragic way last November [a serious sin was exposed in one of the church leaders]. I came to the month of May exhausted mentally, emotionally, and spiritually—and awash with self-pity. It was a very dangerous time for me. I had a funeral on the Friday afternoon before I drove down to McLean Presbyterian Church to speak, and somehow the self-pity and soul sorrow deepened even more during the funeral service. I also felt frustrated from every direction, with no reserves to combat my sense of being locked in. So Rose Marie prayed for me and read the Word as we drove down to Washington. We spent the night in a hotel near the Beltway. Before I went to sleep I knew that no human power could deliver me from the state I was in. So I simply decided to go to sleep and forget about it all.

In the middle of the night I was awakened by the insistent pressure of a verse of Scripture speaking to my mind. It was Matthew 11:29, "Learn of me, for I am gentle and lowly in heart." Mysteriously the Spirit used that verse to clear my mind of the sorrow which had so come to prevail in my life. Next morning Rose Marie asked me, "How are you?" I answered, "Just fine. The self-pity is gone." And it was. Christ gentled my spirit and cleansed it. "Learn of me, for I am gentle and lowly in heart," became a gift that He gave me.

I do thank you for your prayers. Who can give any explanation other than prayer for this deliverance? The powers of darkness were really after me. The big guns were firing and the mists were thick, and I was in peril of my life.

It also helped to get away from my burdens here. We visited the Smithsonian and saw a beautiful movie about flight. A terrific soaring film, that did much to lift up our vision to the majesty of Him who made all things. It made me see how I had been making my relatively minor problems into major ones. At the funeral, I had preached on Romans 8:28 and the theme of "Letting Go." Unfortunately I had become so identified with the work that I couldn't let go. I was caught up in the idolatry of work, an obsessive preoccupation with fulfilling my own unhumbled religious ego!

So as I watched the film on the history of flight, I moved from worshipping the work to worshipping the God of the work. I let go of the earthly and soared with the vision of the heavenly. Not that my soaring was perfect, but at least I was in the air getting my vision back. We spent the two days after speaking at McLean, visiting the National Art Gallery and the Smithsonian. It was really valuable to get away. It was used of God to release both Rose Marie and me from oppression. . . .

You have been much in our prayers and especially during the past weeks as we have had newspaper reports of unsettled security matters in your area. We have recently raised up a shield of prayer for you.

I have been really sorry for the burden the Land Rover has been and know that it has hindered the work. I realize I should be a better fundraiser and will try harder to get more wheels to you. To help you understand the situation a bit better, we often find ourselves in the position of making choices. . . . [Jack goes on to discuss the hard choices that the mission makes in deciding whether to concentrate on getting people into the field or on making sure that funds are available for the needs on the field.]

My concern is that such matters not cut the nerve of your joy in Christ. We must all cultivate overflowing thankfulness for one another. We are so deeply grateful to God for putting you in the harvest field and . . . we believe you are doing a fine piece of work.

All of us in the home office have been making every sacrifice to help you . . . It is also important that you see our weaknesses and slips as part of God's humbling master plan for conforming us to the image of a gentle Christ. I do not say that to excuse our failings, but in international communications you just do have failures to connect and delays.

A family here at New Life, for instance, has been really upset with the bank regarding the telexing of money for Australia. It's very upsetting, but the family is learning to see it as Satan's attack but [also] God's way of discipling them to live by faith.

Live, then, my dear brother, by faith. Pray the same for me. Love conquers all.

In a gentle Jesus,
Jack

God's Appointments Sometimes Are Our Disappointments

To the wife of a missionary who has been deeply hurt by the people to whom they are ministering. She and her husband are on furlough in the United States.

July, 1985

Dear Jackie,

Greetings in Christ! The summer has gone speeding by like the movement of a swallow's wings. We just had most of a week at the shore, and it went and is already almost forgotten.

But it has been an excellent time. . . . It is a joy to know that you are getting a good rest and a time to meditate and get more deeply rooted in Christ. We do pray much for you. . . .

I also want to encourage you to look to Christ with confidence. Obviously that can sound trite, especially when the light in the darkness is not very bright. But it seems to me that Christ is speaking to you, and one of the things He is calling you to is a surrender to His will. I think that is hard to do, especially when His will seems to have had so many rough things in it for you. The last six months . . . was kind of a death for you, and I suspect many things turned out in ways that were deeply disappointing to you.

God's appointments sometimes are our disappointments, and when that happens it is hard to trust in God. The feeling we have is: "Well, what is He going to do next to rob me of my hopes and values?" But I think that getting to know God does not come out of skill in being able to evaluate my experiences. Instead, it must come from my understanding God Himself as He is revealed as a Father of all love in the self-giving of His Son. I want to ask you to focus your faith on that love for you. Not to try to rationalize that love in relationship to your experiences but to submit to it as sheer grace for you and simply rest in the knowledge of John 3:16. God loves. . . .

281

Get to that center, and then the experiences will be seen in a new light. Start with the experiences, though, and you will never find the center in God.

How do you start? I think Phil [an elder at NLPC] made an excellent point in talking about Abraham's faith. He noted in his Sunday night teaching that Abraham's trip to Egypt had been made without consulting with God. He did not even tell God his fears and doubts. But then Phil noted that the scene in Genesis 15 opens with Abraham bringing his doubts to God. He said, "How can this be?" The advantage of bringing our doubts in this way is that faith begins by confessing our doubts to God with the confidence that He will deal with what we cannot deal with. Paradoxically, Phil added, faith is just a wanting to have God's help and being honest enough to admit that this desire is not even all that pure and the promises of God are not all that bright in our eyes. I do hope these thoughts bring encouragement to you.

Do keep praying for us. I'll be writing George [Jackie's husband] soon. Greetings to him and the children.

Most affectionately,
Jack

The Love of Jesus Is Unalterable

To a pastor friend whose church has just split and more than half the church has left.

April, 1987

Dear Greg,

Warm greetings in the Lord Jesus.

Here it is the day before Rose Marie and I leave for Ireland, and my intention to visit with you is still not fulfilled. I am really very sorry. Please forgive me, for I do count you as a very good friend in Christ, a brother whom I respect very much.

I would have liked to have sat down with you for prayer and for doing what I could to share the load that must have come upon you during these past months. This brief letter must serve as a poor substitute for a time of fellowship together. But I especially want you to know that you have been in my prayers, often with the Lord giving me ardent intercession for the burden that you and your family have borne at this time. I believe I can say that the Lord Jesus has given my prayers the wings of love to carry you before the throne of God in heaven. This freedom in praying for you has given me the confidence that Christ will carry you through a difficult time. I do believe that He will bring you through it all greatly strengthened. . . .

My prayer is that God will give you what I have always seen in you in the past, a gentle, forbearing spirit. I have also prayed that He would give you specific guidance for the future. You are a man with many graces, much experience and wisdom, and Christ will certainly use you in His service in the days ahead.

In brief, it seems to me that what matters in this situation is for you to have the assurance that Christ will show you His direction for your life. . . . I know for myself that is always enough—to know and do Christ's will. My prayer is that He will give you the grace to discern it clearly and much peace in following it out. This is not so easy after one has been traumatized by a hard series of experiences. You must have all kinds of questions in your mind about your life and calling, and concerns about God's own government of your life and His

283

church. But as the pain eases remember that Jesus loves you very much and that His love is unalterable. I love you too and want to assure you that I too have felt the rod, smarted under it, and then come to bless God for the wounds it left. Granted, this did not come about without a severe struggle of soul in the night, but it did come, and today I look back on the dark hours as the sweet woundings of a loving Christ. May it always be so for both of us.

Try not to sit too long, though, on the problem. Somehow by grace you need to discern God's will and embrace it with positive action steps. Faith must be joined with courage: dare to move forward even though you cannot see what lies ahead. The forest path may be dark, but the child puts his hand in his Father's hand and then fears no evil. Nothing that walks in darkness can match my Father's strength. Just keep your hand in His. Trust Him.

Christ be with you. If you want to write us, we can be reached at Malaga Media Center, Apartado 570, Malaga, Spain. We shall be there working on a new book and recharging our batteries by soaking in the Word and spending time in prayer. We have been through a most arduous time, with much blessing, but we are in great need of sitting at Jesus' feet and listening to Him.

In His grace,
Jack

Shift Your Trust from Yourself to God

To a fellow cancer sufferer. One of the members of NLPC asked Jack to write to a friend who was recently diag-nosed with cancer and was very afraid of chemotherapy.

Jack often gave out this letter along with a pamphlet he wrote ("How to Cope with Personal Crisis") while he was on chemotherapy.

June 24, 1988

Dear Mrs. Jones,

Though I have never met you, I have heard that you have cancer and would like to hear from me. You know that I also have recently suffered from this disease—about the hardest time in my whole life. So I think I understand you. Most important, do not think of yourself as a victim. You are *not* a defeated person.

Fight despair by doing everything you can to maintain normal life and work. Struggle to keep yourself active and occupied. Develop your sense of humor and creativity. If you do not have the strength to do your ordinary work, find some new tasks to do. Even if your "work" is only to drink a cup of tea every morning at 10:00 do it and enjoy it. And if you have the opportunity, prepare a cup of tea for someone else. Don't spend time thinking about yourself. Keep exercising your body, and keep serving others even when the only thing you can give is a smile.

However, do not suppress your inward struggles with cancer. Learn that a powerful hope can grow in you as you become honest with God. When the symptoms of your illness frighten you or chemotherapy makes you nauseous, pray and tell Him how you really feel. Admit that you are desperate. Acknowledge the truth if your *misplaced confidence* has been in yourself and not in Him. But shift your trust *from yourself to God.* He's a lot bigger than you are! When you are feeling well, it's easy to say, "I confidently believe that God will help me." But what you really mean is, "I can handle my own affairs with a bit of assist from God." So give up presumptuous self-reliance. Discover the power of a living faith placed in a mighty God! To trust Him, do two things:

1. Ask Christ to show God's love to you.
2. Read my pamphlet "How to Cope with Personal Crisis" at least three times.

Dear friend, make Christ your only hope. Trust in Him and trust your life to Him. Take this loving Lord into your heart. Your security will not be in yourself or medical technology or diet but in God alone. He will shepherd you in His mighty love through every trial that comes your way. Be of good courage!

Cordially yours,

C. John Miller

Trust Him All the Way

To a couple whose child is seriously ill in the hospital.

April, 1989

Dear Kyle and Pam,

As soon as we heard about Susan and her serious health problem, we prayed for her and for you. Our hearts were moved with compassion for little Susan and also for you. It must be very hard to see how helpless she is in the face of what happened. Our prayers were earnest, and we felt much comforted after we had begun to pray.

We prayed for healing for Susan and also for God to do a deep work of grace in her heart. We also prayed for you to be comforted and strengthened and built up in Christ Jesus. Things like this can be hard to understand, but as God opens our hearts through prayer, we have a submission to His will that can bring us a peace unlike anything else we have experienced. May God cause your peace to abound as you surrender Susan to Him in faith. My prayer is that God will sustain you with an understanding that He really has Susan on His heart. Trust Him. Trust Him all the way, for Susan is His and her life is under the control of His perfect plan. This definitely comes in when His plan does not seem to fit with what we had planned. For us we long to see our children abounding in life and health, but sometimes that isn't His plan. It can be very hard to surrender to what God is doing.

I especially think of the way Hannah surrendered little Samuel to the Lord and how God used that in her life and in his. I would encourage you to read the story in 1 Samuel 1 and 2. There you learn that in her weakness she received grace that made her strong.

We love you very much and will keep on praying for you and Susan. We hope soon that we will hear good reports of her progress and health and your growth in Christ.

Much love in Him,
Jack and Rose Marie

Do Not Take Your Identity from Your Suffering

To a man whose wife, Anne, had recently left him. Jack and Rose Marie were counseling with him and his wife.

June, 1989

Dear Gary,

Since I won't get to see you before Friday, I want to take this opportunity to assure you of our love and prayers—and to secure yours for us. We really need your prayers desperately. . . .

But we do want you to know how this whole thing has deepened our love for you and how much our hearts reach out to you. In that spirit, let me encourage you to remember that Jesus loves you and far better than ourselves understands the terrible pain that you are going through. In your circumstances I do not think anyone can fully enter in but the Savior who passed through the agony of Gethsemane and Calvary.

It will be easy for you at this time to feel utterly forsaken, because in relationship to your wife that is the reality. You have been forsaken in an awful manner, and only gradually does your wife begin to see what she has done. That makes it even harder. It would seem that any idiot could grasp [this], but don't forget the awful blinding power of sin when it goes deep into a life, and it goes deep into all of our lives. Such sin cannot endure suffering. Anne has admitted that she cannot endure suffering, and she has made you suffer so terribly. So now you suffer for her, and we suffer for her. We die at the sight of her blindness, and yet in all of it are so profoundly rebuked by the same blindness in ourselves to God's surpassing love in Christ.

The whole thing makes me hate sin, mine, Anne's, and everyone else's, as I see what it did to my Lord on the cross and in Gethsemane.

We do mean to urge you not to take your identity from your suffering and having been made a victim, even a mutilated one. That is what has happened to you, but that is not your identity. Your identity is defined in Ephesians as being *in Christ*. You are first of all forever defined by your being in union with your most faithful friend, even the Son of God, who saw you perishing in your sin and blindness and then gave His precious life for you. He sees all of us as betrayers of His love, grace, and laws. And yet He found it in His great loving heart to die for the treasonous, faithless ones. For me and for you.

Do remember your identity. Soak in Ephesians if you will. See yourself as a new person. Hurt and wounded, yes, but not controlled by that hurt, but controlled by your Savior in whom you live and move and have your being. I don't have any great counseling formulas, only Jesus. Only Jesus, Gary. Only Jesus. Remember Jesus and see yourself, your wife, your family, and all the rest of us from that standpoint. See Anne through Jesus' eyes as you pray for her. See how desperately needy she is. . . .

Only believe, only believe, says Jesus. Dear brother, we love you. Pray for us.

Most cordially in Jesus,
Jack Miller

This World Is Not Our Home

To the elders at NLPC regarding the letter to Andrew that follows and the sin of restlessness.

June, 1990

Dear Fellow Elder:

Enclosed is a lengthy letter to Andrew Gates. Andrew is an old-time New Lifer who has AIDS. His condition has been worsening, and he is taking steps to move in with James Helwig. Several other members of the church have been giving him guidance and practical help. He is deeply thankful for this love. I believe that Jesus is really speaking to Andrew in his suffering. . . .

The letter to Andrew is based upon some strong meditation/medicine which derives from Psalm 84 and that wise man Augustine. In the letter I mention its content as also issuing from my struggles with health in Nairobi. All of this is true enough, but the letter has roots in another burden of mine. It has to do with the restlessness of this generation; people everywhere seem to be trying to build a permanent home in this world and do it just as fast as they can.

Incredible restlessness everywhere! These are tough times in which to do evangelism and pastoral work just because people are madly pursuing their secular illusions.

I hope I am wrong but it seems this restlessness is reflected in our own lives within the church. God, I believe, has really hit me over the head to get me to repent of it, and I do not think I can yet say the battle is won. Pray for me that my heart will repent more deeply of this great evil.

But the battle is everywhere. When I arrived in Kenya I was amazed to find that John [a Kenyan pastor] was about the busiest pastor I have seen in a long time. To the praise of God's grace he has committed himself to slow down. The pastors in Switzerland were in the same rat-race. Amazing. I entreated them to reconsider. Restlessness in the world, and everlasting stirring in the church members and leaders.

My gut feeling is that much of this activity is based upon the unconscious notion that this world is a pretty permanent place, an arena where we can make our home, build our reputations, get ahead in our ambitions, secure the right education, establish the right programs, etc. Well, I want to raise the question: Are we looking for demonization in the modern world in the wrong places? Is this restlessness fleshly and also demonic in its power over hearts in our time? I suspect this restlessness has roots in hell. Consider its subtlety. Who can repent when he is going at warp speed? For how can you repent if you do not have time to see where you are going wrong?

George [Jack's copastor at NLPC] and I are concerned to give leadership in the area of repentance in our church and the community. Well, dear brothers, pray for us to be still and know God. We shall pray that for you too.

In Christ's love,
Jack

God Is My Home

To a young man who is dying of AIDS.

June, 1990

Dear Andrew,

Warm greetings in Christ! Thank you for the telephone call the other night, and your willingness to share with me your current burdens. It meant a lot to me to hear how the members and deacons of New Life Church have been helping you. I glorify Christ for pouring out such a spirit of love on our members. In an age of me-firstism I am deeply encouraged by what they have been doing in serving you.

Rose Marie and I will be praying that the AZT drug will really help you and that the side effects will be minimal and that you will endure the hard times without turning in on yourself. Andrew, fight the battle; don't give in to self-preoccupation!

We are also praying that James [Andrew's counselor] will be able to help you wrestle with the issues of self-centeredness that you see in the two fellows who live with you. I am glad that you were deeply shocked by their blindness to their own me-firstism. Think about it! Today self-worship is an epidemic. Actually the battle in your home is cosmic in its implications. We are in a fight to the death with the powers of darkness right here on this issue. You see all the ways your two friends take advantage of you in your weakness—and their failure even to see their own egocentricity and exploitation. You are feeling the raging of the kingdom of self, and believe me the blinding power of the devil is behind it all!

You are right to hate what you see in your friends. It's evil stuff. But now let's get into the fight by repenting of the same egocentricity in ourselves! How many times has my own self-centered heart grieved my heavenly Father and wounded others! Remember what Jesus said in Luke 6:42: "First take the plank out of your eye, and then you will see clearly to remove the speck from your brother's eye."

Are my friends so preoccupied with self that they sin against me without even knowing it? I think yours do this to you. But will you join me in crying out to God for grace to pull the planks out of our own eyes first—before we correct others. For you, your challenge comes now. It's so big you cannot escape seeing it; you must either look away from yourself to Christ and others or cave in. So seize the opportunity to serve Christ with a God-centered heart.

Andrew, we love you. You are shining for Jesus. Now let's shine brighter for Him in the days ahead by caring for others with a reckless abandon that is the gift of the Spirit of the Father.

I'd also like to continue the thoughts I began to share with you in my letter from Kenya. My idea is that we can grow together and experience much peace and joy by helping each other.

So here come some of my meditations "out of Africa."

I'm really interested in what goes into being happy. Everybody wants to be happy, but very few ever attain it, not even Christians. Here are some thoughts about what goes into it.

First let me talk about appearances. It naturally appears to our minds that suffering and disappointments destroy our happiness. Experience would seem to confirm this conclusion. We all have found ourselves dreadfully unhappy in our sufferings and in our losses.

But this is only appearance. Wisdom says that appearance and reality are not the same. For suffering can put us in a position of insight which non-sufferers never enjoy. That new perspective can give us a fulfillment which goes beyond our sweetest dreams. That fulfillment consists in being almost forced to rest in God or perish in despair.

Consider my cancer or your AIDS. Each person's suffering is unique, but I think I have some feel for what you are going through. No outsider can understand how powerful is the impulse just to lie down and quit—or to give in to fears and despair when you hear the word "cancer" or "AIDS."

For me the month of October in 1987 was a time of heavy-duty anxiety. Happiness? There seemed to be no place for it. The onset of lymphoma really branded my mind so that my emotions were sensitized, even sometimes dominated, by the whole experience. On the one level, I was easily moved to fear by any fever, tightness of my belt through adding a little weight, or any feeling of unusual tiredness. You may know these are all symptoms of lymphoma—and of a thousand other things. On a deeper level, there was the haunting question of God's dependability, my security in Him. My troubling question was, "If He let me have lymphoma, what is coming next?" And will He permit it to come back?

It seems to me that God gave me some answers in Kenya to my questions. Just before the attack on the team at Muru I had a week in which I had a severe back problem that could have meant I had a mini-heart attack, and at the end of the week I had a fever for two days. It was a painful time also for my spirit. Was I being abandoned by God? But meditating on Psalm 84 proved to be water flowing in the desert. I was especially helped by verse 4: "Blessed are those who dwell in your house; they are ever praising you."

God is my home, and I do not need to fear if my American doctors are far away. I can accept—albeit reluctantly—the idea that my severe back pain is the prelude to a major heart attack. God is my home.

What does that mean? God is my home. In what way? I think it means that as I lose my other "homes" in this world I find that God is there to receive me. But I would add, God is there as I want Him for myself as my God. This is how Psalm 84 begins. It reads, "My soul yearns, even faints for the courts of the Lord."

Bring together my yearning heart and a God who alone can satisfy that heart. That is true home comfort for the life. Augustine says, "If you have a house of your own, you are poor; if you have the house of God, you are rich. In your own house you will fear thieves; in God's house God himself is the wall. Blessed, then, are those who dwell in your house. They possess the heavenly Jerusalem, without distress, without pressure, without diverse and divided boundaries. All possess it; and each singly possesses the whole."

Augustine's insight? If you have made your home this world and whatever you can possess in it, you are always in danger of being plunged into insecurities, fears, and losses. But make God your dwelling place and you have unlosable treasure. And a deeper kind of happiness.

My fever had hardly left when the Mission to the World (PCA) team in north Kitwi was attacked by terroristic bandits and two of the women missionaries were physically brutalized . . . they were in deadly peril. For a time they were constantly threatened by death, and all they could do was pray for courage to endure a terrible end. When the bandits left the mission, these women were in profound shock. They came to me for help, and it appears that what I was able to share was used by the Lord to restore them to hope and courage. Their memories are also being healed. Personally I found talking and praying with them helped me too. It was an opportunity for me to wrestle with the meaning of Psalm 84.

I asked you if you would be willing to read my new book and make suggestions and criticisms, etc. I need your help—not that you need to edit it or anything like that, but because I need your friendship and encouragement and partnership. You think you have all the pain you can bear, but yours will be lessened as you bear mine, and mine will be lessened as I bear yours!

Writing the book has been a painful undertaking. More so than I had imagined. The book is not about cancer, but about the change of perceptions that can come into the life when one suffers intensely.

Still, recalling memories of my struggle with lymphoma was part of the writing. Tough, but good for the soul in the long run.

As I write and serve others I now understand things better. The week of October 5–12, 1987, was a part of my memory: the remembrance had a good side and a negative aspect. My questions were, will the trauma of that week ever leave? Should it leave? What did I learn that was eminently precious during that time? Is there anything about this intense suffering that is crippling me? And if so, what do I do about it?

I am now of the view that God wanted me to find Him as my home in order to live at peace in this present temporary home. Augustine explains it well: "Let our God be our hope. He who made all things is better than all things. He who has made beautiful things is more beautiful than all things. He who made what is mighty is mightier; and he who made what is great is greater. Whatever you have loved, he will be that for you. Learn to love the Creator in the creature; the maker in what is made, lest you grasp what he has made and lose him by whom you too have been made."

For me, though, I can discover God as my hope only as He reveals Himself to me by faith. Believing is the cause of knowing; knowing (including self-analysis) is not the cause of believing.

Believing in God as my sovereign Father is where it all begins. Therefore I must believe in order that I may come to understand; the reverse is not the way to go. I cannot by my struggles, experiences, sorrows, come to know God. Job tried this route and ended up completely confused. In Elihu's words, Job's reasonings led him to "condemn God so that he might justify himself." I must not labor to analyze my experience and so out of this knowledge come to believe in Him.

There is a reason for starting with trust in God and not with the complexities of our introspection. Whether we know it or not we often try to understand God from a distance. We are viewing the center from the standpoint of a remote circumference. Or worse, we have assumed a position in which we are trying to be the god of God. Like Job we have virtually put Him on trial, and then are left mystified that communion with Him has disappeared.

What is there to do, Andrew, when you cannot do anything? Believe and keep believing!

Once again let me offer my struggles as an illustration of what I am trying to say. I was left with a deep wellspring of fears after my encounter with lymphoma. I felt like I had died during those days. The former Jack Miller was gone from this world. How could I live again? By facing my questions with my own wisdom? Impossible! I am convinced today that most people have a dark heritage of fears in their inner self that has never been faced. Intense suffering simply exposes what was there all the time. But Jesus is very much concerned to help us face up to these fears and deal with them. There is certainly no power in us to do so.

While in Nairobi I went through the Gospel of Matthew and counted twenty passages where Jesus commands us to believe, not to fear or worry, to get rid of despair and doubts. We can do so as we ask the Father for grace to admit our deepest fears. But don't expect a real conversation with the Father to be painless. I mean that grace comes to us as we know we lack it.

In Nairobi I had to cry out to God that I could not handle the fears. Just could not do it, and would He please help.

In ourselves we simply cannot find the courage to face ourselves honestly. How can I admit that my condition is desperate? But I did. I told God that left to myself, I would perish. No man—or woman— likes to say that. It seems like a total loss of—well, everything that matters—dignity, hope, and independence. But, in reality, to speak so plainly to the Father is to begin the move to the Father's house.

Can you believe it? In our apartment in Nairobi peace came to me once again. Here I was sweating away with a fever and with peace in my soul. I was at home in my Father's house and accepting the temporary character of my present home. I had experienced the paradox of faith expressed in Psalm 84. Those who live in God's house are always on the move in this world. Those who live in God's house are pilgrims: God's homeless people who are always at home in Him.

They have learned:

"Blessed are those whose strength is in you, Who have set their hearts on pilgrimage."

And:

"They go from strength to strength, Till each appears before God in Zion."

I have written such a long letter to you not to tax your patience, but because of Jesus' love to all of us. You are not alone. We are with you in your struggle, and so is Jesus. I just want to share my joy in that love and the power of that love to release us from the worst kinds of spiritual homelessness. He is bigger than all our crippling fears and doubts.

In myself I don't have a lot of advice to give you about many things. How do you handle AIDS or lymphoma or AZT? By now you probably know more about these issues than I do. But let me round out the picture of what God says to us in our yearnings. Did I seem to contrast faith and knowledge? Let me qualify that just a little. Faith has in it a knowledge, a content supplied by the gospel of Jesus Christ.

That content is my hope. I am a sinner. A life-threatening disease makes me very much aware that what matters is not what people think but what God thinks. And God knows the vileness of my heart. Oh, how sweet that makes the sound of the gospel. In the gospel I come to know and rely on something that is very powerful. It's the blood of the Lamb of God, and what that blood says about the nature of God. It says that the Father has welcomed me at the price of the death of His Son, Jesus, my precious Savior. It isn't empty words from God. It is the blood of the One who is almighty. He shed His precious blood to buy us sonship, a place in the home of our holy Father. His blood spells pardon, acceptance, assurance, comfort, the Spirit of adoption praying in us. It teaches our hearts that the Father's rule of our lives is good.

Those who live in God's love will be praising Him all day long! Would I have ever tasted this happiness without suffering?

Soon I expect to have six chapters completed in my book and need feedback. Will you become a prayer partner with me for this writing? Again, please read it and see how big a sinner I am and admire the grace which has constantly delivered me.

I look forward to seeing a miracle of grace in your life and in mine. We have prayed for you. Be at peace in the walk of a son of the Father. Be at home in the God of all mercies! . . . I think we are all going to be very happy in Jesus.

In His glorious grace,
Jack

Life for Others Comes out of Our Dying

To the elders at NLPC. This is Jack's report on a mission trip recently completed.

July, 1991

Dear Session:

Matt and Lisa, missionaries from Canada, had moved into a small village in Spain, not far from where we were staying. The village people seemed indifferent to religion and Christ. In their minds Christ was remote, powerless, and irrelevant. These attitudes are often typical of the European world.

Then this couple told God that they were willing to make any sacrifice in order to see these villagers turned to Christ.

In early November of last year Peter, their twelve-year-old son, rode his bicycle into a cement truck. Peter died in the ambulance on the way to the hospital. The truck driver went into shock, the villagers were stunned. Though the Canadian couple grieved deeply, Christ comforted them powerfully, and they gave testimony to their faith that Peter, a born-again believer, was with Jesus in heaven.

"Peter's death opened our pueblo [village] to Christ. Two people committed themselves to Christ soon after the funeral," Lisa told us. Through a death Jesus became powerful in Spain. The village is now open to hearing about the Son of God in an entirely new way.

The Father spoke deeply to my own heart through these Canadian Christians who stayed next door to us for two weeks. I was so moved by the power of the Lord's working in their lives that I went up to their village and attended a party that they held for some of their Spanish friends.

I came away convinced that the gospel becomes powerful in our lives and in the lives of others when we love them enough to suffer for them. Life for others comes out of my dying (2 Cor. 4:12). We don't naturally die for others; we don't want to get involved in their problems and certainly not in their messes. We do not want to be seen as foolish and frail in their eyes, and yet this is the way of Christ's power.

In Switzerland our team [a group including both Swiss and American Christians] and Rose Marie and I met for prayer and mutual humbling before I spoke in June in one of the state churches. I knew the audience would likely include evangelicals, liberals, and just secular non-Christians. Who was sufficient to speak to these competent Swiss whose country seems to work so well? We humbled ourselves, confessing our self-dependence, pride, and lack of love. We died as we prayed. In our weakness we felt the resurrection power of Christ. As I spoke in the evening about moving from misdirected thirsts to thirsting for Christ, I found myself going through a death and a resurrection. Before I asked for a response at the end of the message, I stopped speaking and waited. While silently looking at the people, I seemed to die. I wanted to die to what they might think of me. To die to any power in me to change them. To die to the desire to glorify myself and to become willing to be thought a fool for Christ's sake. I then said, "You have heard me say that we suppress our confusions and pretend that we have no misdirected thirsts. Actually we thirst after everything but Christ. We demand others meet our needs and do not know that we do not give what we demand from others. We do not face up to our inability to love others, our coldness. We dislike the messiness of close personal relationships."

I said that in each of us there is an ugly human energy driving us away from God, a reactive allergy to God and His holiness, a refusal to submit to His control, and a treasonous disloyalty to His person and laws. The hard truth: "This is sin against a holy God and therefore makes us the subjects of His wrath."

I went on, "Now is the time to move from this world of self and wrath and put yourself under the blood and righteousness of Christ." I then invited those who wished to admit they were deeply confused, knew they were bad sinners, to join me in repentance and faith by standing to admit their total need.

I had never heard of Swiss people in this kind of setting standing up to confess their sinfulness and need of a Savior. But my dying was now completed. It was entirely in the hands of the powerful Son of God, and He is alive!

Three people stood up. Was this all? Then ten. Then thirty, fifty, eighty, and perhaps a hundred or more. I poured out my heart in prayer for them. Christ was on the move.

That was Wednesday evening. By Sunday evening God had powerfully blessed the testimony and work of our team, and after I preached I was tired. But Jane [one of the team members] took me by the hand and said, "Please don't stay with the Christians but come to the door and talk with non-Christians."

A young Swiss man was leaving. After greeting him, I asked, "Did you understand the message?" He answered that he did, but acknowledged that he had never "put his weight on Jesus." After the pastor and I talked with him for over two hours, he was unexpectedly wrought upon by the Son of God. He resisted, we prayed, waited— died if you will. Then while the gospel was being explained to him, he suddenly repented and believed it.

He then confessed his faith before several of us gathered in the pastor's home. He said thoughtfully, "I believe Jesus is raised from the dead for me and He died for my sins. The big barrier in me—it is gone!"

I would like to tell you more about our time in Switzerland, but must quickly move on to the ministry in London, the first two weeks in July. God had prepared me by the pattern of death and resurrection.

We arrived with two teams, with over twenty people on each team. One was based at Clapham Junction and worked with Providence House, and the other was based in Ealing and worked with the International Presbyterian Church. This Ealing team also reached out to the Asian community in Southall. I was also slated to speak twice for outreach times in Cole Abbey, a church located in the London business center.

Both teams went through a dying, especially the first week. Here we were, unknown quantities in a world that is established and running along its own lines, and we represented an outside force. But Christ intervened, humbling us and reviving us and those among whom we labored.

One of the biggest breakthroughs was our establishing lasting friendships with our hosts. Christ knit our hearts together in love. The second breakthrough was the welcome we received doing things that we would not naturally like to do—like witnessing from door to door. Our hosts were surprised that so many people welcomed us. One church member in Ealing said, "We have never had success at calling door to door. This is something new; I can't remember its happening before."

The second week in Clapham the door-to-door calling had such an impact that forty visitors came to one church service in response to invitations. When can you remember that happening in the U.S? And in England where 1,000 people a week stop attending church? The street ministries were powerful, so much so that Satanists that came to disturb our dramas and preaching simply fled away. The Asians in Southall willingly stopped to hear Bob Heppe preach using a sketchboard. . . .

People prayed. That is the cause of this working. But behind it all was authority—that of the Son of God. All the glory is His! Praise Him!

In His grace,
Jack Miller

Leaning on Jesus Is the Essence of Maturity

To a young couple whose child has just been diagnosed with a progressive disease.

December, 1993

Dear Peter and Shelley,

Rose Marie and I want to let you know how concerned we have been for you during this time of difficult trial. We have been praying for you and bearing you up before God, asking Him to provide you with grace of the Spirit to persevere. We just want to let you know that we love you and are encouraged by your example.

What can we say at a difficult time like this? We don't have any advice, but we can share with you what God has been teaching us about having childlike faith. Rose Marie and I have been meditating on Matthew 18. The disciples ask Jesus, "Who is the greatest in the kingdom of heaven?" Jesus answers that the greatest in the kingdom of heaven is the one who becomes like a little child. We often take Jesus' words for granted because they're familiar to us. Often we really don't hear them. But what He has said is utterly astonishing. Who could believe in our competitive world that the most important person is one who is virtually helpless? I can accept that somewhat intellectually. But practically to lean upon Him the way that a child must lean on us for care is utterly contrary to my human nature. I don't even want to be put in positions where I have to lean heavily on Him and say, "Lord, I don't know what to do." Could it be that leaning on Him completely in utter helplessness and finding life and strength through Him for my helplessness is the essence of maturity?

Jesus, you turn my world upside down! When I submit to You, Lord, it suddenly occurs to me that I am seeing the world right-side-up. And somehow mysteriously the pain of not knowing what to do becomes the joy of the child of God. And I say, "Ah Lord, if I don't have to be in charge anymore, then I can drop a lot of burdens. I don't need to worry, or plan, where planning makes no sense. I am free to sit at Your feet and to listen and be taught, and learn about Your plans." At such times I often see new ways of doing things. The various things that Satan meant to use to destroy me become opportunities for serving Christ joyfully, boldly, and freely. Then my heart knows a peace and quietness. I find myself saying in spite of myself, "Your will, not mine, be done." In Your will I find perfect peace. What a mystery of grace!

I don't know how this may apply to you, but it comes from hearts that are deeply sympathetic. May grace abound in your lives together, and may Thomas shine as Jesus' star forever and ever. Thanks again for the grace you have shown in tough times. We love you.

In His grace,

Jack

Appendix

Recovering the Grand Cause

This paper was written by Jack Miller in 1993. It came out of discussions with his son-in-law Bob Heppe about the need to address again the issues of introversion in the church. At this time Bob and Jack were planning to start a missionary training center in London. This document was part of the packet that was developed for that center. Jack died before those plans could be realized.

Me-Firstism in the Church

We believe that the Grand Cause of the gospel has been substantially compromised in the last decade. Among evangelicals the gospel has been rightly understood to mean that Christ is for us, but this "Christ for us" has frequently been used as an excuse for self-centered thinking and living. All too often we are left with a wimpy Jesus who is hardly able to meet our needs—much less dislodge the powers of darkness that are deeply entrenched all about us. We have been so busy thinking and worrying about ourselves that we have lost touch with the awesome Lord of the Great Commission.

According to a well-known pollster, the expressed goal of 56 percent of those attending evangelical churches today is remarkably self-oriented: They believe that the primary reason for existence is "personal satisfaction and fulfillment." It's not just nominal Christians who live for the here and now. The astonishing thing is that the majority of evangelicals do not seem to even consider that there might be something wrong with making meeting one's own needs the purpose in life. George Barna reports: "The fact remains, however, that even among the groups involved in religious endeavors, the majority agree that life is about personal satisfaction and fulfillment."[1]

Christ for us means little because all we need from the Lord is a bit of propping up on the way to making ourselves the possessors of the American dream.

To such persons, the Apostle Paul's passion for identifying with Christ's suffering runs absolutely counter to what they believe is the purpose of their lives. For them life finds its meaning in fulfilling the needs of number one.

In another major shift in values, four out of five Americans now subscribe strongly to some form of prosperity doctrine, and 96 percent "agree to some extent with it."[2] Prosperity is now viewed as a fundamental human right, and according to Barna, "Born-again Christians hold the same view as non-Christians on this matter."

The Loss of the Biblical Teaching on "Lostness"

This "me-firstism" is closely allied to a warped theology about the sinful nature of man and his eternal peril. A whopping 77 per-

1. George Barna, *The Barna Report: What Americans Believe* (Ventura, Calif.: Regal, 1991), p. 92.
2. Ibid., p. 107.

cent of evangelical Christians agree with the statement: "People are basically good."[3] We are faced with a radical crippling of a grace theology here within the church. If we are all good people, then we are not bankrupt sinners desperately needing grace. Instead, we have become self-righteous attorneys defending our own goodness.

We have become those whose subtle pride leads them to wish to be seen as right before people without deep concern for being righteous before God. We are a generation of folks who were only half lost, and that may explain why so many professing Christians seem only half saved.

Win and Charles Arn in their book *The Master's Plan for Making Disciples* say flatly, "The biblical concept of 'lostness' has disappeared from the conscience of most churches and most Christians." They conclude their solemn indictment with these words, "Little remains of the first-century Christian's burning conviction that without Christ, every person is forever lost."[4]

We conclude: If one believes that the purpose of life is about "personal satisfaction and fulfillment" and that "people are basically good," it should not surprise anyone to discover that the whole idea of lostness has vanished from the consciousness of ththe typical evangelical. He or she is too preoccupied with self to care very much about others, and even if the caring is there, it would hardly make any difference. Good people hardly need the gospel anyway; so what's the fuss all about?

The Blunting Effect of Me-Firstism and the Loss of "Lostness"

One lethal result of these trends has been the virtual explosion of guilt, shame, and fear among Christians—and the apparent inabil-

3. Ibid., p. 89.
4. Win and Charles Arn, *The Master's Plan for Making Disciples* (Pasadena: Church Growth.

ity of the gospel to touch these feelings of inward chaos. This has become the age of the orphan. This pathetic figure tries in vain to escape from guilt by denying deep sinfulness and ends up hopelessly entangled in the very thing he or she denies.

This state of affairs goes a long way toward explaining the blunting of evangelistic and missionary passion. Many church members and leaders have never experienced the gospel's reviving power. It hardly seems good news to us. Therefore we are not likely to think that it can do much for those who dwell in the darkness of the harvest field.

It should not be surprising, then, that many evangelical missionary agencies are no longer growing. At a time when the opportunities are so great, many missions want to grow, but are not finding the missionary recruits. Paul McKaughn, executive director of the EFMA, is reported in *Mission Frontiers* as having said that "2/3 of our missions . . . are not growing at the present time" and that "it is almost the same figure in IFMA."[5]

Now Is the Time to Declare War . . .

Our conclusion is that the gospel has been presented so exclusively in terms of personal fulfillment, with the realities of depravity and God's judgment retreating into the background, that Christians have lost touch with the Grand Cause.

The Grand Cause has lost its wonder, the glory has departed. Yes, it is still honored by our lips, but the vision of a whole church totally committed to what Christ is totally committed to has faded from the minds of many of us.

But now is the hour for rediscovery. We begin with our own repentance. Join us. We ourselves admit that our own self-centered pursuit of comfort has again and again eaten up our zeal for reach-

5. *Mission Frontiers* (Nov–Dec., 1991).

ing the lost. Here, then, we express our repentance for our egoism and cold apathy in the face of the Great Commission.

We further confess that the Scriptures teach that Christ is for us in the gospel and freely justifies and adopts us as sons and gives us the Spirit of adoption. But we must not stop here. We must be for others with the same intensity that Christ was for us. We must get back our joy by having a holy disregard for personal safety. We reject the status of civilians and the mind-set of the civilian. We are soldiers/sons of God.

Therefore we gladly renounce me-firstism, and then bend our ears to hear the voice of the ascended Commander-in-Chief.

The Son of God tells us that the kingdom always comes with overturning force, and requires a forceful response from us. He has declared war on the world and the devil. He aims to "set the world on fire" and bring peace to the heart, but war to the evil in ourselves and the world. For us this means that we must throw away our lives for Jesus as we take the gospel to the lost. This intelligent carelessness is our true security. Anything less is dangerous compromise. We who once were enemies have been justified by faith. We must not fall asleep in self-preoccupation and comfort zones. Instead, justification is meant to release us for the battle.

What is the battle? To risk unpopularity by preaching the cross as a real cross on which a real Savior shed real blood for real sinners headed for a real hell. The battle is giving up the pretence that we are all nice people. The battle is taking the gospel to the lost with radical devotion. The battle is to own nothing in order to own Christ. The battle is to have no righteousness except the righteousness of God through faith in Christ. The battle is to attack the dark places of the earth with all the energy of the Spirit and the conquering gospel of the substitutionary death of Christ.

Such a declaration of war can issue only from a work of grace. Therefore we pray for our heavenly Father to grant a heart willingness to sacrifice everything, that the Great Commission might be fulfilled speedily as it applies to our generation. We pledge ourselves to this cause, to reach all the people of the world for Christ with the message of the cross.

Rediscover the Grand Cause—Taking the Gospel to the Dark Places of the Earth

We are talking about the Grand Cause, about finding our lives as we lose them for this cause in our generation. Since we have muddled about so badly, let us now seek grace with new intensity so that we may discover afresh the practical implications of the call of Christ to take the gospel to the sin-darkened nations. Let's pray together.

Prayer: Our God, thank You for giving us a grand cause through the self-giving of Your beloved Son. We confess that our sluggishness is so great that Your grand cause will not be fulfilled in our generation, unless You overpower us and change our deepest motivations. By Your grace, set us on fire with the love of Christ. Make the words of the gospel become life in us; pour the hot words of John 3:16 into our coldness until we melt and crack and dissolve under the burning power of the cross. Fill us with the love of God as we go with the gospel to the ends of the earth through the door of London. Above all, make us willing to endure all suffering because our minds can never forget Jesus' dreadful pains in his death for us.

Several key elements of Christ's Grand Gause are set forth below for emphasis:

Find the Key Concepts in the Grand Cause

The Grand Task—going with the gospel to the lost: To fulfill the Great Commission, possibly in our generation (Matt. 28:18–20).

The command to go to the nations with the gospel is not one command among many; it is the master command of Jesus the Master. If we do not obey this command, we are living out of accord with our whole reason for being in this world.

The Grand Privilege—experiencing empowerment through suffering: To seek grace in prayer in order to welcome suffering as the vehicle for realizing this task.

There is no power without prayer and there is no power in prayer without a resolve to endure all things for the sake of Jesus. A wise Christian writes, "The place of suffering in service and of passion in mission is hardly ever taught today. But the greatest single secret of evangelism or missionary effectiveness is the willingness to suffer and die."[6]

The Grand Missionary Power: To fulfill the Great Commission by rejecting every form of self-reliance in order to rely on Christ's missionary presence, the Holy Spirit (Matt. 28:20).

The power of faith comes from relying on the Spirit as we self-consciously reject everything else on which we rely, including abilities, spiritual gifts, experience, training, organization, and reputation, in order to put all hope in the working of the Spirit of grace.

The Grand Method: To pray with one mind together. We activate the power of the Holy Spirit to reach the lost in our generation by laboring to foster intense and self-conscious oneness in corporate prayer (Acts 1:1–14; 2:1).

Revival is entirely a gift of God, but the working of God comes to expression through our ongoing mutual repentance, a bold love expressed by a common willingness to confess and forsake our sin together, and self-consciously seeking a deepening oneness with our fellow ambassadors. This kind of renewal issues only from a close

6. John Stott, *The Cross of Christ* (Downers Grove, Ill.: Intervarsity, 1986), p. 322.

walk with Christ, the Lord of the gospel, through taking much time to pray together.

The Grand Obstacle—the ignoring of grace: To ignore grace is in every generation the greatest barrier to the fulfilling of the Great Commission. In our generation this blindness takes at least three virulent forms:

1. A self-righteous attitude:
Grace is viewed, unconsciously, as something to be received by human choice and self-effort, because people are basically good.

We have seen that in the U.S. a majority even of evangelical Christians (77 percent) believe that people are fundamentally good (George Barna). On this view, grace is propping up of human virtues, and leads straight into self-righteousness based upon human achievement through self-effort.

Therefore, grace becomes something that makes one morally superior to other people. Faith for serving Christ is little more than disguised will-power. Will-power cannot endure suffering long-term and leads to fierce judging of others who do not seem to have the will-power to do right.

Concerning the life of self-effort, Herman Bavinck has said, "Many are prepared to admit that they are justified by the righteousness earned by Christ. But they suppose, or they behave in actual practice as if they thought, they must be sanctified by a kind of sanctification brought about by themselves."[7]

2. An uncontrolled tongue:
If grace is seen on a deeply felt level as a human attainment, then the religious person will boast in successes and feel overwhelmed by defeats. Defensiveness in human relations in the church and on the mission field is inevitable. Quarrels or at least distanc-

---

7. Herman Bavinck, *Gereformeerde Dogmatick*, IV, p. 233.

ing follows. Thus a self-righteous attitude leads to an uncontrolled tongue, one that fails to praise God in order to glory in self and freely spreads bitter and bad reports about others.

Dan Herron, WHM missionary, says, "There is no greater problem in the local church and on the mission field today than Christians spreading bad reports about one another."

Countless Christian families and churches today are torn apart—or at least marred—by a ruthless use of the tongue. The greatest need today is for "a new tongues movement" which will emphasize controlling the tongue and using it exclusively for praise and speaking the truth in love. This is the language of the sons and daughters of God.

3. A self-indulging attitude:

Human will-power always fails. It is a human attempt to do God's work with our own resources. But working out of self-dependence is guilt-inducing and exhausting. It impels the egoist to seek relief in pleasure and self-fulfillment, to use the good things of God as drugs to escape from reality. Self-fulfillment then takes over as the person's grand task in life leaving the person burdened with suppressed guilt and shame.

Unfortunately the person seeking self-fulfillment never finds happiness. Instead, his inner life shrivels and dries up. But let this person look away from self-interest, fight self-preoccupation, and set the affectional life on Christ and His cause. Christ is alive; He is the giant Son of God. He walks through the earth. Those who walk with Him know that Christ and the cause of the gospel really do introduce us to the deeply satisfying love of God.

The Grand Message of Pure Grace: To declare first to ourselves and to our own consciences the saving message, and to let it control our imaginations until we can see how great and glorious is our forgiveness through the blood of the Lamb. Then we take the message

315

to the lost with all the joy and energy that comes from a fresh taste of the forgiving power of the blood of the Lamb.

We as the chief of sinners expect to see this gospel conquer the lost. Did it not conquer us? Most certainly. Then we preach the all-conquering message of "Christ and him crucified," in much "weakness and fear, and with much trembling . . . but with the demonstration of the Spirit's power" (1 Cor. 2:2–4).

Joyfully we pledge ourselves to give our hearts, our minds, our time, our bodies, our money, and all that we have to this Grand Cause. As we major in taking the message to the dark places of the earth, we share Charles H. Spurgeon's confidence in its conquering power.

He declared: "Oh the power, the melting, conquering, transforming power of that dear cross of Christ! My brethren, we have but to abide by the preaching of it, we have but constantly to tell abroad the matchless story, and we may expect to see the most remarkable spiritual results. We need to despair of no man now that Jesus has died for sinners. With such a hammer as the doctrine of the cross, the most flinty heart will be broken; and with such a fire as the sweet love of Christ, the most mighty iceberg will be melted. We need never despair for the heathenish or superstitious races of men; if we can but find occasion to bring the doctrine of Christ crucified into contact with their natures, it will yet change them, and Christ will be their King."

C. John (Jack) Miller taught practical theology at Westminster Theological Seminary, was Director of World Harvest Mission, and led mission trips to several countries. He was founding pastor of New Life Presbyterian Church outside of Philadelphia, from which sprang several other congregations in the Philadelphia area. His other books including *Repentance and Twentieth Century Man, Outgrowing the Ingrown Church, Powerful Evangelism for the Powerless,* and, with his daughter Barbara Juliani, *Come Back, Barbara.*

Timeline
OF JACK MILLER'S LIFE
AND MINISTRY

1928   born in Gold Beach, Oregon
1943   leaves home and finishes high school in San Francisco
1950   marries Rose Marie Carlsen
1951   their first child, Roseann, is born
1952   their second child, Ruth, is born
1953   their third child, Paul, is born
       graduates from San Francisco University (B.A. in
           philosophy/history)
       begins studies at Westminster Theological Seminary
1954   their fourth child, Barbara, is born
1955   leaves seminary and begins teaching at Ripon Christian High
           School in Ripon, California
1959   ordination as an evangelist in the Orthodox Presbyterian
           Church
       begins church plant in Stockton, California
1960   their fifth child, Keren, is born
1961   begins work on doctorate in English literature while
           continuing to pastor
1963   leaves Stockton church and begins work as consultant for the
           Center for American Studies, Redwood City, California
1964   moves to Pennsylvania and begins work on finishing M.Div.
           from Westminster Seminary
1965   finishes work on M.Div. and begins to pastor at
           Mechanicsville Chapel, Mechanicsville, Pennsylvania
1967   begins teaching at Westminster Theological Seminary in the
           practical theology department
1968   receives doctorate in English literature from University of the
           Pacific, Stockton, California
1972   leaves Mechanicsville Chapel

1973   starts New Life Presbyterian Church in his living room
1975   *Repentance and Twentieth Century Man* published
1977   first mission trip to Ireland
1979   first mission trip to Uganda
1980   *Evangelism and Your Church* published (available now as
        Powerful Evangelism for the Powerless, republished in
        1997 a year after Jack's death)
1981   begins full-time at New Life Presbyterian, stops teaching at
        Westminster Seminary
1983   World Harvest Mission formed with Jack as director
        Jack has a heart attack in Uganda
        New Life plants its first daughter church—New Life
        Philadelphia
1986   *Outgrowing the Ingrown Church* published
1987   *Come Back, Barbara* published
        Jack almost dies from lymphoma
        New Life Presbyterian plants second daughter church, New
        Life Dresher
1991   mission trip to Spain
1992   leaves New Life Presbyterian Church and starts full-time at
        World Harvest Mission
1993   mission trips to Poland and Russia
1994   mission trip to Ukraine
1995   mission trip to London
        stroke in United States
1996   writes *A Faith Worth Sharing* while suffering heart problems in
        Spain
        speaks in Germany at mission conference
        dies in Spain after open-heart surgery